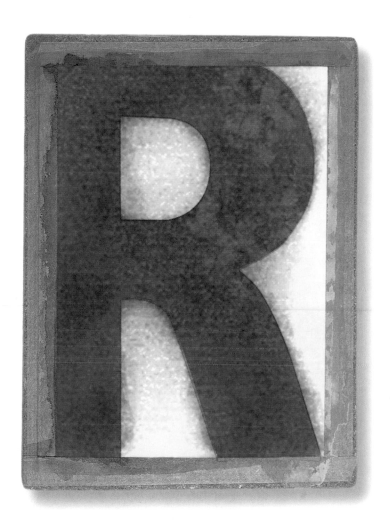
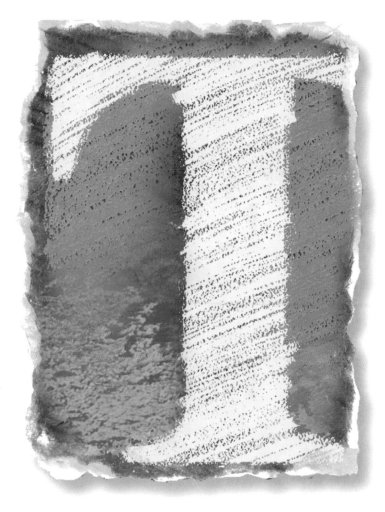

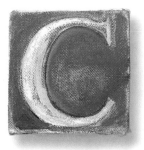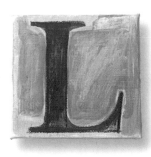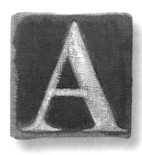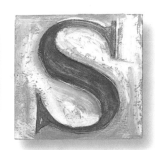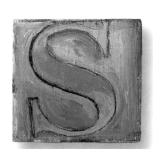

GENERAL EDITOR: SIMON JENNINGS

First published in hardback in 1999 by
Collins
an imprint of
HarperCollins*Publishers*
77–85 Fulham Palace Road
Hammersmith
London W6 8JB

The Collins website address is www.collins.co.uk

Collins is a registered trademark of HarperCollins Publishers Limited

This edition first published in paperback in 2002

07 06 05 04 03 02
9 8 7 6 5 4 3 2 1

Concept, design and editorial direction by Simon Jennings
Produced, edited and designed at the
Inklink Studio, Greenwich, London.

General editor: Simon Jennings
Consultant editor: Sally Bulgin
Publisher The Artist *and* Leisure Painter *magazines*
Emma Pierce *Technical Advisor – Winsor & Newton*
Carolynne Cook *Education Advisor*
Head of Art, Impington Village College, Cambridge
Cathy Gosling *Editorial Director – HarperCollins*

Text editors: Albert Jackson and Peter Leek
Illustrations editor: David Day
Assistant designer: Amanda Allchin
Studio photography: Ben Jennings
Indexer: Mary Morton

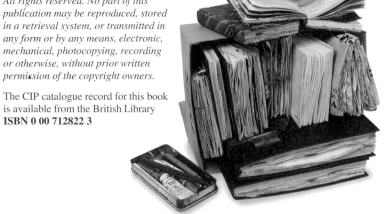

The CIP catalogue record for this book
is available from the British Library
ISBN 0 00 712822 3

Colour origination by Colourscan, Singapore
Printed and bound by Rotolito Lombarda, Italy

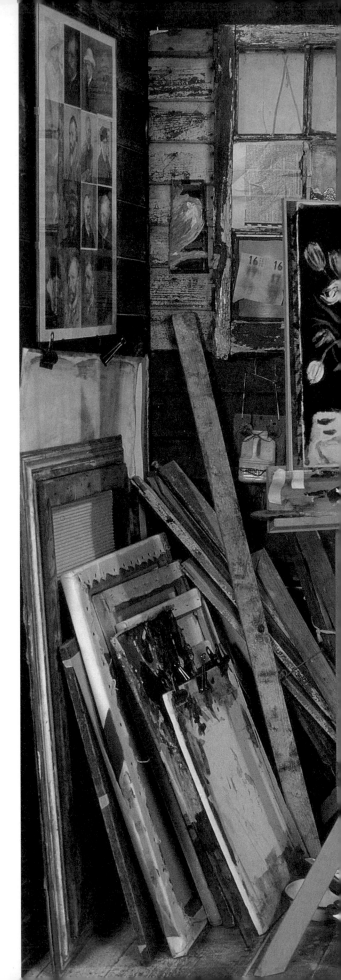

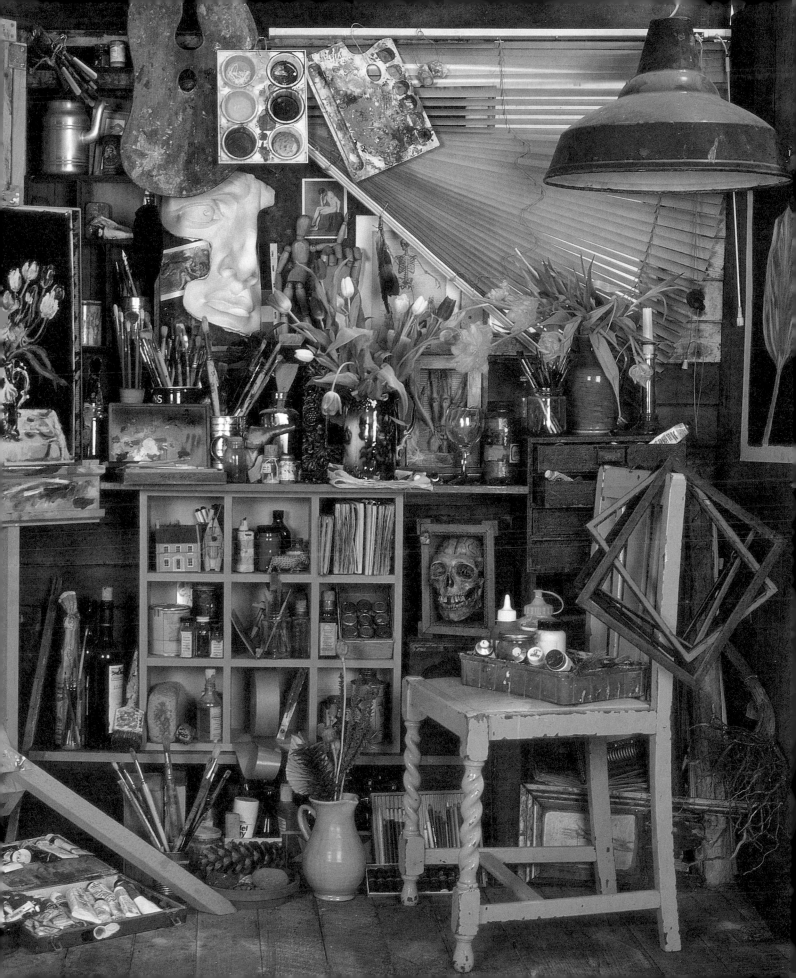

ACKNOWLEDGMENTS

This book represents the work of many hands. The editors and producers of *Collins Art Class* would like to thank the following artists for their advice, contributions and support.

Alastair Adams is a professional painter, designer and illustrator. His work is widely accredited, having been exhibited on numerous occasions, including twice at the National Portrait Gallery, London. In 1999 he was the recipient of the Daler-Rowney Award at the National Acrylic Painters Association Annual Open Exhibition, and the year before was presented with the Spectrum Paint Award.

Ray Balkwill decided to concentrate on painting full-time in 1990. Since then, his work has been exhibited widely, including numerous solo exhibitions. With his wealth of teaching experience, he runs painting courses and demonstrations. He is also a contributor to magazines, including *The Artist*, *International Artist* and *Pastel Artists International*.

Jennie Dunn is an instinctive painter who, rather than follow a traditional art-school training, sought out private tutors whose work she admired. Her work is frequently exhibited and is collected in Germany, Holland, America and the Far East. Jennie Dunn reviews and demonstrates new products for Winsor & Newton, and writes for *Leisure Painter* magazine.

Timothy Easton worked as a sculptor for many years before returning to painting. His work has been exhibited in many parts of the world, including America, Germany and Luxembourg. He is the recipient of the Elizabeth Greenshield Memorial Foundation Award from Montreal, Canada, and in 1996 was awarded the Winston Churchill Travelling Fellowship. Timothy Easton is the author of *Oil Painting Techniques*, published in 1997.

Sharon Finmark is an artist, writer and teacher. After training at Saint Martin's School of Art, she illustrated magazines, books and national newspapers. Since the 1980s she has been engaged as a visiting lecturer in the UK and Canada. She is also the author of two books from the HarperCollins *Learn to Paint* series, and has contributed to a number of articles on painting and drawing.

David Griffin is an ardent marine painter. From the age of seven, when he used to ride the free ferry across the River Thames, he has been passionate about all things nautical. David Griffin was trained at Saint Martin's School of Art during World War II. His pictures have found their way into private collections in Europe, South Africa, America and the Far East, and have appeared in numerous exhibitions.

Ken Howard, a graduate of the Royal College of Art, was appointed Official Artist in Northern Ireland in 1973. A member of the Royal Academy and the Royal Watercolour Society, Ken Howard has enjoyed considerable success and acclaim. His work is collected and exhibited widely, and he has won a string of major awards, including first prizes in the Lord Mayor's Art Award and the Hunting Group Awards.

Nick Hyams studied painting and drawing at Camberwell Art College and was awarded a fine-art degree in 1979. He has successfully undertaken commissions and has exhibited in numerous mixed shows. He has also appeared on European television to discuss his work. Nick Hyams is a qualified art teacher and is currently lecturing at a number of adult institutes and colleges.

David Jackson is a demonstrator and lecturer, and runs painting workshops in Ireland, France and the UK. His paintings have been exhibited in solo and group shows, and he is a regular contributor to the Royal Institute of Painters in Water Colours and the Royal Watercolour Society. He is also a companion member of the British Watercolour Society. David Jackson was the winner of the Eva Pollycott Award in 1996.

Ella Jennings graduated in textile design. As a post-graduate student, she specialized in tapestry weaving, and subsequently worked on many commissions at the world-famous West Dean Tapestry Workshop. Her designs have been exhibited widely, and she was the winner of the Simon Jersey Textile Design Award in 1997. As a qualified art teacher, Ella Jennings is currently passing on a wide range of skills and disciplines.

John Lidzey left teaching in the late 1980s to become a full-time professional watercolourist. He was awarded the Daler-Rowney Prize at the Royal Watercolour Society Exhibition in 1992 and, two years later, was a prizewinner in the *Sunday Times*/Singer Friedlander Watercolour competition. He writes regularly for *The Artist* magazine, and is the author of several books, including *Watercolour Workshop* and *Learn to Paint Light in Watercolour*. His work may also be seen in a video entitled *Watercolour Workshop*.

Debra Manifold specializes in painting urban landscapes, interiors and historical buildings. In 1995, she was elected a full member of the Pastel Society. She has exhibited at scores of galleries in the UK, Canada and France, including a solo show in London in 1998. Debra Manifold is the recipient of the Willi Hoffman Guth Award at the Pastel Society Exhibition and the 1999 Daler-Rowney Premier Award.

Kay Ohsten turned to watercolour painting with a commission for over 100 landscapes, which were completed in just three months. With this body of work behind her, she undertook to document the redevelopment of her home town, producing more than 400 works of art. Kay Ohsten has pioneered an unconventional approach to watercolour painting, characterized by bold use of colour and texture.

Ken Paine travelled the world, developing his portraiture and character studies that have become his life's work. He is a member of the Pastel Society and the Société des Pastellistes de France. He is the recipient of many awards, including first prize at the International Pastel Exhibition in France and was the 1989 Master Pastelliste of Société des Pastellistes. His biography, *Ken Paine – His Life and Work*, by Michael Simonow, was published in 1997.

Peter Partington is a versatile painter, but he is perhaps best known as a wildlife artist. He has been elected to the Society of Wildlife Artists; and the International Museum of Wildlife Art has several pieces of his work in its collection. He is an art teacher and the author of *Learn to Paint Birds in Watercolour*, *Learn to Draw Wildlife*, *Learn to Draw Farm Animals* and *Learn to Draw Birds*.

Jackie Simmonds is a successful painter whose work is exhibited and sold throughout the UK and America. She is a Pastel Society award winner and a recipient of the Chevron Art in Nature prize. Jackie Simmonds runs painting workshops, has made six teaching videos, and is the author of *Pastels Workshop*, *Learn to Paint Gardens in Pastel* and *Pastels Workbook*.

Shirley Trevena taught herself to paint exuberant watercolours that are now her hallmark. In 1994 she was elected a member of the Royal Institute of Painters in Water Colours, and in her first year won the Winsor & Newton award for the most outstanding contribution to the annual show. Shirley Trevena is a regular contributor to magazines and books. She is also a highly successful publisher of prints, posters and greeting cards.

Valerie Wiffen graduated from the Royal College of Art, having won the prestigious Drawing Prize. Her career has been wide-ranging – she is an art teacher, lecturer and demonstrator, with works shown at the New English Art Club, the Royal Academy Summer Show, and a one-person show at the West Dean College Gallery. She writes regularly on technical matters and is the author of several books, including *Learn to Draw Still Life* and *The Perfect Drawing*.

Colin Willey was among the finalists in the Winsor & Newton Young Artists Competition at the Royal Institute of Oil Painters Exhibition. His work has been shown to much acclaim at numerous venues, including the Royal Society of Marine Artists Exhibition and the Laing Landscape Exhibition at the Mall Galleries, London.

John Yardley has an enviable gift for capturing light and vitality with a few deft brushstrokes. Elected to the Royal Institute of Painters in Water Colours in 1990, John Yardley is a regular contributor to its annual exhibitions. He holds tuition courses in painting, and has produced two videos. He is also the author of *Watercolours – A Personal View*. His work is the subject of *The Art of John Yardley* by Ron Ranson.

CONTENTS

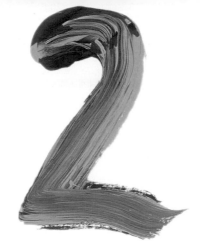
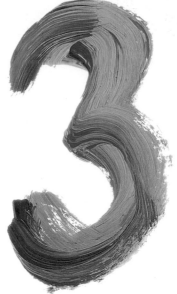

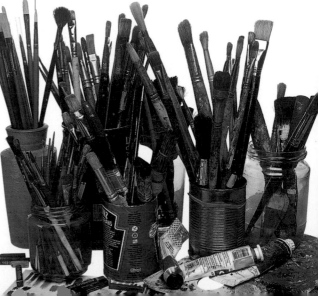

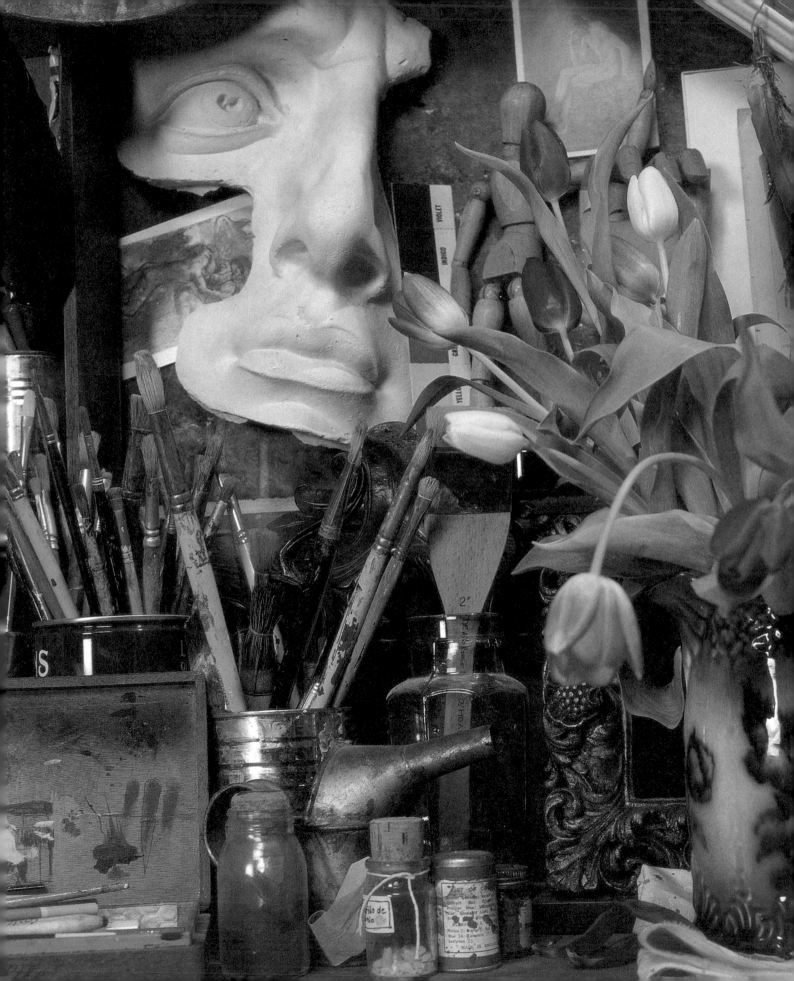

COLLINS *ART CLASS* is about the activity of painting and about communicating ideas, images and impressions via a painted surface. In the making of this book, many teachers and artists have been consulted and observed in the act of painting. One widely held view that came through loud and clear was that there are no hard-and-fast rules. There are, of course, methods to learn and materials to experiment with – but when it comes to the defining moment of painting a picture, the artist is alone. This can be a tremendously liberating state, and one to which many people aspire: to be alone without rules, relying on your imagination, with the space and time to do as you wish. And at the end of it all, there is something to show for it.

The downside of this freedom and solitude can be the very fact that you are on your own. With a blank canvas in front of you, what are you going to do if your creative imagination dries up? What if you suddenly find yourself without a clue about how to get going with a painting? What if you are confronted with a technical problem with paint, brushes or canvas? What can you do if a painting starts going hopelessly wrong? Indeed, what should or could you paint? And what materials should or could you use to paint with?

The aim of this book is to supply answers to such questions and to provide an opportunity to see how a number of artists with a wide range of skills and techniques have responded to the challenge of painting a variety of pictures. There is no substitute for practical experience and the confidence that it brings, but COLLINS ART CLASS enables you to make the initial steps by tapping into a rich seam of creative activities, from the simple basics of painting and drawing to advanced life-painting techniques.

Using this book

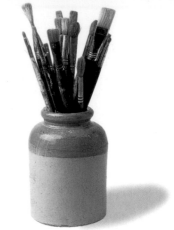

COLLINS ART CLASS is a practical book that is designed to be accessible, reassuring and inspirational. It is structured like a real art school, with numerous studios and painting rooms in which professional artists hold one-to-one tutorials on a wide range of subjects. You are invited to attend all the classes, but can move through the course at your own pace and take from it what you will. Simply decide for yourself what skill level suits your stage of development as a painter.

The object of the book is to create the real-life experience of learning to paint, interspersed with helpful exercises, tips and back-up information. Practising artists pass on their valuable experience, and share with you the challenges and solutions that come with painting a picture.

Finding your way around
You choose the subjects you are interested in and the direction in which you want to proceed. The ☞ **SEE ALSO** cross references direct you forwards or backwards page by page – from project to project and to other sections that you might find helpful or, in some cases, essential.

COLLINS ART CLASS IS DIVIDED INTO THREE SECTIONS:

SECTION ONE
WHERE SHALL I START?
THIS IS THE FOUNDATION of the book. It introduces you to the various genres, what media to use and what subjects to paint, using a comprehensive gallery of paintings for inspiration. It also includes tips on how to get started – collecting resources and references, keeping a sketchbook and starting points for paintings – plus suggestions for working outdoors and organizing a studio.

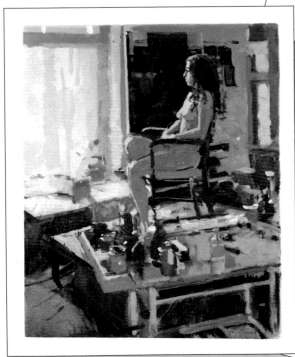

Large-scale examples of paintings
Pin-sharp photographs allow you to see every brushstroke on the finished painting.

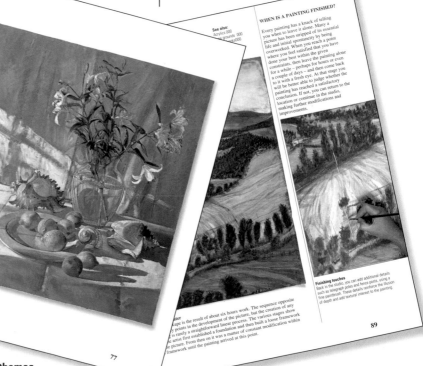

Subjects and themes
All the popular painting subjects are covered, including landscape, still life, figure painting and portraiture.

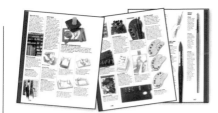

SECTION TWO

WHAT SHALL I PAINT?

THIS IS THE CORE of *Collins Art Class* – where the contributing artists spell out their tips and techniques, using specially commissioned paintings that cover the major subjects outlined in *Where shall I start?*

This part of the book begins with basic exercises and simple subject matter to get you started, and introduces you to the skills and terms associated with painting in various media. The curriculum gradually builds up to ever more ambitious projects, until you find yourself painting life studies in the studio and constructing paintings from imagination.

Here you will find still lifes, interiors, gardens, landscapes, buildings, animals, figures, portraits – just about every type of painting you might want to tackle, and in all the commonly used media from watercolour to oil paint.

As well as the major projects, you will find a wealth of suggestions and ideas for details that you might want to include in your own work. Browse through the sections on trees and foliage, skies and weather, water and basic perspective. And make use of the bridging sections – on painting hands, feet and facial features, bringing a landscape to life, and trying out different poses – to help enrich your life painting, outdoor work and portraiture.

SECTION THREE

WHAT ARE THE BASICS?

THE REFERENCE SECTION – which contains detailed information on materials and techniques – is designed to back up the core of the book. If you are familiar with the terms used by the artists and contributors, then you won't need to consult this section very often. However, if there's a reference to a technique or piece of equipment that is new to you, this section of the book will put you in the picture with a succinct description and helpful advice.

1 Teaching points

Lists the main skills and points covered by a particular exercise or project and what you can hope to achieve. For further detail and support, refer to *What are the basics?*

2 Project heading

A clearly defined heading introduces each topic or exercise. Refer to the gallery pages in *Where shall I start?* for further examples and alternative approaches to the topic in hand.

3 Running heads

These identify the section you are reading and the main subject area under discussion.

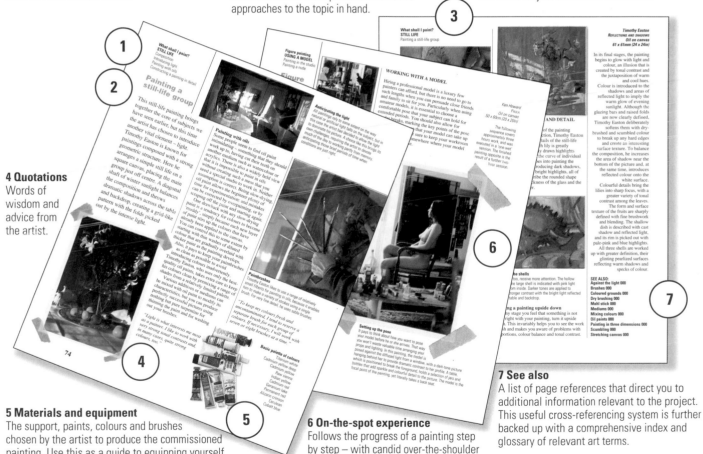

4 Quotations

Words of wisdom and advice from the artist.

5 Materials and equipment

The support, paints, colours and brushes chosen by the artist to produce the commissioned painting. Use this as a guide to equipping yourself when creating similar works.

6 On-the-spot experience

Follows the progress of a painting step by step – with candid over-the-shoulder photographs taken on location and in the studio.

7 See also

A list of page references that direct you to additional information relevant to the project. This useful cross-referencing system is further backed up with a comprehensive index and glossary of relevant art terms.

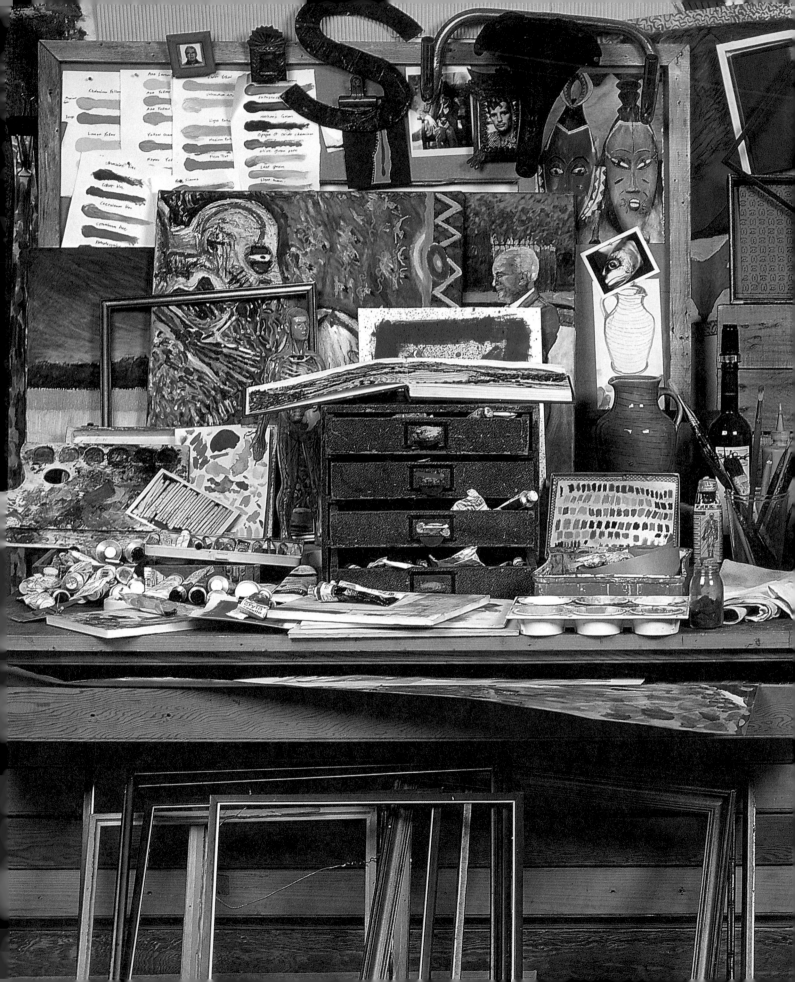

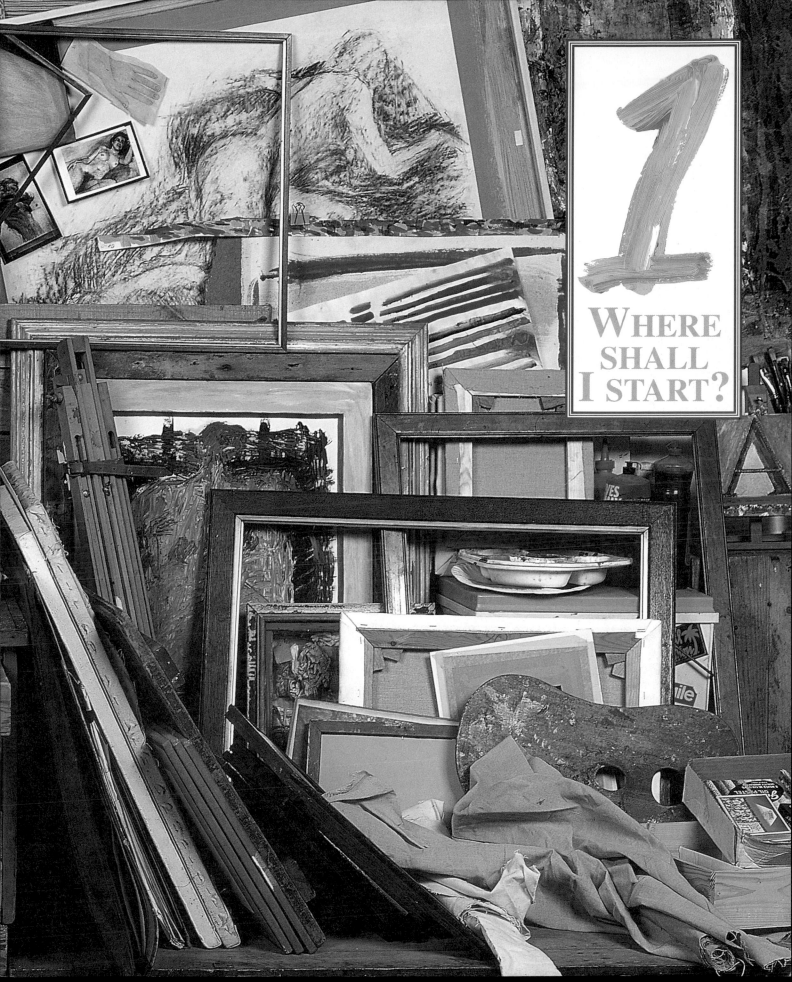

1
WHERE SHALL I START?

Where shall I start?
INTRODUCTION
Drawing for painting

Starting to paint

Where shall I start? A difficult question but an easy answer – you have taken the first step by picking up this book and leafing through the pages. Maybe you are returning to painting and have not picked up a paintbrush since leaving school, but have a warm memory of a rewarding and engaging pursuit. Or maybe you are an absolute beginner whose experience of landscape painting is to put blue at the top, brown in the middle, and green at the bottom. This book covers many levels of ability, but this page is aimed at the absolute beginner rather than the painter whose interests have been focused and techniques honed through years of dedication and experience.

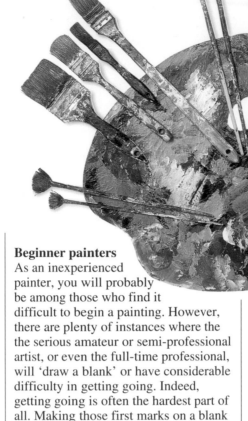

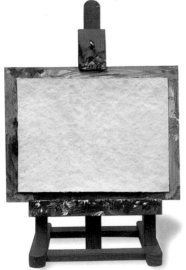

A blank canvas
Many people are influenced by an object, an idea, a photograph, a scene or situation, or something that just catches their eye. Even a dream or an experience can inspire a painting.

Beginner painters
As an inexperienced painter, you will probably be among those who find it difficult to begin a painting. However, there are plenty of instances where the the serious amateur or semi-professional artist, or even the full-time professional, will 'draw a blank' or have considerable difficulty in getting going. Indeed, getting going is often the hardest part of all. Making those first marks on a blank canvas can be a daunting prospect. If you feel daunted, you will not be alone.

Many of the artists who have contributed to this book have remarked that there are no rules in painting. This seems to be particularly true of getting started. There are all sorts of ways to begin a painting, but the desire to do so is the most important requirement – once you have made a start, you can pick the route you want to go down.

Professional advice
Among the words that kept cropping up during interviews with the professional artists who contributed to this book were expressions such as 'choices', 'freedom' and 'satisfaction'. These key words point to the fact that, although painting is not an easy process, it is an enjoyable and rewarding one. They also imply that there are a number of steps you can take to help you get started – and that, combined with perseverance, these steps gradually lead towards a pleasing finished painting.

Opposite and on the following pages you will find a variety of practical hints and suggestions for choosing subjects and how to start a painting.

Getting started
So, in order to get started, what shall I do? From the outset try to avoid setting yourself up for disappointment. Choose a subject and a medium that you feel comfortable with, one that you feel you can handle. Don't try to run before you can walk – but by the same token don't be too timid or too 'tight' in your approach, or scared to try an unfamiliar medium. Be bold and confident, and remember that it is *your* choice. You have decided to paint and what to paint; you are not in a competition, and you aren't under any pressure or under an obligation to anyone other than yourself.

Shine through
Choose a subject that is enjoyable and interesting. Be open-minded in your approach. Let the painting sometimes lead you – celebrate the accidental brushstroke, the chance blending of colours, the misplaced or quirkily drawn object. Painting is not photography; if you want to get an exact copy of a scene or an object, go out and buy a camera.

Let your own style and personality come through. Painting is an opportunity for you to be yourself, and will give you an opportunity to convey feeling and atmosphere. Do not be afraid of paint or colour. Artists' paints are relatively expensive materials and you may be reluctant to squander them – but many a potentially good amateur painting has been spoilt through lack of boldness in the application of paint.

☞ SEE ALSO
Choosing your medium 20
Classic themes and approaches 26
**Collecting resources
and references 18**
Keeping a sketchbook 16

First steps

Many painters like to start by making
pencil or colour studies and sketches.
Some make meticulous drawings and
transfer them to canvas; some put in the
simplest and most basic of drawn lines;
some make a thin wash drawing with
a brush; and others prefer to jump right
in with brush and knife and pure neat
colour. Shown right is a selection of
photographs of the first steps taken in
the creation of four paintings.

Charcoal drawing

Artist Ken Howard (see page 138) follows a
traditional approach and makes a very simple yet
measured charcoal drawing of the salient points
before proceeding with a brush and laying in the
dark areas (top row).

Brush drawing

Timothy Easton (see page 72) likes to make a
fairly detailed neutral-colour brush drawing   of
the whole composition before he starts laying in
the colours (second row).

Valerie Wiffen (see page 132) starts with
a water-soluble coloured pencil and quickly
proceeds to simple brushwork, drawing in thin
washes to lay in what she calls 'sightlines'
(third row).

Pencil drawing

Pencil line tends to be the favoured drawing
medium of watercolourists – often drawn in
lightly, and sometimes erased so that it is barely
noticeable. Here, using a photographic reference,
Kay Ohsten (see page 112) plots a light yet
accurate pencil-line sketch to serve as the basis
for her landscape painting (bottom row).

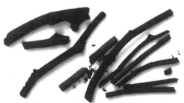

Charcoal

This is the preferred drawing material for plotting
a painting on canvas. Its soft friable consistency
glides over the grainy textile surface of canvas,
making a strong positive line that responds
instantly to the pressure applied and creating
thick or fine lines. It has the merit of being fast
and spontaneous, and is easily obliterated by
opaque mediums such as oil and acrylic paints.

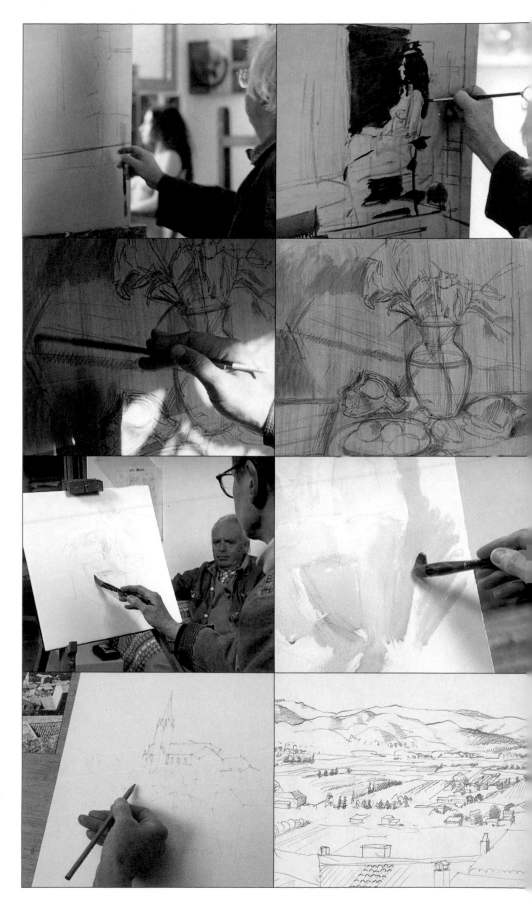

☞ **SEE ALSO**
Acrylic paint 162
Capturing water 110
Gouache 161
Painting outdoors 34
Painting skies 100
Watercolour paint 161

Keeping a sketchbook

An artist's sketchbook takes on many guises. It can be a means of recording fleeting impressions, colour notes and compositions for turning into paintings. It can be a portable scrapbook in which to collect interesting pieces of printed ephemera and pictorial references. It can be a notebook for observations and ideas that, one day, may provide that essential spark of inspiration. And if nothing else, a sketchbook gives you somewhere to develop and practise your drawing and painting skills.

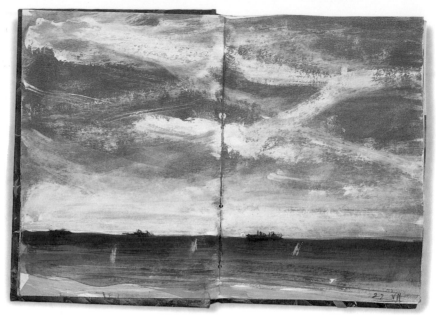

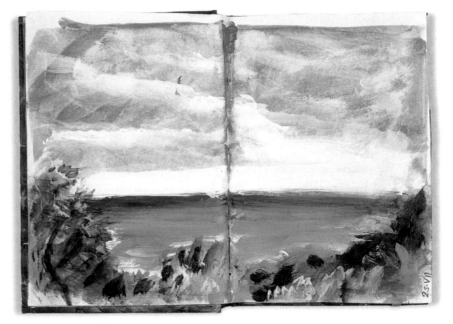

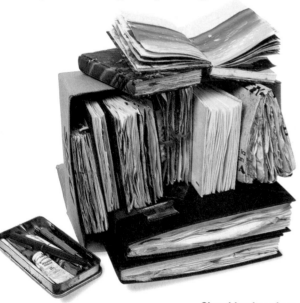

Sketching in colour
Water-soluble paints and pencils have obvious advantages, particularly when you are sketching outdoors. Illustrated here are pages from a sketchbook in which the artist was able to make simple colour studies of changing weather and varying light conditions from a single viewpoint. Colour sketching provides the ideal opportunity for experimenting with style and technique.

Simon Jennings
SEA AND SKY STUDIES
Mixed media on paper
15 x 21cm (6 x 8¼in

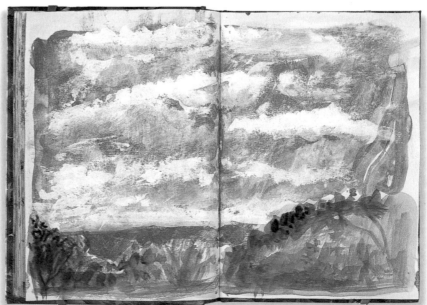

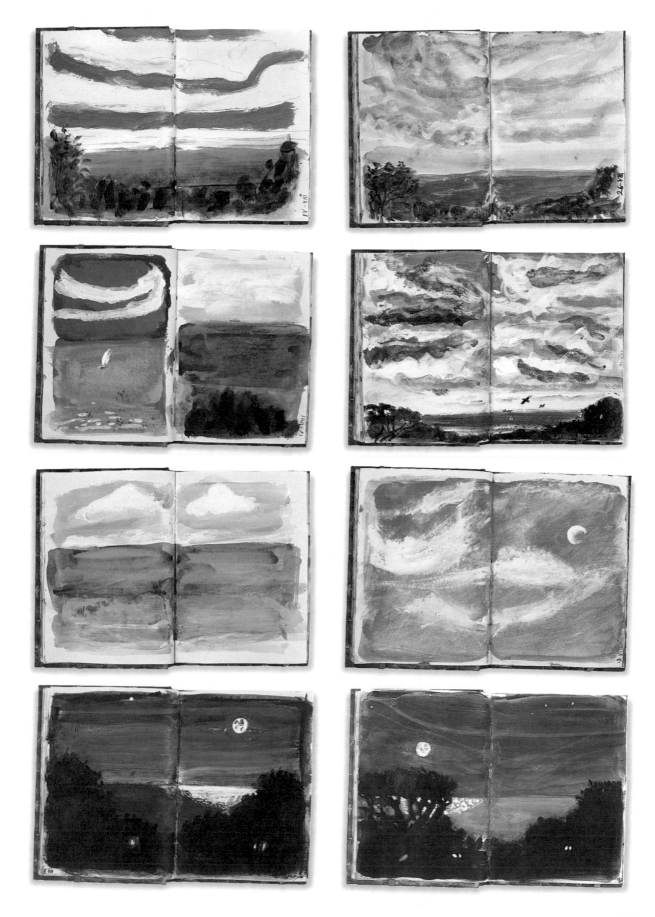

17

Collecting resources and references

Objets trouvés
Cheap to obtain and fun to collect, other people's junk makes fascinating subjects for still-life paintings.

Artists are invariably avid collectors of what to the uninitiated eye is nothing short of junk. Accumulating anything and everything of interest is a fascinating and often amusing way to build an invaluable resource of objects for the still-life table. Printed ephemera and reproductions can inspire ideas for paintings and provide visual information that may be difficult to acquire first-hand. They also constitute a rich yet inexpensive source of material for collages.

In the world of art, 'copying' is a time-honoured way of learning to paint and draw. Traditionally, students were encouraged to make studies of what were known as 'antiques' – plaster casts of statues from antiquity, usually including *Venus de Milo*, Michelangelo's *David* and fragments of the Parthenon frieze.

An organic theme
The human form features prominently in this selection of objects. We see an artist's full-figure manikin and hand, a plastic kit of the human body, and an acupuncturist's model. Together, they represent a convenient source of reference for figure drawing, obtainable at little cost. In the box there is a mummified frog found in a cellar, and a pigeon's skull retrieved from the garden.

☞ SEE ALSO
Collage 54, 185
Composing a picture from imagination 152

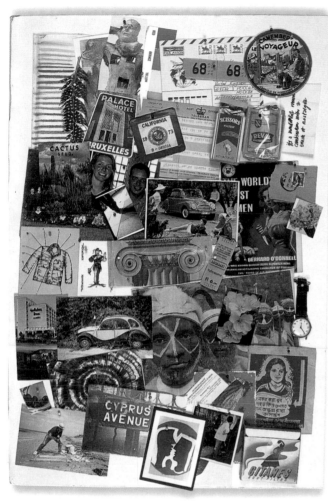

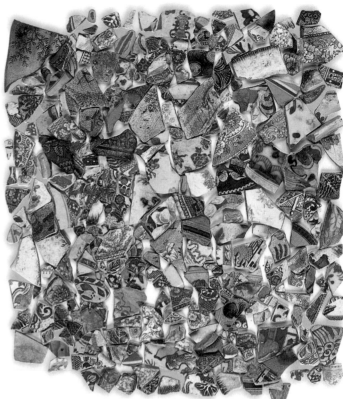

A lively interest in the world around you is an essential grounding for good observational drawing and painting. Training yourself to see with an artist's eye develops an awareness of form, colour, texture and pattern, without putting brush to canvas.

Eventually students would progress to copying Old Masters in museums and galleries. In addition, a sound knowledge of human anatomy was required before pupils were allowed to set foot in the life room. In many ways, students sought to become accomplished artists by learning to see through other people's eyes.

Today these traditional approaches to teaching have mostly been superseded by a quest for free expression and personal exploration. However, whilst slavish copying is not recommended, it is always of value to see how other artists have tackled particular themes, and you may be able to pick up useful tips on methods and materials along the way.

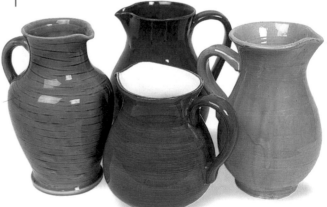

Looking for the unexpected
A trained eye can spot potential in unexceptional material. Inexpensive china and pottery can make a colourful theme for a still-life painting; and discarded shards that have no intrinsic value take on a new and surprisingly rich quality when viewed en masse.

Choosing your medium

The seemingly infinite variety of styles and painting techniques stems not only from the immense diversity of the human race, but is also strongly influenced by the availability of a vast range of art materials. Within each medium, every colour has its own characteristics to be discovered and exploited; and when different binders are used, those colours take on quite different personalities. Here are some hints and tips on how to choose a painting medium that will suit you and the way you like to paint.

Your personality
The first thing to consider is you. Think about what it was that first attracted you to painting. Was it a particular painter's work, for example? Or was it a strong desire to create images of things that give you pleasure?

Choosing the medium used in pictures you like not only fuels your enthusiasm but will make it possible technically to achieve the result you are after – you'll never create a Monet cathedral by using watercolour!

Your temperament is also a consideration. If you are a careful, fastidious person who cannot be hurried, you'll probably find painting architectural studies in watercolour more appealing than, say, abstract expressionism – whereas a bubbly extrovert may have an affinity for the latter.

Space and equipment
Personal circumstances are always a deciding factor in a person's choice of medium. Having a spare room or a warm shed to work in will probably avoid complaints from the family about

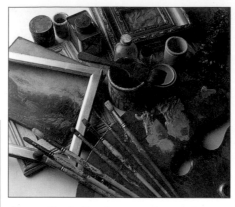

the smell of oil paints or solvents, but unless the space is roomy you won't be able to paint large canvases. Bear in mind that you will need well-organized storage space, too.

Even though it will accommodate less equipment, some artists prefer to work in a small studio because it gives them the excuse to dabble in private, only emerging when they feel confident enough to show their work. Others take pleasure in elaborate preparations before getting down to work – indeed, many a lovingly crafted home-made easel or palette has been produced without any sign of a single painting!

Perhaps you are the type of artist who is attracted to painting outdoors. Without doubt, watercolour is the most easily portable medium – but with a little planning, even oils can be taken and used on location.

The cost of getting started
Surprisingly, cost is rarely a major priority. Even art students, who have little disposable income, will buy what they need for their paintings. But cost may be the deciding factor between one medium and another – and if you can get started for a small outlay, it means you have nothing to lose and all to gain.

Millilitre for millilitre, acrylics are the cheapest; but because watercolour goes further, it does not necessarily cost more in the end. When starting out, oil painting is the most expensive, because you need more accessories. Whatever medium you choose, buy just the quantities you are likely to use in a year or two. Although many colours will last decades or more, if you don't keep the caps scrupulously clean you'll find that the paint dries out. Larger volumes are for prolific users.

Generally there are two qualities available within each medium: students' and artists'. Always buy the best-quality colours you can afford – they not only make painting more enjoyable, quicker and easier, but in some cases they are the only colours that will actually work with certain techniques.

If you've been encouraged to join an art class or accompany a friend on a painting trip, it may be best to go with the flow and choose the medium that the other artists are using. This will get you started and make it easier to learn from your colleagues. You can always break out into other media later on.

Most important, don't be deterred by negative thoughts or criticism. Forget your schooldays, when someone else was always better than you. Now you have the opportunity to blossom, with a more mature approach and enthusiasm that may produce results you never thought possible

Watercolour
This is the most popular of all painting media. Its great appeal is its immediacy – a small paintbox, a sheet of paper and a brush, and you're away. And you only require water to paint and clean up with, which also makes watercolour painting feel easy. It is such a popular medium that even when professionals specialize in other media, you'd be hard-pressed to find one that doesn't use watercolour from time to time.

Being compact and lightweight, watercolours are highly portable. You can paint on top of a mountain, or even on a bus. You need very little storage space, and a single portfolio will house dozens of paintings.

Watercolour does, however, have some hidden pitfalls, and it is a lot more difficult than it looks. You have to learn not to fiddle and overwork a painting, and to develop the knack of building up a painting without mistakes. Using the best paints certainly makes it easier; and good-quality watercolour paper is a must, otherwise your colours will be flat and lifeless. Cheap, thin paper will cockle.

When you begin to paint regularly, and especially when making larger pictures, you will find that sable brushes are worth their weight in gold. They carry as much colour as you need for one wash and respond sensitively to the slightest movement of your hand.

If your budget is limited, buy one large sable brush, rather than several small ones. It will point well for painting details, yet still have plenty of colour-carrying capacity.

Although most watercolourists use both tubes and pans, they tend to favour tube colours because you can mix stronger colours more quickly and in larger quantities. However, pans are easier to carry around, and are useful for applying the finishing touches to a picture. It's also more convenient to buy pans of colours you use infrequently.

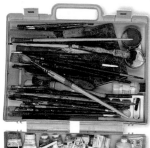

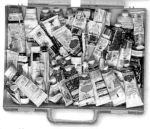

Acrylics

The second most popular medium is acrylic paint, primarily because it is so extraordinarily versatile. If you want to stick to just one range of paints, acrylics are for you. They can be applied straight from the tube, or diluted with water. You can even use them to paint your own picture frames or decorate your furniture.

Unlike other painting media, acrylics are made in different consistencies. Generally there are two types available: tube colour and pot paint, also known as 'concentrated'. Tube colour has a soft paste-like consistency, similar to oil paint. By comparison, acrylic paint sold in pots is more fluid, but it is just as good in terms of colour strength.

Concentrated acrylics should not be confused with the lower-priced craft colours – which are likely to be less permanent, and have lower pigment strength and fewer artists' colours in the range.

Liquid acrylics are available, too. In actuality, these are inks that are most often used by artists for mixed-media techniques, rather than as a medium on their own.

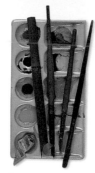

Gouache

This type of paint was not available commercially until the 1930s. In the 19th century it was known as 'body colour' and was achieved by mixing Chinese White into other watercolours, to make them opaque. Body colour was used to give extra solidity and for highlights when painting watercolours, or to create paintings from solid colour.

Today the best-quality gouache is highly pigmented, giving dense, matt, opaque colours that flow well and dry without streaks. Gouache is particularly popular with designers and illustrators, because strong, matt colours are most suitable for reproduction. Watercolourists tend to use Permanent White gouache for strong highlights. Gouache on coloured pastel paper is a popular combination among wildlife artists.

Oils

Oil paint is, without doubt, the professional's medium. Art galleries prefer oils to acrylics, and so do the public. Its popularity amongst patrons can largely be attributed to its 500-year history, and the fact that the majority of famous pictures have been executed in oils.

With painters, its appeal lies in its marvellous buttery consistency, its evocative smell and its versatility. Oils not only produce better glazes than any other paint medium, they also retain brush and knife marks exceptionally well.

Oil paint is not as difficult to handle as you might think. However, you will have to buy a number of accessories, and you need plenty of storage space for drying and keeping pictures. If you are well organized, you can keep clutter to a minimum, but a lot of painters seem to get more paint on the carpet and doorknobs than on the canvas. A word of warning for oil painters: don't ignore the technical rules. If you fail to follow the correct techniques, you can go badly wrong.

Water-mixable oil colours

The most exciting development in painting since the emergence of acrylics in the 1960s has been the introduction of water-mixable oil colours. Stringent regulations concerning the use of solvents had led to a decline in the use of oils in art schools. And as more and more people took up painting as a leisure activity, they too found oils less appealing because of the strong smell of white spirit and turpentine. Water-mixable oil colours were the answer. They have all the characteristics of traditional oils, but are both diluted and cleaned up with water.

Alkyds

These fast-drying oil colours are touch-dry within 18 to 24 hours instead of the usual 2 to 12 days. They are also more transparent than conventional oils, making them excellent for glazing. Alkyds are also perfect for painting outdoors.

Oil sticks

Oil colour can be blended with waxes to make solid painting sticks. They are wonderfully expressive, but are used up quickly if you paint large canvases. The best-quality oil sticks are superior to oil pastels, which have lower pigment strength and lower permanence.

Pastels

Although termed a painting medium, pastel technique is similar to drawing. Pastels are available in ranges comprising hundreds of pure colours. Large colour ranges are necessary because, unlike paints, pastels cannot be mixed to create secondary and tertiary colours.

Colours can be blended, however, either physically on the paper or by means of hatching. Pastels are opaque and work best on coloured backgrounds, which tend to unify a picture and sometimes help suggest a particular mood.

A disadvantage of pastel paintings is their dusty, fragile surface, which makes them difficult to store safely. This fragility is reduced by applying fixative – but don't apply fixative heavily, or the colour change will be too great. The best way of storing pastel paintings is within picture mounts, which are an extra cost but prevent the finished paintings from rubbing against each other.

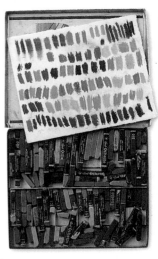

Soft pastels

The best pastels are soft and creamy, transferring just the right amount of colour to the paper. Larger pastels are preferable to the small-diameter sticks, because they break less easily and apply more colour with each stroke.

Hard pastels

Hard pastels are also available, though in more limited ranges. They are good for final definition and for applying highlights, and are particularly suited to linear work.

Water-soluble pencils and crayons

Water-soluble pencil is another drawing medium that beginners sometimes find useful in bridging the gap between drawing and painting. However, the results are not the same as those achieved by applying a conventional watercolour wash, and the quality of the pigments is not as high as those used for the best watercolours.

Thicker water-soluble crayons are also available, which are capable of producing broader marks and denser hatching, making them more of a painter's medium.

☞ SEE ALSO

Where shall I start?
MATERIALS
Choosing your medium

Appreciating the visual qualities of paint

Whatever other reasons you might have for choosing a particular medium, its visual qualities are surely the most compelling. It's not that one medium is more attractive or in some way superior to another. It has something to do with the way you feel about a picture when you look at it, and how it makes you want to paint your own pictures, using a similar medium.

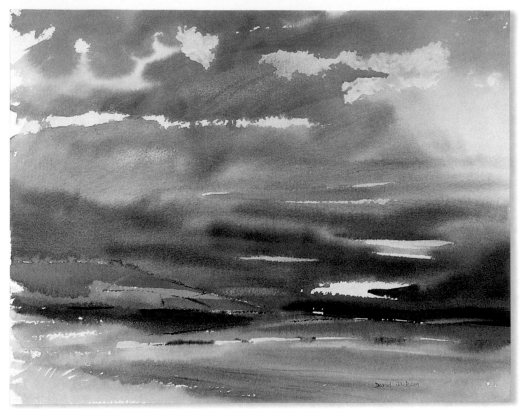

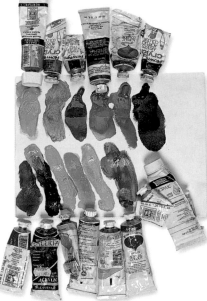

Versatility

Acrylic paint is a relative newcomer that seems to be loved and despised in equal measure. Nevertheless, its versatility as a medium has to be acknowledged. It can be applied in thin veils of fluid colour, similar in appearance to watercolour, or as thick impasted brushwork that resembles oil paint. But acrylic paint behaves quite differently from the two more-traditional painting mediums – especially in that it dries very, very quickly.

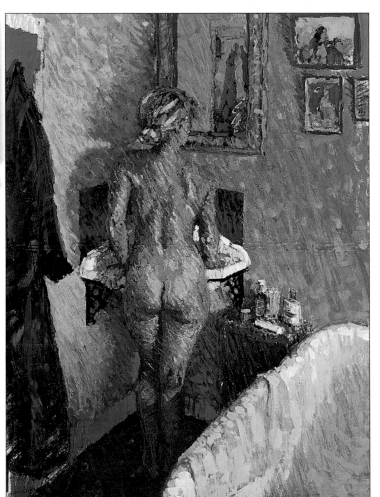

David Jackson (above)
TOWARDS WASTWATER
Watercolour on paper
46 x 58.5cm (17 x 23in)

Hugo Grenville
GIRL AT THE BASIN – MORNING
Pastel and distemper on board
91.5 x 68.5cm (36 x 27in)

Painting in various media

For the watercolour (opposite), the artist has employed the conventional wet-in-wet technique, whereby paint is applied as thin staining washes. When dry, the paint is nothing more than flat colour on paper.

In the bold landscape painting (right), we see the other end of the textural scale with the application of an opaque buttery medium, in this case oils. The paint has distinct physical properties in the form of clearly defined knife marks and brushstrokes. Similar surface textures can be created using acrylic paint.

The lively figure study (opposite) relies for its effect on mixed-media – traditional home-made distemper and soft pastel. The small juxtaposed marks of bold colour create the illusion known as optical mixing.

The beach scene (below) is painted in pastels, which have been blended and softened to give an overall painterly effect of colour and tone.

The sketches of a village street (bottom right) have been executed in tempera, a fast-drying water-based medium with good opacity. Gouache and acrylics are ideal, too, for sketching on location and for making colour notes.

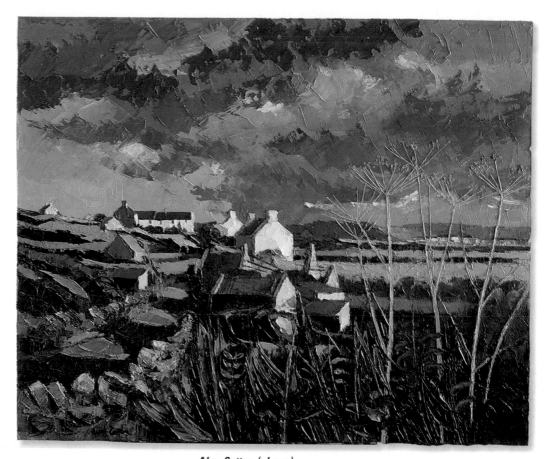

Alan Cotton (above)
CO. KERRY – COTTAGES
AT VENTRY HARBOUR
Oil on canvas
76 x 91.5 cm (30 x 36in)

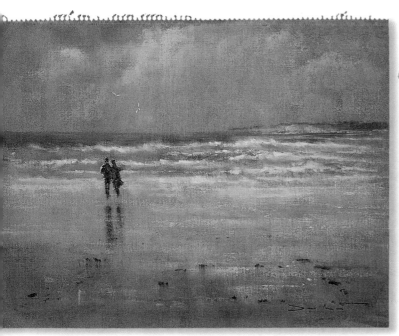

David Mynett
WET SANDS
Pastel on sketchbook page
30.5 x 40.5cm (12 x 16in)

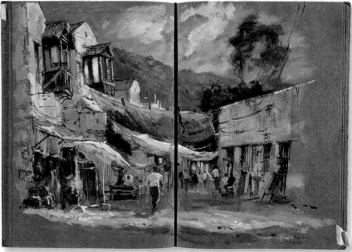

David Mynett
KALKAN – SOUTHERN TURKEY
Tempera on sketchbook pages
30.5 x 40.5cm (12 x 16in)

23

Where shall I start?
A PLACE TO WORK
Planning
Equipment
Lighting
Easels
Storage

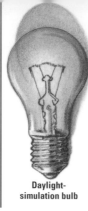

Organizing your studio

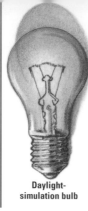

Daylight-simulation bulb

Every artist dreams of having a dedicated studio for his or her sole use, but that is not an essential requisite for good painting. You can work almost as well in a shared space, so long as there is room for you to leave your paints and materials set out ready for you to resume work when the mood strikes you. With a little planning, it is easy to provide a practical solution to meet your needs, but a studio should be stimulating as well as efficient – and for that, you need to stamp your own personality on the place.

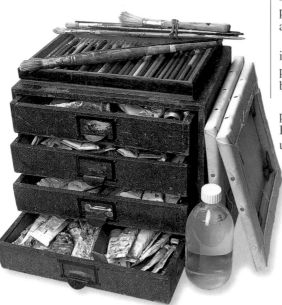

Artificial lighting

Good lighting is essential to prevent eyestrain and to render colours accurately. When levels of natural light are low, you need good artificial lighting, preferably ceiling-mounted fluorescent lamps fitted with blue-tinted daylight tubes. To provide an even spread of light and avoid any problems with shadows, install at least two fluorescent fittings. For table-top work, use an adjustable lamp, also fitted with a daylight bulb.

Natural lighting

Natural light from a large north-facing window is ideal (south-facing in the Southern Hemisphere), since it provides even, neutral-coloured illumination that remains constant throughout the day.

Workstations

If you don't like to work flat on a table, support your paintings on a table-top easel. Made from wood or metal, this type of easel can be adjusted to different angles and folded flat for storage.

Most artists set out their painting materials on the worktable. But a mobile storage box or trolley may be more convenient, since you can move it from table to studio easel.

Storing materials and paintings

Ideally, works on paper should be laid flat in a plan chest or, if space is limited, stored in a strong portfolio. For added protection, interleave your work with acid-free tissue paper.

A bank of shallow wall-hung shelves is useful for storing reference books, props, boxed materials, storage pots for brushes, even wet canvases.

Store your stretched canvases in a partitioned rack mounted on castors. If there is room, you can park the rack under your worktable.

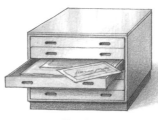

Plan chest

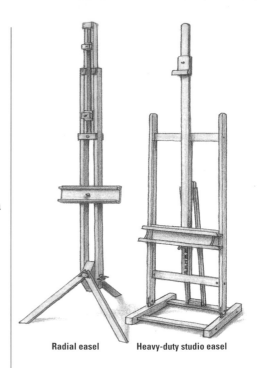

Radial easel   **Heavy-duty studio easel**

Studio easels

If you plan to produce large paintings, you will want to buy a floor-standing studio easel. Heavy-duty easels, usually made from wood, have a strong base frame. Less expensive versions, in wood or aluminium, have tripod legs. All easels are adjustable in height and angle, so that you are able to sit or stand while you paint. If you work from a wheel-chair, tripod designs allow you to get closer to the painting.

To avoid throwing your shadow across the work, set up the easel so that the light source is to one side and over your shoulder.

All-purpose studio (opposite)

A well-equipped studio can be installed relatively cheaply in a spare room or small outbuilding. Your first requirement is a dry, adequately heated space that is light and airy. Since it is practically impossible to paint without creating a mess, it pays to make surfaces easy to clean. Plain white-painted walls make the most of available light, and can be washed down when necessary. Choose a smooth floorcovering such as sheet vinyl or tiles, or sealed strip-wood flooring. Have a sink installed, or make sure there is a water supply close by. Get a large bin for waste, and put flammable rags in a metal bin with a tightly fitting lid.

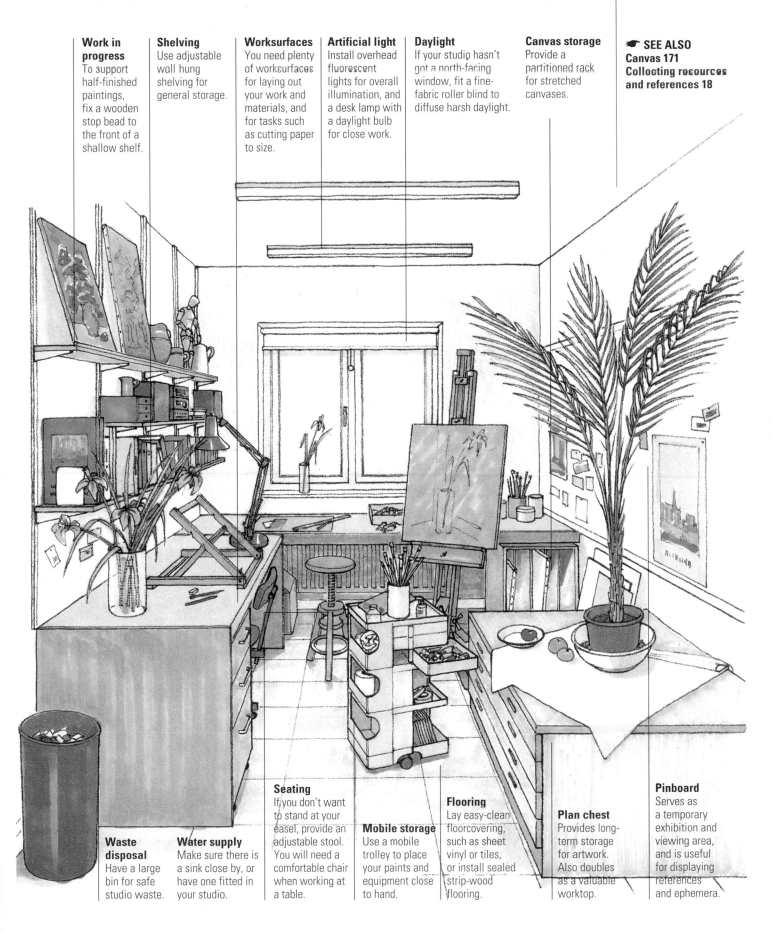

Work in progress
To support half-finished paintings, fix a wooden stop bead to the front of a shallow shelf.

Shelving
Use adjustable wall hung shelving for general storage.

Worksurfaces
You need plenty of worksurfaces for laying out your work and materials, and for tasks such as cutting paper to size.

Artificial light
Install overhead fluorescent lights for overall illumination, and a desk lamp with a daylight bulb for close work.

Daylight
If your studio hasn't got a north-facing window, fit a fine-fabric roller blind to diffuse harsh daylight.

Canvas storage
Provide a partitioned rack for stretched canvases.

☞ **SEE ALSO**
Canvas 171
Collecting resources and references 18

Waste disposal
Have a large bin for safe studio waste.

Water supply
Make sure there is a sink close by, or have one fitted in your studio.

Seating
If you don't want to stand at your easel, provide an adjustable stool. You will need a comfortable chair when working at a table.

Mobile storage
Use a mobile trolley to place your paints and equipment close to hand.

Flooring
Lay easy-clean floorcovering, such as sheet vinyl or tiles, or install sealed strip-wood flooring.

Plan chest
Provides long-term storage for artwork. Also doubles as a valuable worktop.

Pinboard
Serves as a temporary exhibition and viewing area, and is useful for displaying references and ephemera.

25

Where shall I start?
GALLERY
Choosing a subject

Classic themes and approaches

When choosing subjects to paint, the majority of artists turn to the classic themes – still life, landscape, interiors, wildlife, portraiture and figure painting. There are, of course, many variations on these themes. Still life alone can encompass anything from a single object to a complex group of fruit and flowers. Townscapes, seascapes, sky studies and gardens are merely different forms of landscape painting. And when artists construct pictures purely from imagination, any or all the classic themes could be combined in a single picture.

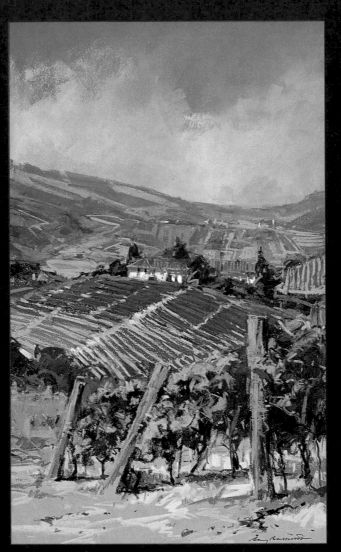

Interpreting subjects
Ranging from a quintessential landscape to a striking nude study, this selection of pictures illustrates how a handful of artists drew inspiration from the classic painting themes. The potential for individual interpretation is further exemplified by a table-top still life, an intimate domestic scene, a view across a sun-dappled garden, and a stylistic representation of an artist's nightmare.

Presented on the following pages is a gallery of pictures that reflect the popular subjects to which artists return again and again. These pictures have been selected to show as wide a variety of painting styles as possible. But whatever you decide to paint, let it be your own choice and be sure to give your personal style full rein.

Ray Balkwill
VINEYARDS NEAR ALBA
Pastel on paper
53 x 35.5cm (21 x 14in)

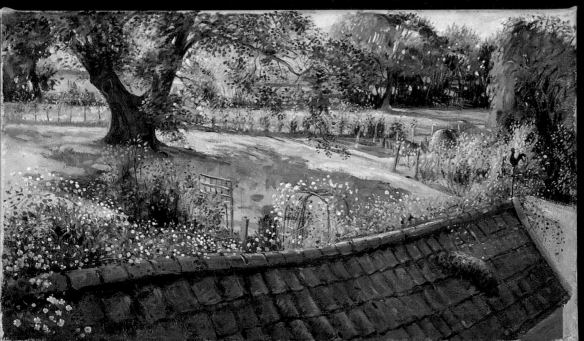

Timothy Easton
ROOF RIDGE WITH ROSES
Oil on canvas
20 x 35.5cm (8 x 14in)

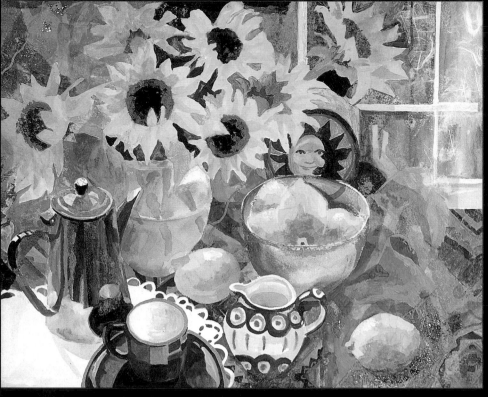

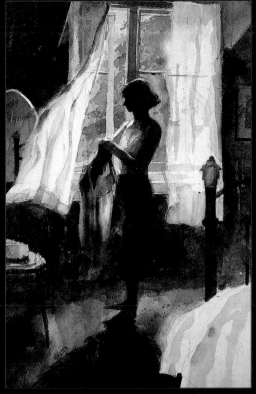

Anuk Naumann (above)
SUNFLOWERS AND LEMONS
Mixed media on paper
35.5 x 53cm (14 x 21in)

John Lidzey (above)
A WOMAN DRESSING
AT THE DELL
Watercolour on paper
50.5 x 35.5cm (20 x 14in)

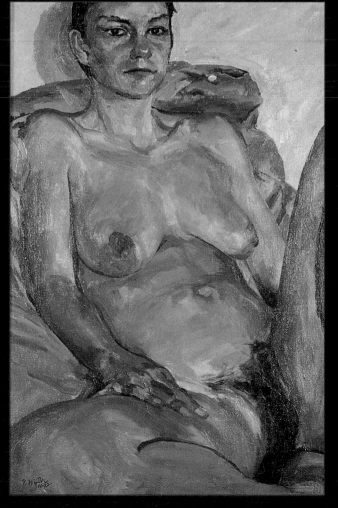

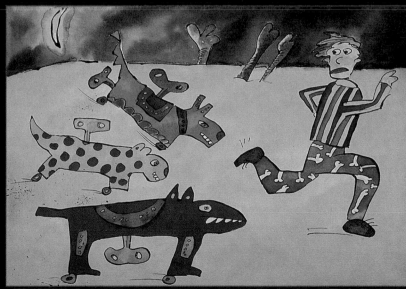

Valerie Wiffen
SAXOPHONIST
Oil on canvas
40.5 x 30cm (16 x 12in)

Chris Perry
CLOCKWORK DOGS
Acrylic on hardboard
56 x 81cm (22 x 32in)

Still life

Painting inanimate objects, either singly or in arranged groups, has obvious appeal – it's so easy to control. You can select and compose the objects at your leisure, pick a background that sets off the still life to advantage, choose the direction and form of lighting that gives you the required mood and, perhaps more importantly, you can take up and lay down your brushes at your convenience.

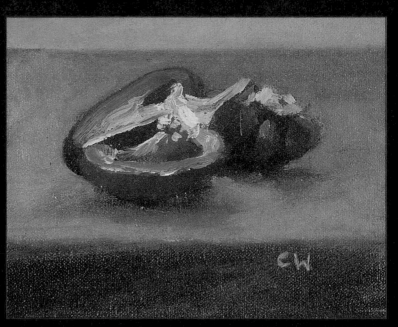

Colin Willey
RED PEPPER
Oil on canvas
5 x 6in (13 x 15cm)

Peter Kelly (below)
THE RED VASE
Oil on canvas
17 x 13in (43 x 33cm)

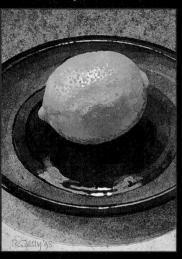

Ronald Jesty
JUST A LEMON
Watercolor on paper
7 x 5in (18 x 13cm)

From a single fruit to a kitchen dresser

Still-life painting offers such a variety of possibilities. Some artists enjoy making careful and detailed studies of simple objects, and will gain tremendous satisfaction from precisely rendering the skin of a fruit. For others, the exhilaration comes from painting more complex arrangements of their favourite flowers and colorful props.

For most painters, the object is to make their still-life paintings look as natural as possible, but a formal arrangement of props can lend a quite different, almost surreal, atmosphere to a painting.

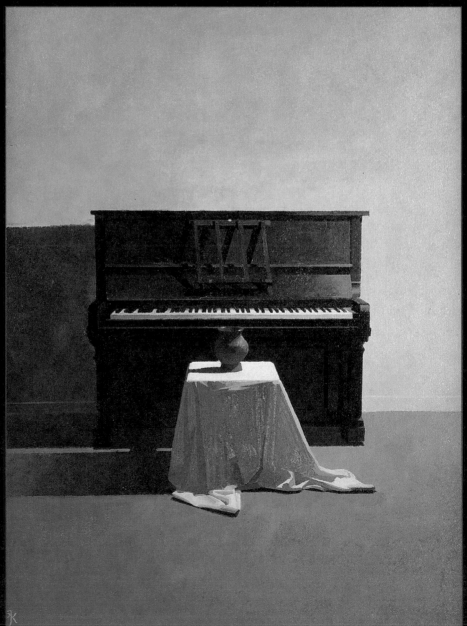

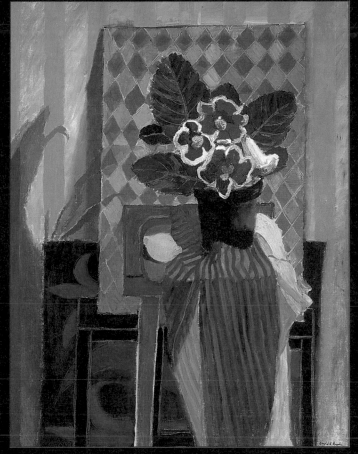

David Martin (right)
STILL LIFE WITH GLOXINIA
Oil on canvas
40 x 30in (101.5 x 76cm)

John Mitchell
STUDIO WINDOW
Watercolor
on paper
13 x 10in
(33 x 25cm)

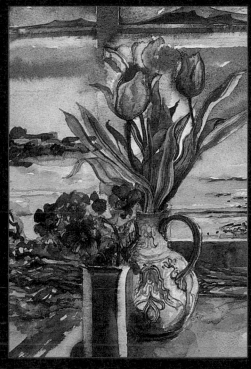

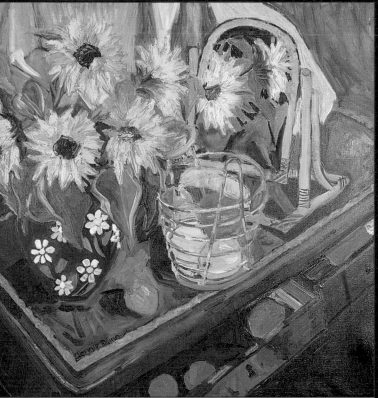

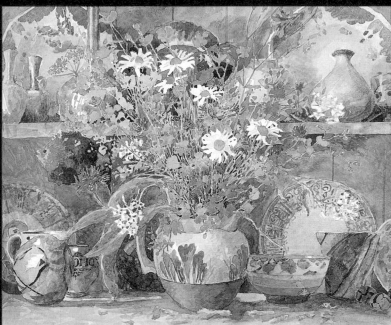

Jennie Dunn (left)
SUNFLOWERS TOO
Oil on canvas
24 x 26in (61 x 66cm)

Annie Williams
THE CROCUS JUG
Watercolor on paper
15 x 16½in (38 x 42cm)

29

Rooms and interiors

Throughout history, artists have painted their familiar surroundings, often providing us with intimate snapshots that reveal the details of their personal lives. But if you are prepared to step into the wider world, there are also exciting possibilities for painting in public spaces, such as pubs, restaurants, railway stations and historical buildings.

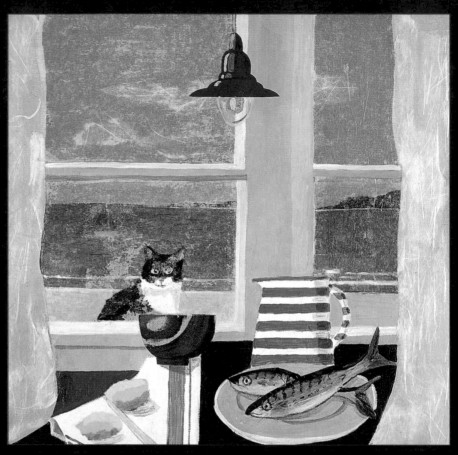

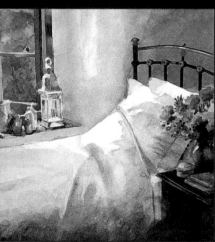

John Lidzey (left)
COTTAGE BEDROOM
Watercolour on paper
30 x 30cm (12 x 12in)

Anuk Naumann (above)
A MACKEREL FOR SUPPER
Mixed media on paper
25 x 25cm (10 x 10in)

Debra Manifold (below)
THE LADY CHAPEL
GLASTONBURY ABBEY
Acrylic on board
53 x 76cm (21 x 30in)

Inside outside

Painting a small corner of your own room is akin to painting a still life – you choose the viewpoint, rearrange the furniture to suit your composition and, if you don't already own suitable props to enrich the scene, you can buy, borrow or even invent them. You can also adjust or supplement ambient lighting to throw shadows exactly where you want them.

When you set up your easel to take in a wider view of an interior, daylight almost invariably plays a part. Strong, even diffused, light from a window can transform a scene, creating bold shadows or shafts of light and bringing the room to life with sparkling highlights and intriguing reflections.

In many instances, an artist uses a window to frame the view beyond, creating, in a single picture, a back-lit still life, an interior and a landscape.

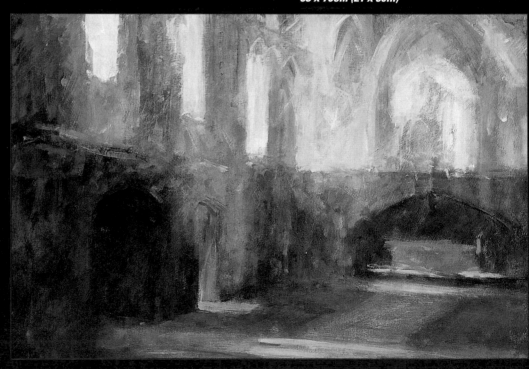

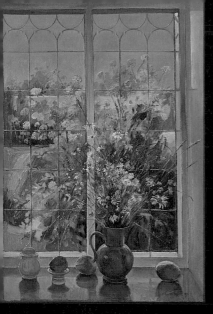

Timothy Easton (above)
SUMMER FLOWERS AT DUSK
Oil on canvas
58 x 40.5cm (23 x 16in)

Gerald Green (below)
INTERIOR
Watercolour on paper
35 x 25cm (13¾ x 10in)

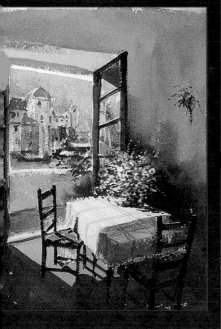

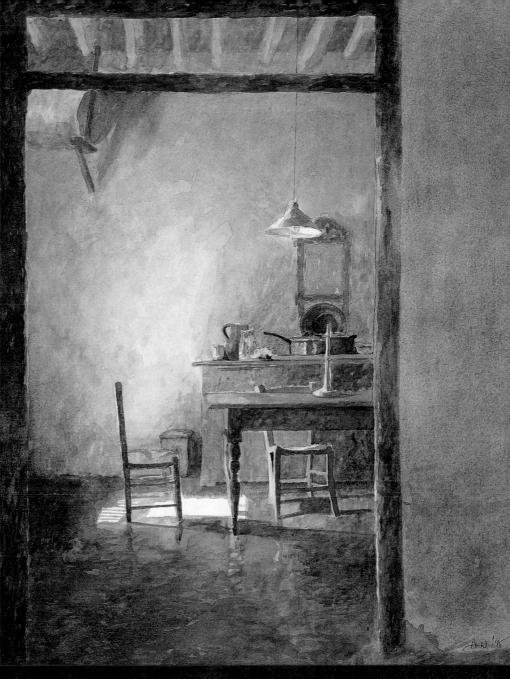

Annie Williams (above)
THE KITCHEN
Watercolour on paper
58.5 x 45.5cm (23 x 18in)

Peter Kelly
TABLE – CHATEAU
CHAMP DE BATAILLE
Oil on canvas
35.5 x 53.5cm (12 x 21in)

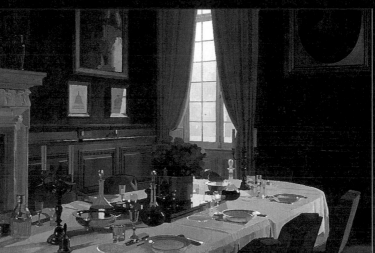

31

Buildings and townscapes

The urban landscape is a fascinating subject for painters. Some beginners find the disciplines of perspective a little daunting, but the opportunities for including a rich variety of colour, texture and copious detail make townscapes and individual buildings irresistible subjects.

Brian Lancaster (below)
THE WATCHTOWER
Watercolour on paper
34 x 52cm (13½ x 20½in)

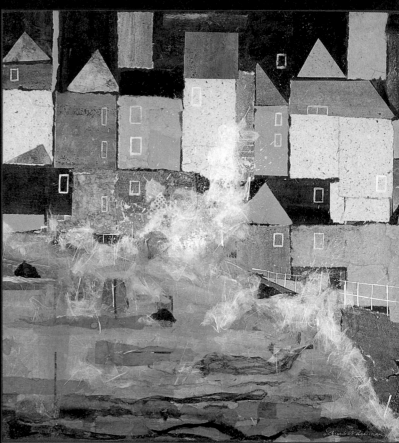

Anuk Naumann
SEAWALL ST. IVES
Mixed media on paper
30 x 30cm (12 x 12in)

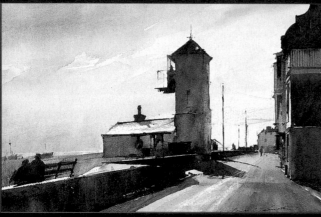

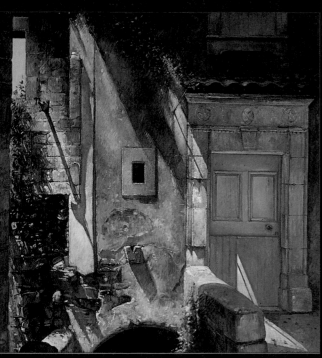

Timothy Easton
NOON SHADOWS
Oil on canvas
76 x 71cm (30 x 28in)

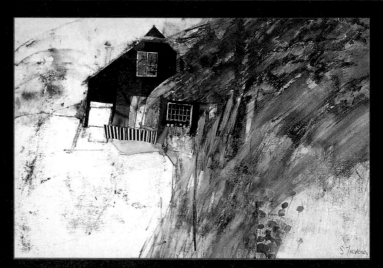

Shirley Trevena
HOUSE BY THE FOREST
Mixed media on paper
27.5 x 39.5cm (10¾ x 15½in)

Buildings make a difference

Look around you, and you can hardly fail to see buildings that could make interesting additions to your paintings. Some merely nestle into a conventional landscape, providing a pleasing contrast to natural forms and colours. In other locations, the buildings might constitute the focal point of a painting, with industrial complexes or street scenes full of life and bustle. Whether you choose to document your own town or village, or bring home sketchbook reminders of a holiday abroad, there are countless opportunities for painting buildings and townscapes.

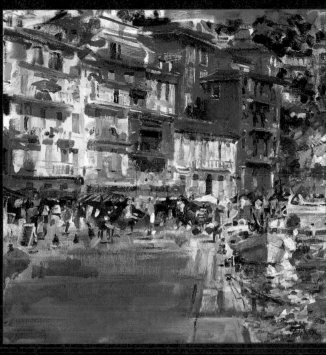

Peter Graham
LA BELLE PROMENADE, VILLEFRANCHE-SUR-MER
Oil on canvas
66 x 65.5cm (26 x 25¾in)

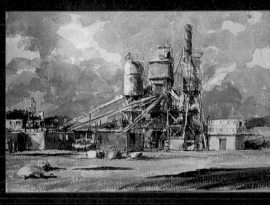

Gerald Green (below)
INDUSTRIAL PLANT
Watercolour on paper
35 x 53cm (13¾ x 21in)

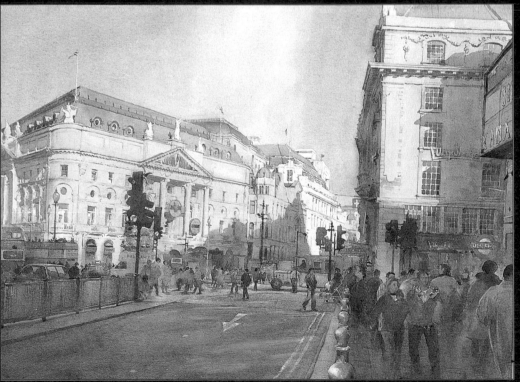

David Curtis
CITY CROWDS – PICCADILLY
Watercolour on paper
57 x 77.5cm (22½ x 30½in)

Painting outdoors

Many inexperienced artists are reluctant to work in public; but once they have overcome their initial shyness, they discover the exhilaration that comes from painting directly from nature. The challenges presented by the weather and fleeting light may force you to develop the ability to work quickly, and you may have to put up with a little discomfort – but it's the sights, sounds and smells of the living landscape that give outdoor painting its singular vitality.

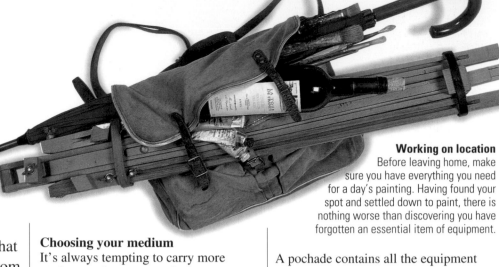

Working on location
Before leaving home, make sure you have everything you need for a day's painting. Having found your spot and settled down to paint, there is nothing worse than discovering you have forgotten an essential item of equipment.

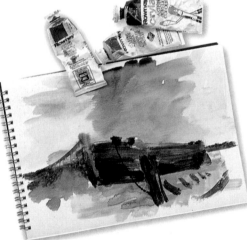

Making a start
Many artists like to record their initial impressions on location, then finish the painting at home. Others like to paint in the studio, using preparatory sketch drawings and colour notes taken on the spot. Although some prefer to work from photographic references, especially as an aid to composition, very few painters rely on photographs for accurate colour rendering.

Choosing your medium
It's always tempting to carry more equipment than you need – but once you have made a few forays into the countryside carrying a loaded rucksack, you soon learn to keep your kit to the bare minimum.

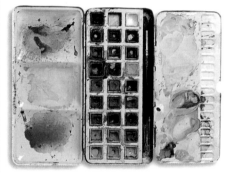

A traditional watercolour box is designed to be portable

Watercolours and acrylics have obvious advantages. Both dry relatively quickly and need only water as a diluent. Unless you want to work on relatively large paintings, a portable watercolour box containing small pans is marginally more convenient than tubes of paint. Some boxes also include storage for water; if not, carry a plastic water bottle to save weight. For expediency, use small tubes of acrylic paint, and buy a stay-wet palette to help keep the paint moist. Cover the palette with clingfilm before carrying it home.

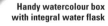

Handy watercolour box with integral water flask

A pochade contains all the equipment you need for oil painting, including a palette. To save cleaning your palette, cover it with clingfilm before you start work; you can then peel it off afterwards and throw it away. Alternatively, use a disposable paper palette.

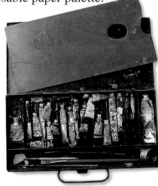

Oil painter's pochade box

Personal considerations
For long sittings, you need to protect yourself from the elements.

In summer, wear a broad-brim hat and a long-sleeve shirt, or protect your skin with high-factor sunscreen cream. It's also a good idea to keep insect repellent in your bag. A sunshade will help keep you cool and protect your painting from glare. If you plan to work for the whole day, remember to take a picnic lunch and plenty to drink.

In winter, wrap up warmly and wear stout waterproof footwear. To keep your hands warm but maintain your sense of touch, wear fingerless gloves.

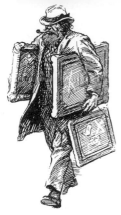

Optimum size

Don't be too ambitious when painting outdoors. Limit the size of your work to about 38 x 50cm (15 x 20in), otherwise your canvas may be awkward to carry and could become unstable, especially in breezy conditions.

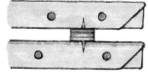

Double-pointed canvas pins

Transporting wet canvases

Insert a double-pointed canvas pin at each corner, and use another stretched canvas or a softboard panel to protect a wet oil painting.

Sketchbooks and drawing boards

A hand-held sketchbook needs no support, but you could utilize a small office clipboard to carry separate sheets of paper. Buy a lightweight folding table from a camping-equipment supplier if you prefer to work flat.

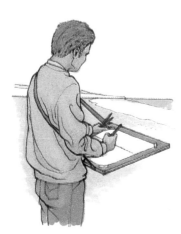

Working standing up

Holding larger drawing boards is tiring. Attach a canvas or leather strap to two corners of your board, and take the weight on your shoulder.

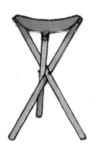

Folding stool

A compact folding stool lets you work in reasonable comfort. Some backpacks are made to carry a folding canvas stool.

Choosing an easel

If you prefer to work standing up, use an adjustable easel. A sketching easel is easy to carry, but you may have to stake the legs to the ground on windy days. A box easel is a sturdier portable platform. It combines a tripod easel with a carrying case for your paints, palette and small canvases. The pull-out drawer is convenient for supporting your palette.

Sketching easel   **Box easel**

A portable studio

Many outdoor painters transport their equipment in large soft bags or haversacks (above); but a compartmentalized toolbox or art box (below), with lift-out or hinged trays, is ideal for carrying all those loose materials that are easily mislaid outdoors. Choose a lightweight plastic box, but make sure it has strong carrying handles.

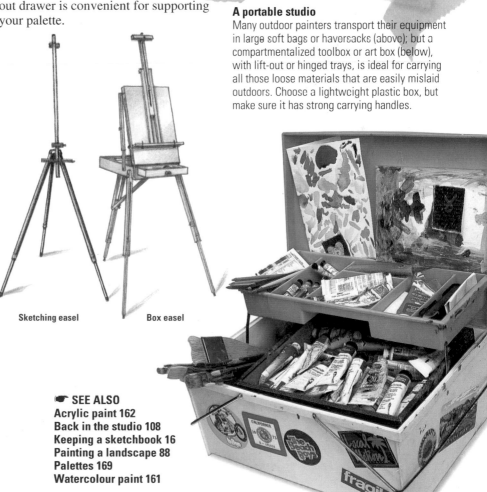

☛ SEE ALSO
Acrylic paint 162
Back in the studio 108
Keeping a sketchbook 16
Painting a landscape 88
Palettes 169
Watercolour paint 161

Landscapes

The classic open landscape has a broad appeal. It not only provides the unique experience of working directly from nature, but also offers challenging opportunities for capturing almost limitless nuances of light and atmosphere. The more intimate 'close' landscape is characterized by comparatively detailed and sometimes colourful imagery, epitomized by a formal garden or dense woodland.

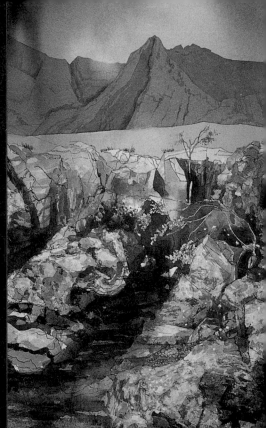

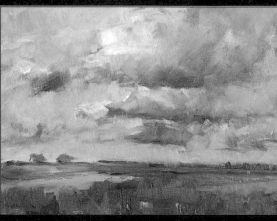

Timothy Easton (below)
BUDDLEIA AND LAVENDER FIELD
Oil on canvas
25.5 x 30.5cm (10 x 12in)

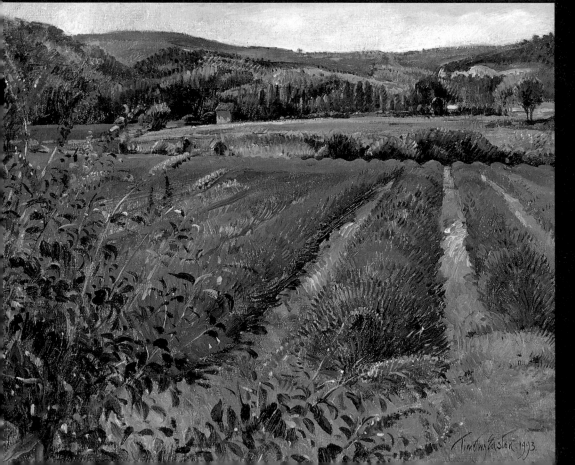

Debra Manifold (top left)
CORNER OF THE WOODS
Pastel on sandpaper
51 x 63.5cm (20 x 25in)

Colin Willey (centre left)
RECEDING CLOUDS
Oil on board
20 x 25.5cm (8 x 10in)

John Mitchell (above)
SGURR AN FHEADAIN
Mixed media on paper
57 x 41cm (22½ x 16in)

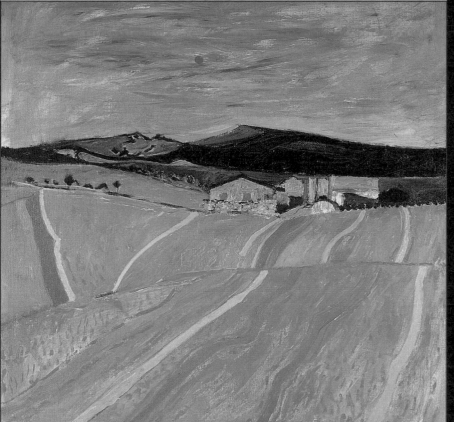

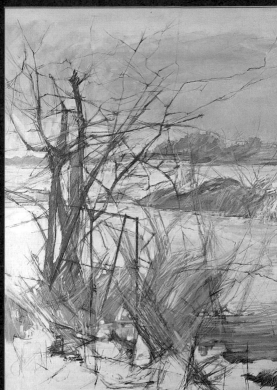

David Martin (above)
After the harvest, Cupar
Oil on canvas
91.5 x 91.5cm (36 x 36in)

The natural landscape

Landscape is a genre that accommodates any style and treatment, from the semi-abstract to highly finished realism. Artists seem able to relax in front of a landscape, re-creating the easy-flowing lines, shapes and textures of nature. Furthermore, there isn't a single medium that does not lend itself to landscape painting, although some are perhaps more suited to studio painting than to working *en plein air*.

John Blockley
Moorland road
Watercolour on paper
30.5 x 46cm (12 x 18in)

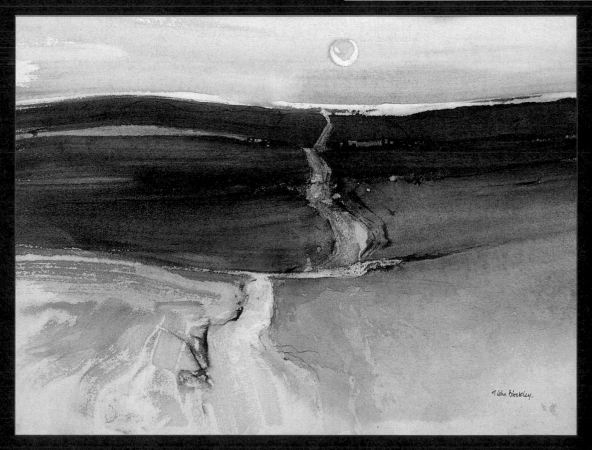

Water and seascapes

There are few landscape artists who have not at some time been drawn to paint seascapes and other scenes featuring water. Whether a tranquil lake or breaking waves, water always adds drama to a picture. In fact, the sea and nautical subjects can be so compelling that some artists make marine painting their life's work.

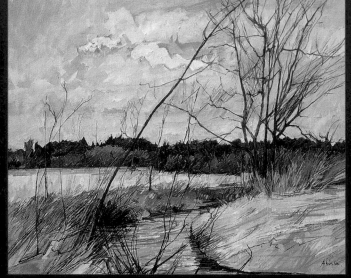

Anthony Atkinson (left)
BEND IN THE RIVER
NEAR LANGHAM
Oil on canvas
63.5 x 76cm (25 x 30in)

Timothy Easton (below)
NETTLE, WILLOWHERB AND LILY PADS
Oil on canvas
25 x 35.5cm (10 x 14in)

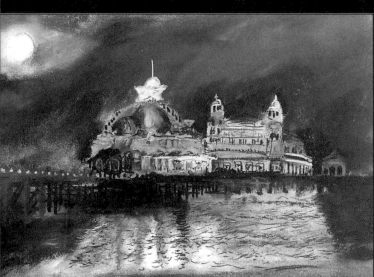

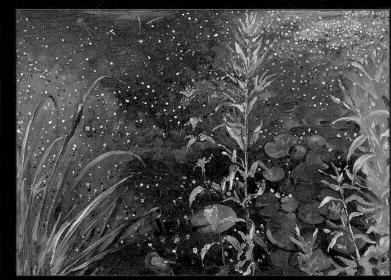

Chris Perry (above)
FULL MOON WEST PIER
Pastel on paper
30 x 42cm (11¾ x 16½in)

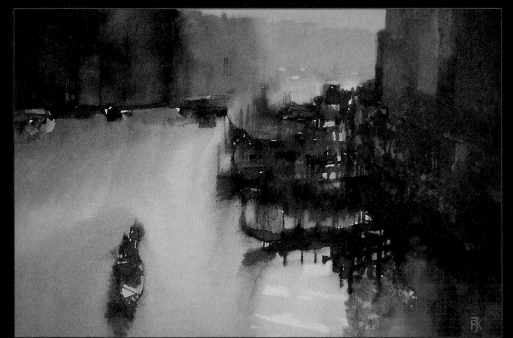

Peter Kelly
SUNLIGHT AND RAIN ON
THE GRAND CANAL
Oil on canvas
28 x 38cm (11 x 15in)

Beautiful obsession

If you are so inclined, painting water can easily become an obsession. From the reflections and play of light across a garden pond to the hypnotic motion of the sea, with its elusive textures of spray and foam, there is so much to paint. Water also provides the perfect foil for other elements in the landscape, be they mountains or buildings mirrored in a flat surface, or waterside plants and trees screened against a backdrop of shimmering colour.

Anuk Naumann (below)
ROUGH SEA
Mixed media on paper
40.5 x 40.5cm (16 x 16in)

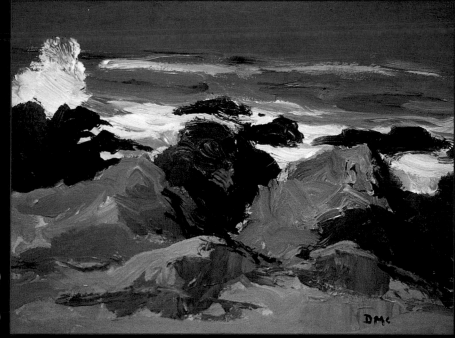

Donald McIntyre (left)
GREEN SEA
Acrylic on board
30.5 x 41cm (12 x 16in)

Brian Lancaster (below)
TIMES OF CHANGE
Watercolour on paper
25 x 34cm (10 x 13½in)

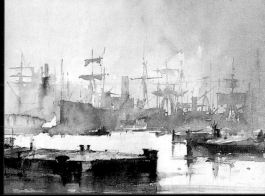

Ronald Jesty (below)
HANDFAST POINT
Watercolour on paper
45.5 x 45.5cm (18 x 18in)

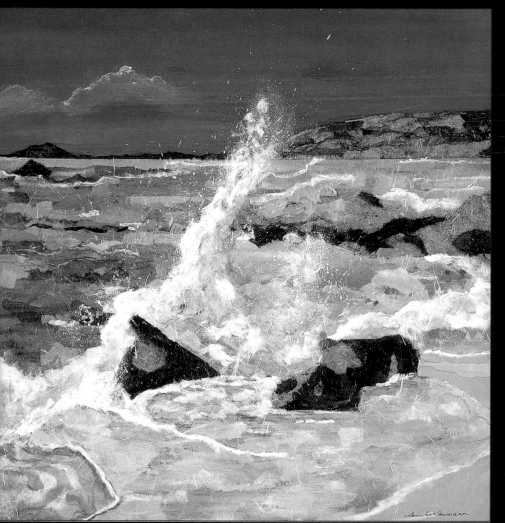

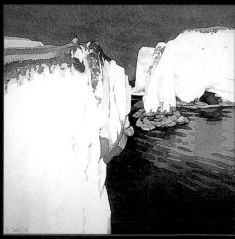

Figures and portraits

Figure painting and portraiture must be among the oldest artistic traditions, and the urge to depict the human form is as strong as ever. There are few subjects that hold such a fascination for artists, and fewer still that offer such a wealth of subtlety and variety.

Painting individuals and groups

You will no doubt want to tackle a nude study or clothed figure, either at a local life-painting class or in your own studio. But it is also worth going out into the street, or into cafés and bars where you can sketch interesting groups of figures and individuals. The workplace and sports clubs offer opportunities for observing people engaged in more-active pursuits.

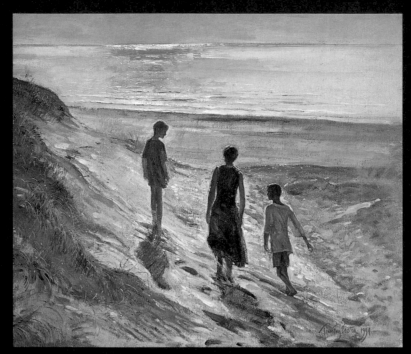

Timothy Easton (left)
DOWN TO THE SEA
Oil on canvas
30 x 35.5cm (12 x 14in)

Debra Manifold (below)
LUNCHTIME AT THE CAFÉ ROUGE
Acrylic on board
76 x 48cm (30 x 19in)

Timothy Easton (below)
RETURNING THE BLADES, HENLEY
Oil on canvas
30 x 25cm (12 x 10in)

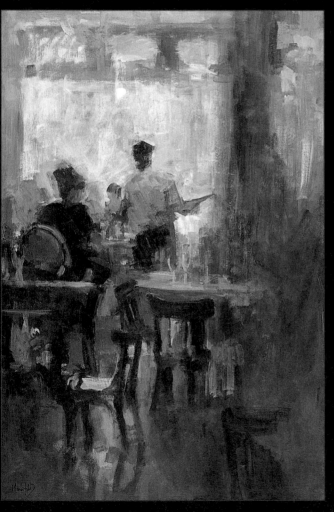

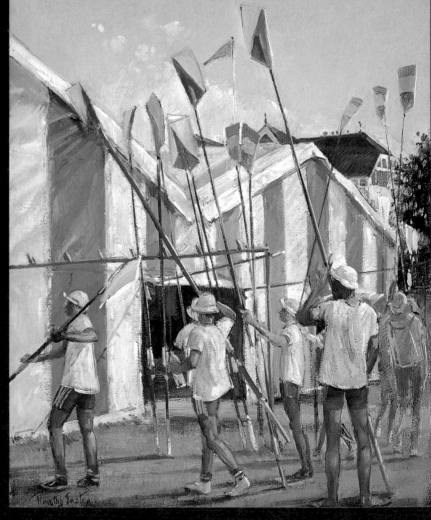

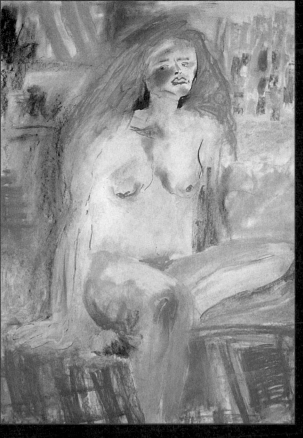

Chris Perry (left)
TINA
**Pastel on paper
84 x 61cm (33 x 24in)**

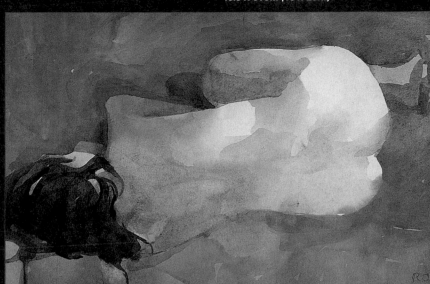

Ronald Jesty (below)
RED NUDE
**Watercolour on paper
40.5 x 51cm (16 x 20in)**

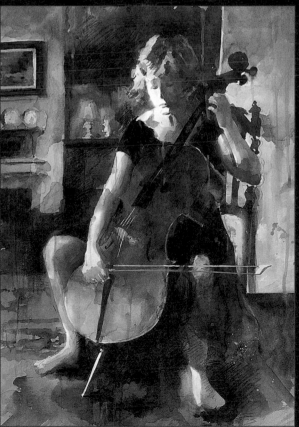

John Lidzey (below left)
ANNA PLAYING THE CELLO
**Watercolour on paper
66 x 45.5cm (26 x 18in)**

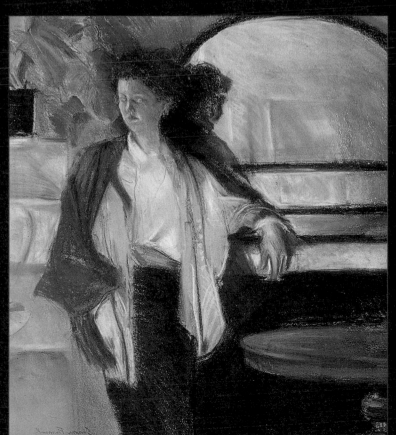

Sharon Finmark (below)
THE MIRROR
**Pastel on paper
132 x 120cm (52 x 48in)**

Where shall I start?
GALLERY
Classic themes
and approaches

Portraits

In the face of strong competition from the camera, paintings of colleagues, family and friends constitute a unique personal record. Although we tend to think of a portrait as being a head-and-shoulders likeness of the sitter, there is much to be said for stepping back to take in the full figure. This may allow you to include a glimpse of the sitter's home, and perhaps incorporate their pets or partner. And don't forget the self-portrait – a time-honoured genre that enables you to work at your own speed and at your convenience.

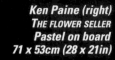

Ken Paine (right)
THE FLOWER SELLER
Pastel on board
71 x 53cm (28 x 21in)

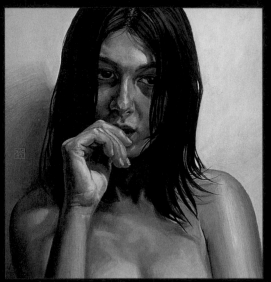

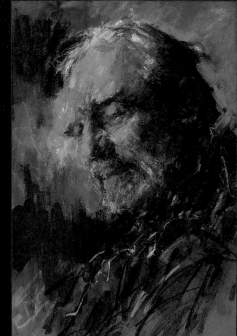

David Cobley (right)
GIRL WITH WET HAIR
Oil on canvas
51 x 51cm (20 x 20in)

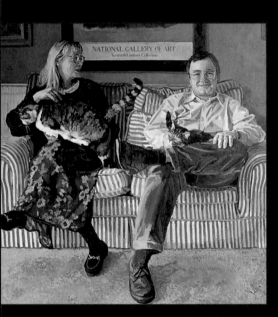

Alastair Adams
MR AND MRS G. POSTON AND CATS
Acrylic on MDF board
101.5x 101.5cm (40 x 40in)

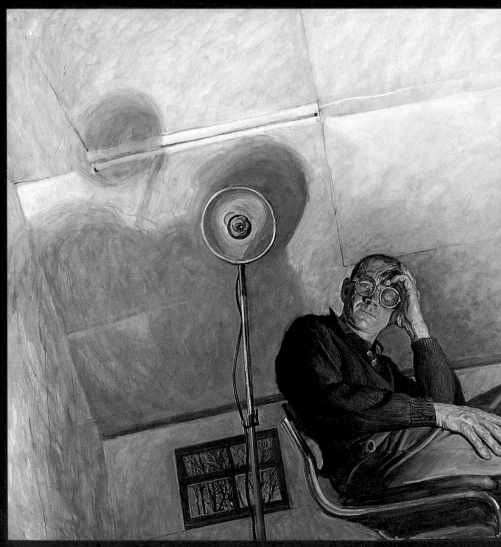

David Cobley
DOUBT – SELF-PORTRAIT
Oil on canvas
168 x 168cm (66 x 66in)

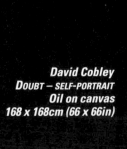

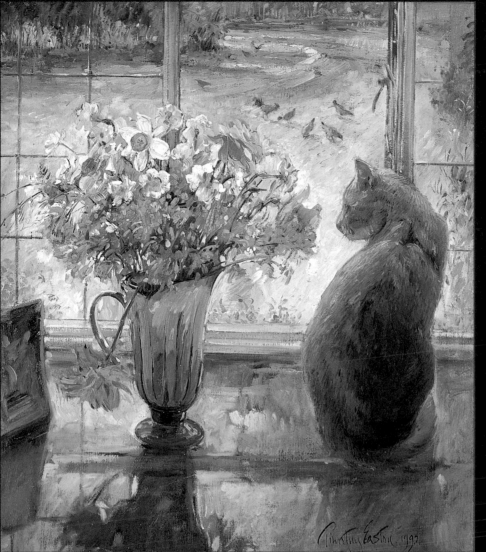

Timothy Easton (left)
STRIPED JUG WITH SPRING FLOWERS
Oil on canvas
40.5 x 35.5cm (16 x 14in)

Wildlife painting

It takes a special talent, and not a little dedication, to capture the unique qualities of animals and birds in their natural surroundings. But there is much to be gained from painting the delightful diversity of wildlife and other animals – including those that are literally on your doorstep, in the form of domestic animals and pets.

Animals and birds

If you are looking for the ideal quiescent model, what could be more perfect than the average domestic cat, who is usually to be found sprawled lazily somewhere in the house or outdoors in the shade?

Birds and other natural-history subjects are often perceived as the preserve of the specialist, requiring a great deal of scientific accuracy and detail – but if you enjoy working outdoors and have an affinity with nature, don't be put off by the apparent difficulties of including wildlife in your paintings.

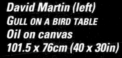

David Martin (left)
GULL ON A BIRD TABLE
Oil on canvas
101.5 x 76cm (40 x 30in)

Peter Partington (below)
MARSH HARRIER SURPRISING COOT
Watercolour on paper
56 x 66cm (22 x 26in)

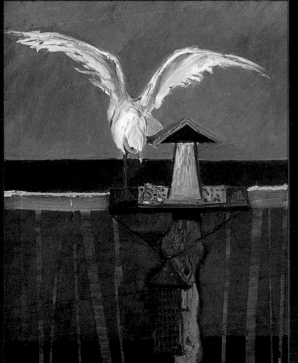

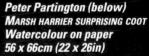

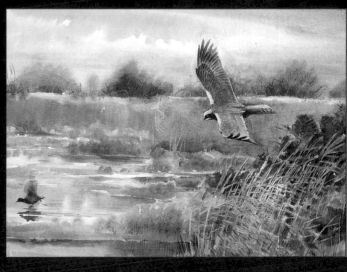

Imaginative painting

Painting pictures from imagination can be very liberating. To what extent you allow fantasy to take over will dictate the degree of your inventiveness. Some artists put together images and references from disparate sources, creating imaginative compositions that are perfectly believable but which exist only in their heads. Other artists take the process much further, putting down their more fanciful thoughts, dreams and surreal visions onto paper and canvas.

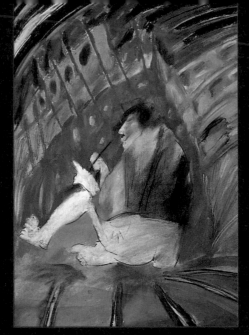

Chris Perry (left)
SCOTT OF THE ANTARCTIC
84 x 61cm (33 x 24in)

Cutting loose

Follow your own muse, and let your ideas and thoughts bubble to the surface. Try developing the first idea that comes to mind and see where it takes you. You may discover that it's not a first idea at all, but a long-lost memory of some past experience, or a subconscious thought that has been lurking in the recesses of your mind, waiting for an opportunity to articulate itself.

Gigol Atler (bottom)
X-RAY HALLUCINATION
Oil on canvas
25.5 x 30.5cm (10 x 12in)

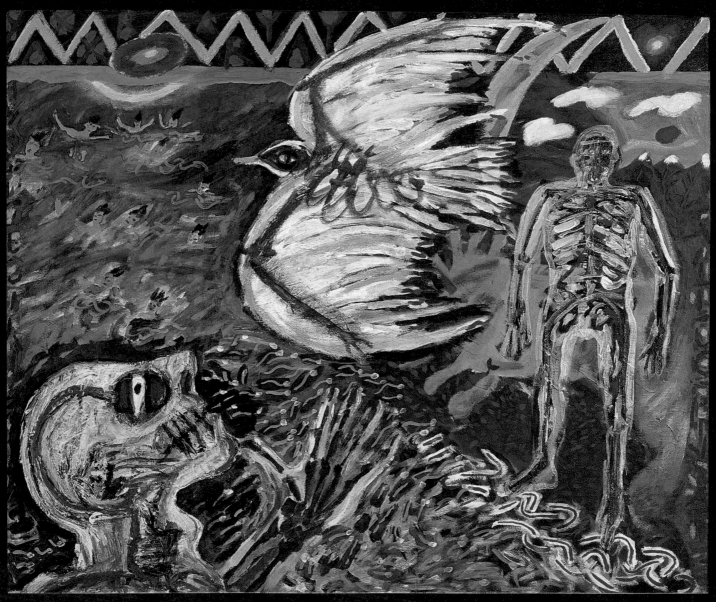

David Cobley
Mr Steven Berkoff
Oil on canvas
122 x 101.5cm (48 x 40in)

Surrealism and abstraction

Conjure with reality to create images that go beyond conventional representation. Go one step further and invent abstract images based on your own experiences and observations, creating paintings of pure colour and pattern.

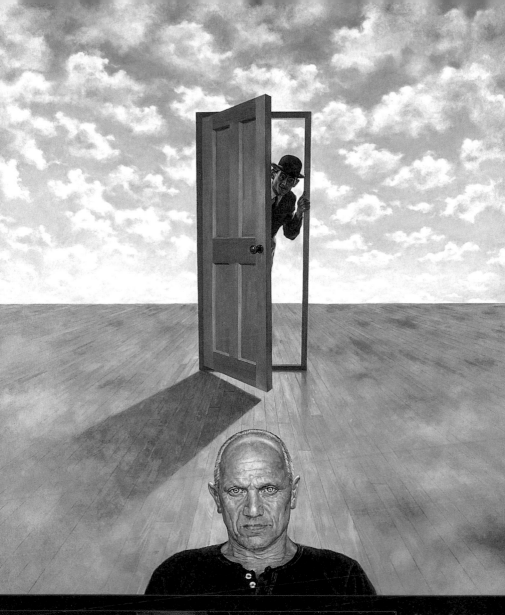

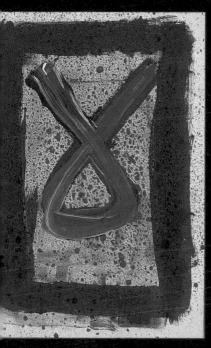

John Ehrlich
RIBBON
Acrylic and gouache on paper
42 x 29cm (16½ x 11½in)

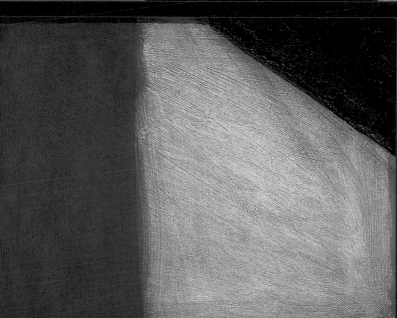

Simon Jennings
RED AND BLACK NO.1
Oil on canvas
20 x 25cm (8 x 10in)

45

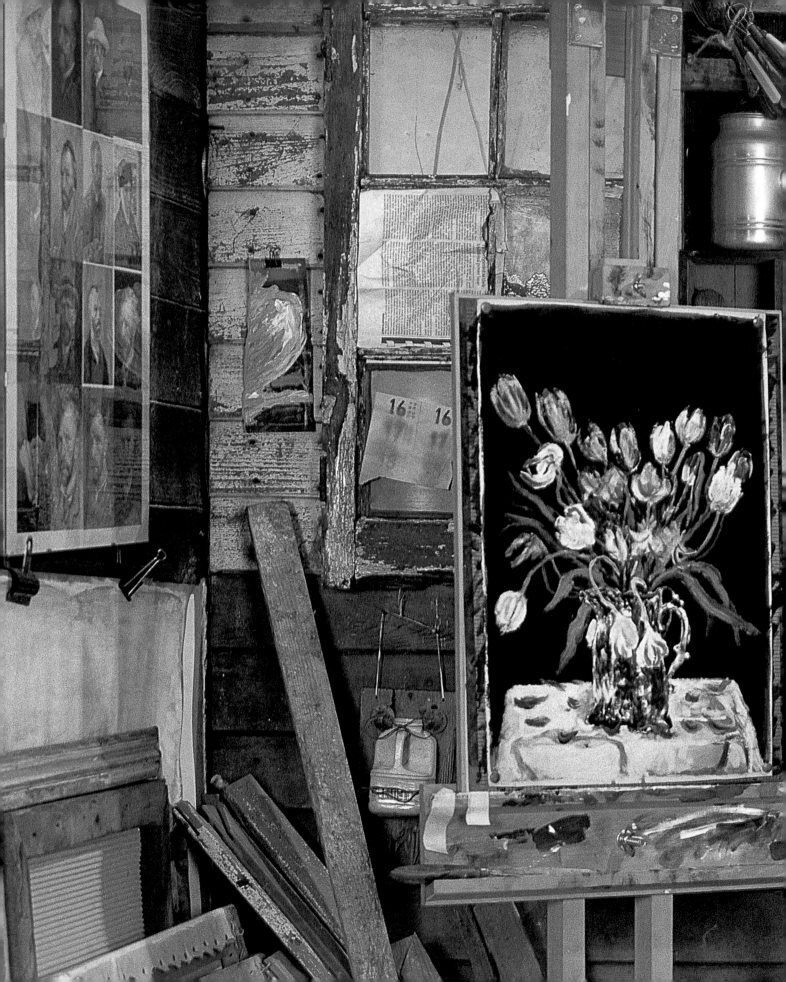

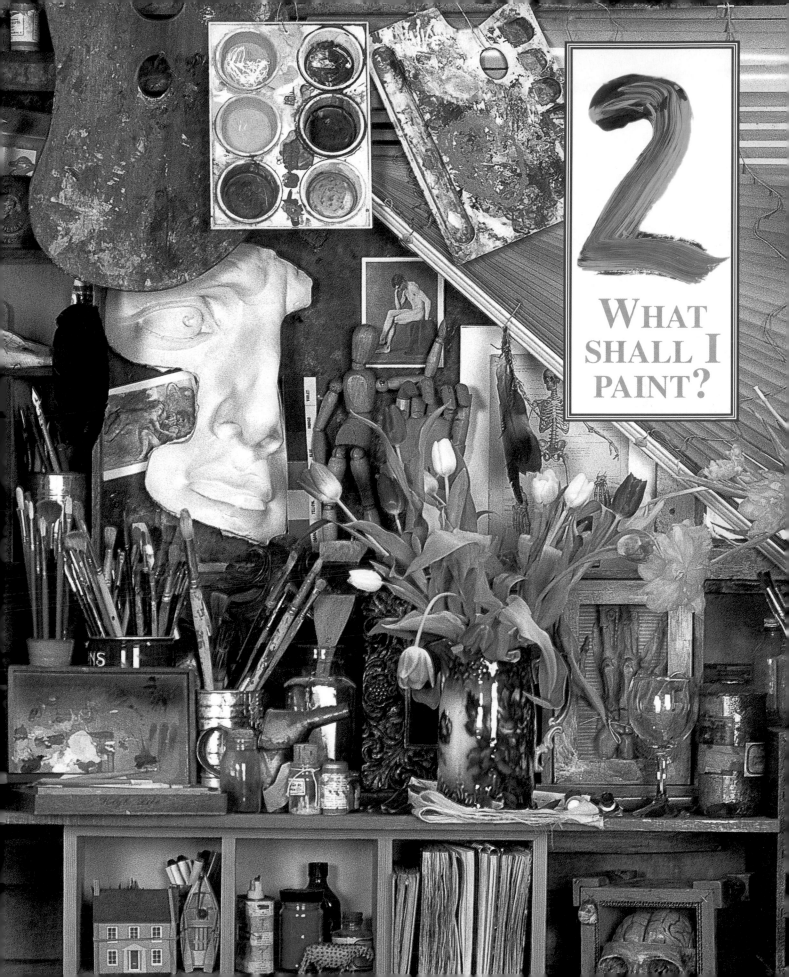

2

WHAT SHALL I PAINT?

The curriculum

This section of the book includes major painting projects interspersed with helpful exercises to get you started and to develop your skills.

It begins with elementary still-life projects, concentrating on single objects and simple groups that introduce the basics of shape, form, colour, texture and composition. There is then a natural progression to a more ambitious still-life painting in oils.

Stepping back from the still-life table, you take in a wider view of your surroundings. Here you are encouraged to paint part of a room and interpret objects in a larger space. Turning your attention to the window, you get your first glimpse of a landscape – but the real challenge here is the notion of painting *contre-jour* (against the light).

Landscape painting is introduced in the form of an enclosed garden, before moving on with a series of open landscapes that initiate you into the challenges and delights of painting outdoors, including trees and foliage, water, skies and weather, and the capriciousness of natural light.

At this point the curriculum moves up a gear to include painting the human form, first with close-up portraits, then with clothed figures and classic nude studies. A step sideways suggests ways of painting a portrait of your pet.

The course rounds off with a relatively ambitious project – composing a picture from imagination, using a variety of sketches and photographs for inspiration.

The direction ☞

A beginner would probably benefit most by starting at the beginning of the section and working systematically through to the end. But, if you prefer, you can begin at any point, moving backwards and forwards as your fancy takes you. To help you with your decision, here at a glance are brief details of all the major painting projects and back-up exercises that make up the curriculum.

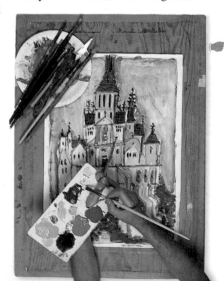

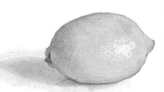

Painting three dimensions
Watercolour ☞ *Page 50*
Painting a single object, focusing on shape, form, tone, colours, light and shade.

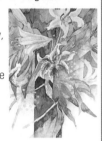

Experimenting with paint
Acrylic ☞ *Page 52*
Exploring the versatility of paint, with a variety of techniques from dry brushing to washes and impasto.

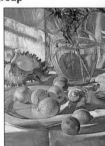

Painting a vase of flowers
Watercolour ☞ *Page 68*
Using colour and texture adventurously, with a strong emphasis on a more flexible approach to composition.

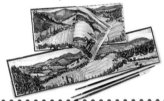

Painting a still-life group
Oils ☞ *Page 72*
Painting a table-top still life that draws on all the previous exercises – we see a painting constructed in detail, from the first marks on the canvas to the finished picture.

Painting trees and foliage
Mixed media ☞ *Page 94*
Depicting trees in close-up and in the distance.

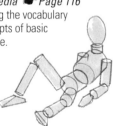

Landscape, on location
Acrylic ☞ *Page 96*
Painting a panoramic view of the countryside, using a warm ground to enliven the conventional palette of colours.

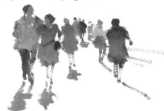

Painting space, depth and distance
Mixed media ☞ *Page 116*
Introducing the vocabulary and concepts of basic perspective.

Putting life into a painting
Watercolour ☞ *Page 118*
Bringing the landscape to life with simple but lively figures.

Experimenting with poses
Mixed media ☞ *Page 136*
Trying out unconventional poses and capturing the essence of figures in motion.

Figure painting in the studio
Oils ☞ *Page 138*
Working with models in the studio, and the development of a full-figure nude study from the very first charcoal marks.

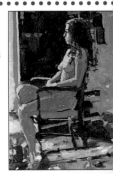

Interpreting colour and pattern
Collage ☞ *Page 54*
Using simple collage techniques to explore the possibilities of colour and pattern with an image of a single flower.

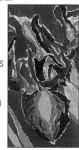

Interpreting surface textures
Mixed media ☞ *Page 56*
An exercise in close observation, looking at ways of capturing the visual qualities of materials from wood to corroded metal.

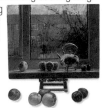

Fish on a plate
Watercolour ☞ *Page 60*
Looking at a still-life object in context, with an introduction to the concept of composition.

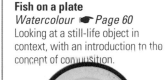
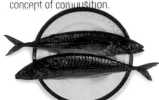

Painting a bowl of fruit
Water-mixable oils ☞ *Page 64*
Taking composition a step further by incorporating a variety of shapes, strong colours and tonal contrasts.

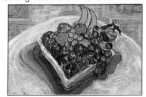

Painting your room
Mixed media ☞ *Page 76*
Painting space and volume in the context of a familiar interior, with special emphasis on capturing atmosphere and light.

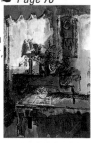

Painting against the light
Oils ☞ *Page 80*
Resolving the problems of painting objects against strong back lighting while creating the illusion of depth beyond the window.

Painting a garden
Pastel ☞ *Page 84*
Painting a landscape without having to travel far from home. With this project we experience for the first time the joys of working outdoors.

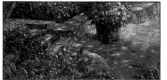

Painting a landscape
Watercolour ☞ *Page 88*
Painting a wide-open space — how to suggest differences in scale between foreground, middle distance and background.

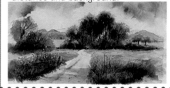

Painting skies and weather
Mixed media ☞ *Page 100*
Incorporating dramatic skyscapes and variable weather conditions.

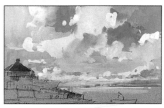

The changing landscape
Oils ☞ *Page 104*
Coping with changeable light and weather, with an introduction to atmospheric perspective.

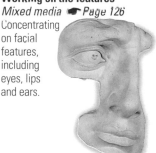

Capturing water
Watercolour ☞ *Page 110*
Ideas and techniques for painting still water and breaking waves.

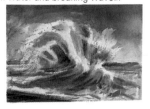

Painting a townscape
Watercolour ☞ *Page 112*
Celebrating the wealth of colour and texture afforded by buildings in a landscape.

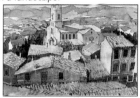

Painting a face
Acrylic ☞ *Page 120*
Composing a traditional portrait, from drawn studies to a highly finished likeness.

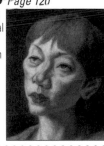

Working on the features
Mixed media ☞ *Page 126*
Concentrating on facial features, including eyes, lips and ears.

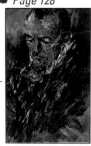

Painting a friend
Mixed media ☞ *Page 128*
Painting more than superficial appearance — here we see how to capture the inner character of a model.

Painting a person
Gouache ☞ *Page 132*
Achieving solidity and form by painting a fully clothed figure in a simple environment.

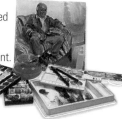

Painting hands and feet
Gouache ☞ *Page 144*
Making studies of hands and feet — an essential precursor to successful figure painting.

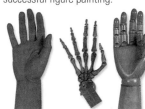

Painting your pets
Mixed media ☞ *Page 146*
Rendering animals on the move, and painting a cat's portrait.

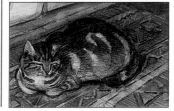

Getting your ideas onto paper and canvas
Mixed media ☞ *Page 150*
Tracing, gridding-up, and projecting images onto a support.

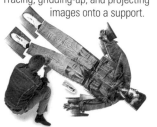

Composing a picture from imagination
Acrylic ☞ *Page 152*
Constructing a painting, using sketches, photographs and cuttings.

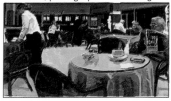

What shall I paint?
STILL LIFE
Painting single objects
Shape and form

Painting three dimensions

Representational paintings are illusions – two-dimensional interpretations of a three-dimensional world. You are about to take up the challenge of creating those illusions. So what is it that makes a painted image believable? To begin to answer this question, we have chosen a lemon as a simple subject to illustrate some basic principles.

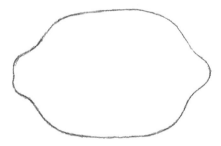

Shape

One of the ways we recognize any object is by its shape – that is, by its profile as it appears against a background. Whether interpreted as a simple outline or as a silhouette, shape helps us distinguish one object from another.

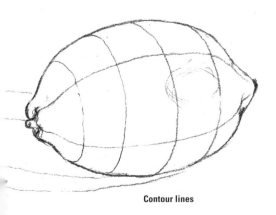

Contour lines

Form

However, an outline provides very limited information about an object. For greater realism, we need to explore ways of conveying three-dimensional form or solidity. One simple method is to draw contour lines representing the surface of the object. This may help you to understand the form of the object, even though it is a somewhat 'mechanical' interpretation.

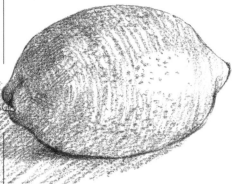

Tone

To create a more realistic image, try making linear marks in the form of hatching and crosshatching to create a tonal image – one that interprets the subject in terms of light and dark. Faceted shapes have clearly defined faces, but rounded forms require a gradual gradation from light to dark. To evaluate tonal values, study your subject through half-closed eyes. This allows you to distinguish the lightest and darkest areas from the halftones.

Light and shade

Light falling upon an object casts a relatively dark area of shadow behind it. Including shadows in your painting helps to create an illusion of weight, because the object appears to be resting firmly on a surface rather than floating in space. Shadows are strongest immediately behind the object, getting lighter as they stretch away.

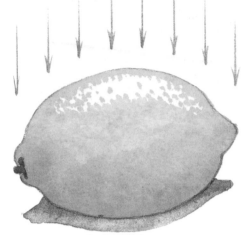

Overhead light

A low angle of light will cast a long shadow, an overhead light a short one. Illuminating an object evenly tends to flatten its appearance, whereas light from one direction exaggerates tonal contrast.

Highlights

Highlights are high-key areas of tone, created by light reflecting back from a surface. Used in conjunction with shadows, highlights serve to enhance the illusion of three-dimensional form. Create highlights by applying opaque paint over laid colour, or mask out areas of white paper before you apply a wash.

Reflected light and colour

Light reflected from a table top, brightens areas of deep shadow. Similarly, the colour of the subject itself may be reflected in the surface of the table. Adding these touches to your painting makes for greater realism.

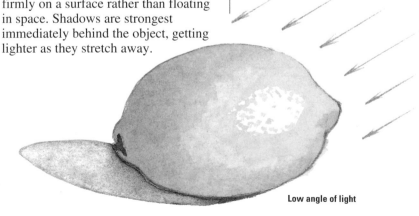

Low angle of light

Local colour

We know that a lemon is yellow – this is its 'local colour'. However, when painting an object, it is necessary to look beyond local colour. The colour that we actually see depends on whether a surface is in direct light, reflected light, or shadow. In this study, the artist has used cadmium yellow, modified with washes of yellow ochre, and a mixture of cobalt blue and burnt umber for the areas in shadow.

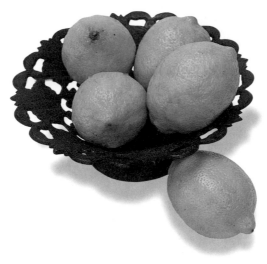

☞ SEE ALSO
Crosshatching 183
Masking fluid 90, 179
Papers 173
Warm and cool colours 158
Washes 180
Wet-in-wet 180
Wet-on-dry 180

Interpreting form

Making drawings and paintings of simple objects is a good way of learning how to interpret solidity and form. This study of a lemon was painted in watercolour on smooth paper.

Modelling with tone

Coloured tones – a mixture of cobalt blue and burnt umber – are used to model three-dimensional form.

Highlights

Created by stippling masking fluid onto the paper before applying a wash.

Reflected colour

A white table top picks up the local colour of the subject.

Reflected light

Reflected light can brighten areas of the subject in shadow.

Cast shadow

A cool grey wash gives the impression that the subject is resting on a flat surface.

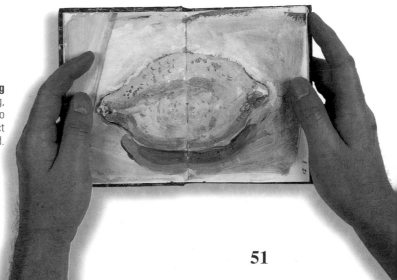

Colour sketching

Before committing to a major painting, make colour sketches of single objects to observe the play of light on the subject and its background.

What shall I paint?
STILL LIFE
Exploring the
versatility of a medium
Paint effects

Experimenting with paint

Before you tackle anything too demanding, experiment with your preferred medium to see just how versatile it can be. Try a wide range of techniques, from simple fluid washes to thick impasto, to discover different ways of interpreting the object you are painting. Being water-soluble and quick-drying, acrylic paint is ideal for experimentation, but be sure to wash your brushes frequently and only squeeze out as much paint as you think you will use in a single session.

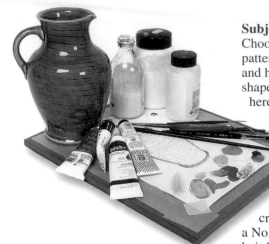

Subject and equipment

Choose a simple object with a surface pattern or texture that is easy to interpret and helps you to see the volume and shape of the subject. The palette used here was opaque chromium oxide (green), light yellow ochre, titanium white, and a little burnt umber for the areas in shadow. Glaze medium, gel medium and texture paste were used to create the paint effects. As well as a small cranked painting knife, the artist used a No.10 round and Nos.2 and 3 synthetic-hair brights (flat short-bristle brushes).

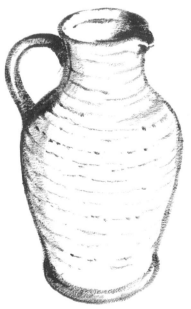

Dry brushing

Try making a brush drawing, using a small amount of undiluted paint and a short-bristle brush. The brushstrokes soon run dry, giving a fresh sketch-like appearance to the work.

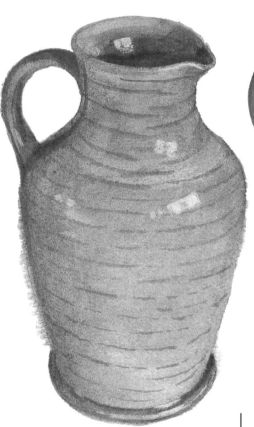

Using diluted paint

Here the paint is diluted with water and applied as washes, wet-in-wet. Draw the jug in pencil, then brush clean water within the pencil outline. Starting at the top, apply a light-coloured wash to the wetted area. Build up the form with successively stronger washes, starting from the darker areas – the colour tends to flow and bleed naturally, creating rewarding accidental effects. Remove excess colour while it is still wet, using a clean damp brush. Create highlights with white body colour.

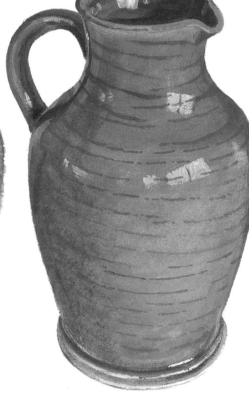

Painting straight from the tube

Mix undiluted paint to match the lightest background colour and brush it over the pencil drawing. Give the painting form, using the paint at full strength or diluted with a little water to model the shape. Blend the tones, and add highlights to give a reflective quality to the surface.

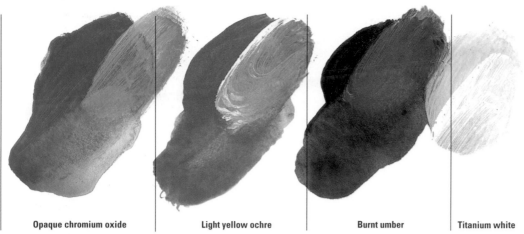

Opaque chromium oxide   **Light yellow ochre**   **Burnt umber**   **Titanium white**

☛ **SEE ALSO**
Acrylic paint 162
Body colour 101
Glazing 176
Knife painting 177
Mediums 164
Paintbrushes 167
Painting knives 169
Washes 180
Wet-in-wet 180

A simple palette
Using just four colours, acrylic paint offers a wide range of possibilities, from translucent washes to strong opaques.

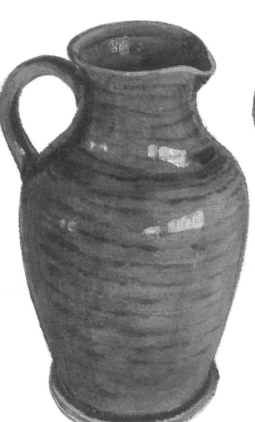

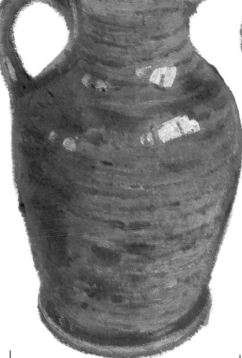

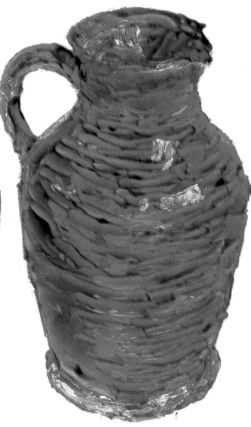

Adding glaze medium
Glaze medium allows acrylics to be used in a similar way to oils. When added in small amounts to undiluted acrylic paint, glossy opaque colours are produced. Adding a larger amount of glaze medium creates thin transparent washes which, when used to overlay other colours, are known as glazes. Here, the paint was applied with bristle brushes, rinsed in water before each change of colour.

Using gel medium
Gel medium, which is thicker than glaze medium, dries to a transparent gloss. It creates a full-bodied paint with a rich depth of colour that can be worked like oil paint. Build up the form of the jug with opaque paint and thin glazes. As acrylics dry relatively quickly, you can soon overpaint the surface to modify the colour or form. Brushmarks left in the extra-thick paint add character to the painting.

Mixing with texture paste
Create a distinctly textured painting by mixing acrylic paints with texture paste. Use a small cranked painting knife to apply the paint, allowing your strokes to follow the curved form of the jug to emphasize its bulbous shape. With acrylic paint, you can work from dark to light or vice versa when building up the form. Although relatively difficult to control, thick paint applied with a knife imparts a sense of freedom and spontaneity to the painting.

53

What shall I paint?
STILL LIFE
Colour and shape
Collage technique

Interpreting colour and pattern

Even a simple painting encompasses a variety of skills. In addition to observing and communicating individual colours and form, a still-life painter has to compose and arrange elements within a given area, and also strive for balanced colour. This picture of a flower concentrates on colour and shape created with paint on paper. Brushes are eventually put aside as the artist employs a collage technique as a simple and effective means of focusing on the colours and shapes evident in this still-life subject.

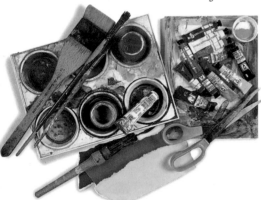

Materials
Use quick-drying, water-soluble colours. Here the artist used gouache, but acrylic paints, watercolours and even poster colours or inks will serve equally well.

Any paper will do. Leftover scraps from sketchbooks and previous projects are ideal, and using papers with different surface textures serves to enrich the finished work.

You don't need scissors unless you want very precise shapes. For this collage, the shapes were torn from the paper. You will need paste and a brush.

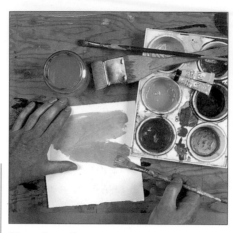

Observing colours
Create your palette of collage materials with paint on paper. Interpret the colours of the object in front of you as closely as possible.

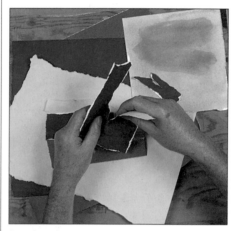

Forming shapes
Tear the basic shapes of the flower from the appropriately coloured paper samples. Simply modify the shape and scale as you go.

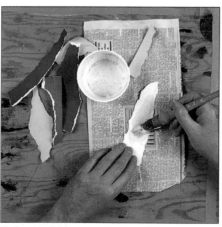

Fixing position
Dry-lay the arrangement onto the background. Then, when you are happy with the composition, paste the various elements in position.

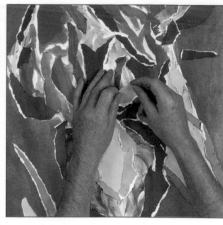

Arranging the collage
Arrange the torn-paper shapes to approximate the form of the flower. Change the shapes and add different colours, gradually building up the picture rather like a mosaic.

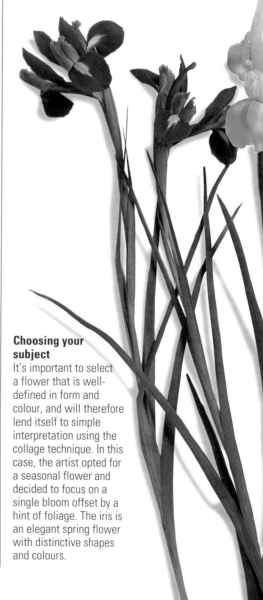

Choosing your subject
It's important to select a flower that is well-defined in form and colour, and will therefore lend itself to simple interpretation using the collage technique. In this case, the artist opted for a seasonal flower and decided to focus on a single bloom offset by a hint of foliage. The iris is an elegant spring flower with distinctive shapes and colours.

A single flower

Making simple collages of single objects will help you to see colour and pattern. This bold interpretation of an iris is made using gouache to colour the paper, which is then torn and arranged on a tinted-cartridge-paper background. The finished work measures 76 x 51cm (30 x 20in). It is an advantage to work at a fairly large scale when making torn-paper collages.

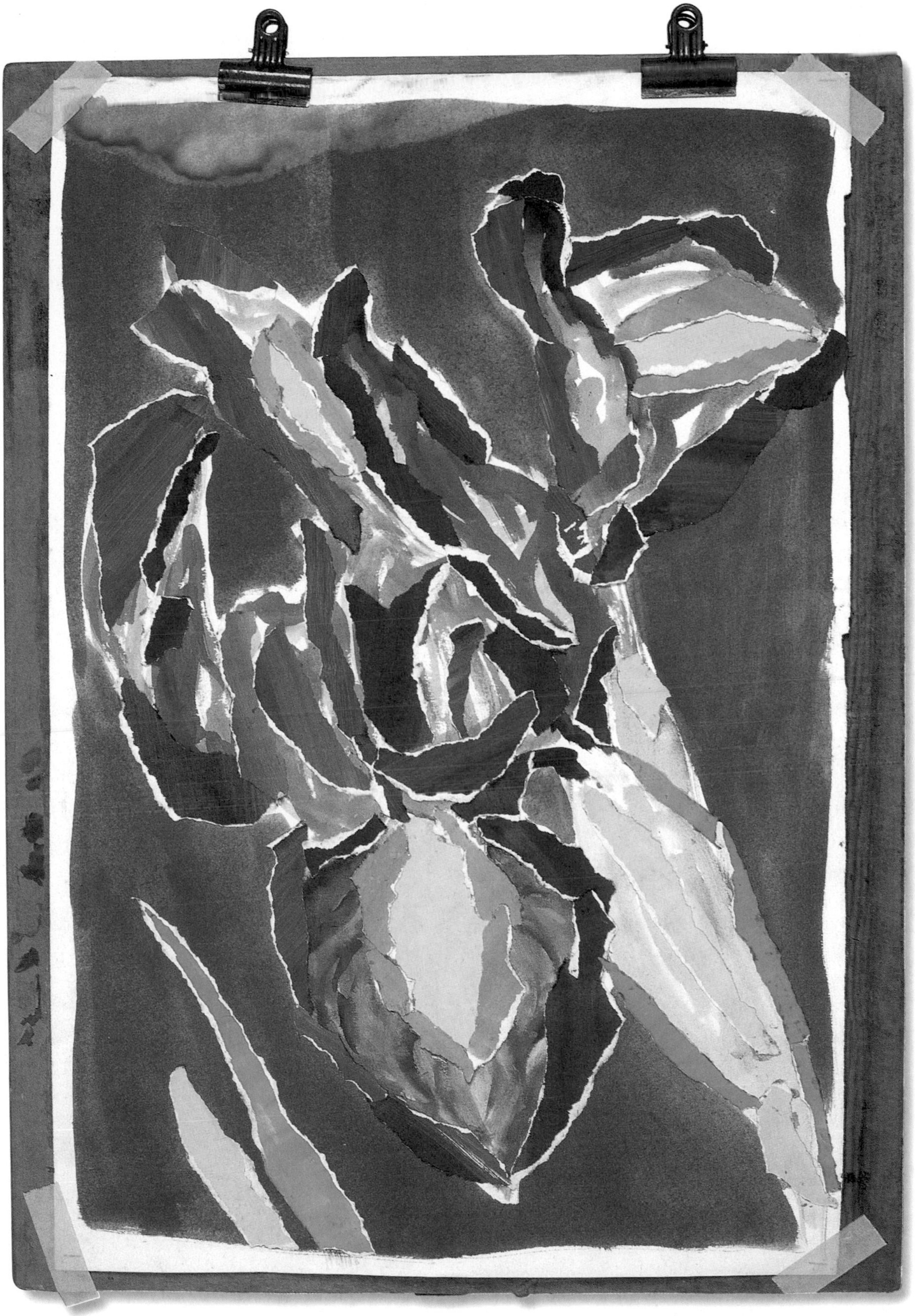

Ella Jennings
BLUE IRIS
Painted and tinted
paper collage
76 x 51cm
(30 x 20in)

☛ SEE ALSO
Collage 185
Gouache 161
Painting a vase
of flowers 68
Papers 173
Shape and form 50
Still life 28
Washes 180

Interpreting surface textures

Each component in a still life has an intrinsic visual quality – hard, brittle, soft, flexible, warm, cold and so on. In addition, the surface of most materials gradually develops its own peculiar character or patina as a result of ageing and exposure. Here, we see a number of ways to capture the essential nature of inanimate objects, using a variety of media. By making a number of studies of different materials, you will begin to build up a repertoire of techniques that will help you with your still-life painting.

WOOD IN PENCIL AND WATERCOLOUR

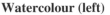

Coloured pencil (right)
Using water-soluble pencils, draw the light wood tones, following the direction of the grain. Build up the colour by crosshatching where darker tones are required. Using a wet brush, blend the pencil lines to make a colour wash. When dry, darken and modify the tones and create the grain pattern of the wood. Use a putty rubber to introduce highlights and clean up edges.

Watercolour (left)
Draw the box in soft graphite pencil. Using yellow ochre, raw sienna and burnt sienna, mix washes that resemble the tones of the wood. For the shadows, mix burnt umber and cobalt blue.

Wet the drawn area and lay a wash of the lightest tone. When almost dry, paint the faces of the box with darker washes. Add streaks to represent grain, and apply a wash for the shadows.

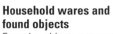

Household wares and found objects
Everyday objects can provide your still-life table with a variety of interesting and challenging surface textures.

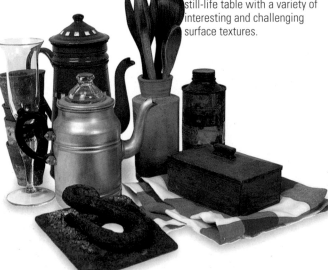

WOOD AND CERAMIC IN PASTEL

Here, soft pastels have been used to depict two contrasting materials – wooden spoons and a fired-clay pot. Draw the still life in soft pencil, then render the smooth surface of the spoons with suitable pastel colours, blended on the paper with a rolled paper stump. Draw the wood grain with pastels, using an eraser to lift off some of the colour.

Render the surface texture of the pot with short diagonal strokes, using colours in various tones to create the cylindrical shape. Let the pastel strokes overlap and blend together.

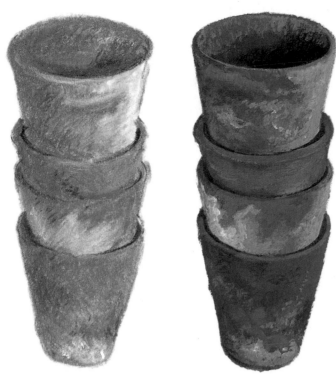

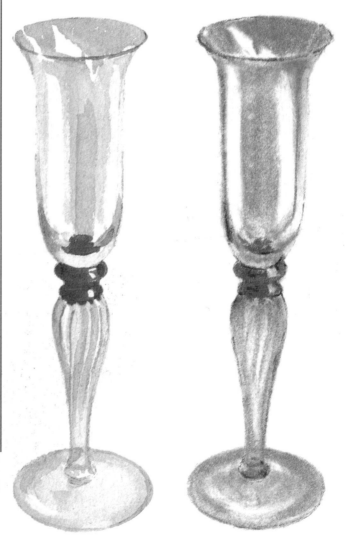

DRINKING GLASS
IN WATERCOLOUR AND PASTEL

Watercolour (below left)
Mix watercolour washes to represent the silver-grey tones seen in glass. Study the shapes of the reflections and block them in with washes, wet-on-dry. Leave areas of white paper to represent the highlights. Carefully outline the darker edges, such as the rim, using the tip of a brush.

Pastel (below right)
It is difficult to be precise with pastels, so use a putty rubber to define the reflections and highlights. A paper stump is useful for blending colours and for drawing fine detail – rub the tip of the stump onto the pastel, then transfer the colour to the work.

CLAY POTS IN PASTEL AND ACRYLIC

Pastel (above left)
Having made a simple underdrawing, depict the colouring and weathered texture of old clay flowerpots by using overlapping strokes of colour. Try not to overwork the colours, or you risk losing their freshness.

Acrylic paint (above right)
Liquid acrylic paint can be used straight from the pot or thinned with water. Apply the colour freely with a flat bristle brush, using a small round brush for detail. Once the surface is dry, overpaint with opaque paint or transparent washes to model the pots and introduce the pale tones of mildew-staining over the terracotta.

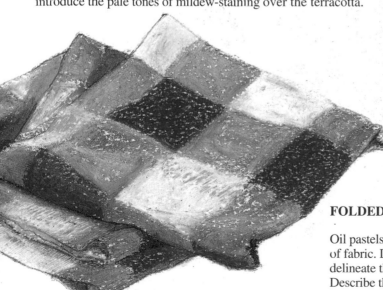

FOLDED FABRIC IN OIL PASTEL

Oil pastels have a paint-like quality, ideal for rendering the folds and texture of fabric. Draw the cloth on a coarse-textured paper and apply colour to delineate the squares, allowing some of the paper's texture to show through. Describe the various tones by overlaying with more pastel, or scrape it back with a scalpel. Use the pointed blade to draw the warp and weft of the fabric.

What shall I paint?
STILL LIFE
Interpreting surface textures

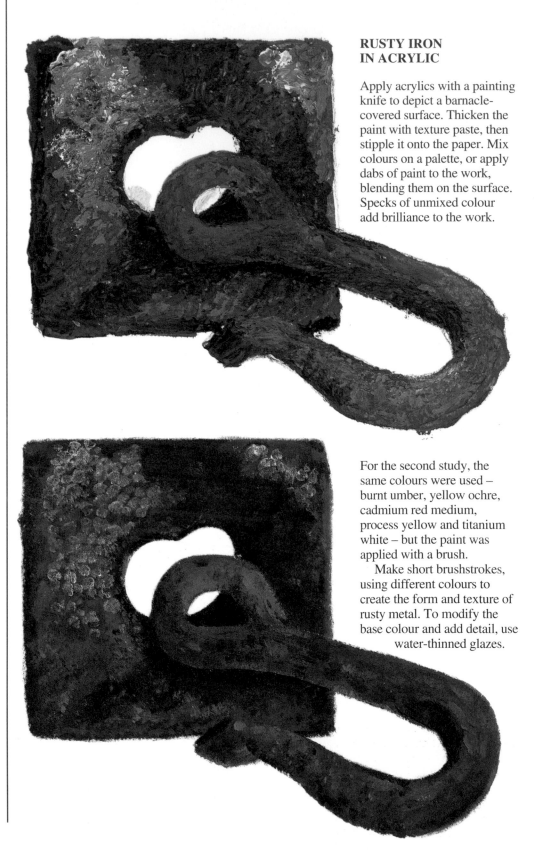

RUSTY IRON
IN ACRYLIC

Apply acrylics with a painting knife to depict a barnacle-covered surface. Thicken the paint with texture paste, then stipple it onto the paper. Mix colours on a palette, or apply dabs of paint to the work, blending them on the surface. Specks of unmixed colour add brilliance to the work.

For the second study, the same colours were used – burnt umber, yellow ochre, cadmium red medium, process yellow and titanium white – but the paint was applied with a brush.

Make short brushstrokes, using different colours to create the form and texture of rusty metal. To modify the base colour and add detail, use water-thinned glazes.

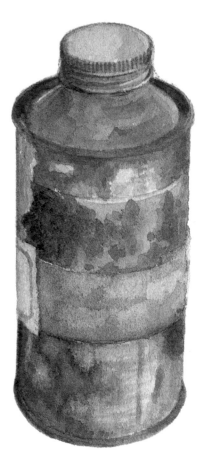

RUSTY CAN
IN WATERCOLOUR

The worn surface and rust patches on this old screw-top can are painted in watercolour. Warm and cool greys mixed from raw umber and cobalt blue are used for the metal surfaces, with washes of yellow ochre, green and raw umber for the old labels and tape.

Make a line drawing of the container, then apply a light-grey wash for the metal. Adopt a similar treatment for the label and tape. Gradually add deeper tones with dabs of colour, wet-in-wet, to build up the form and character of the surfaces.

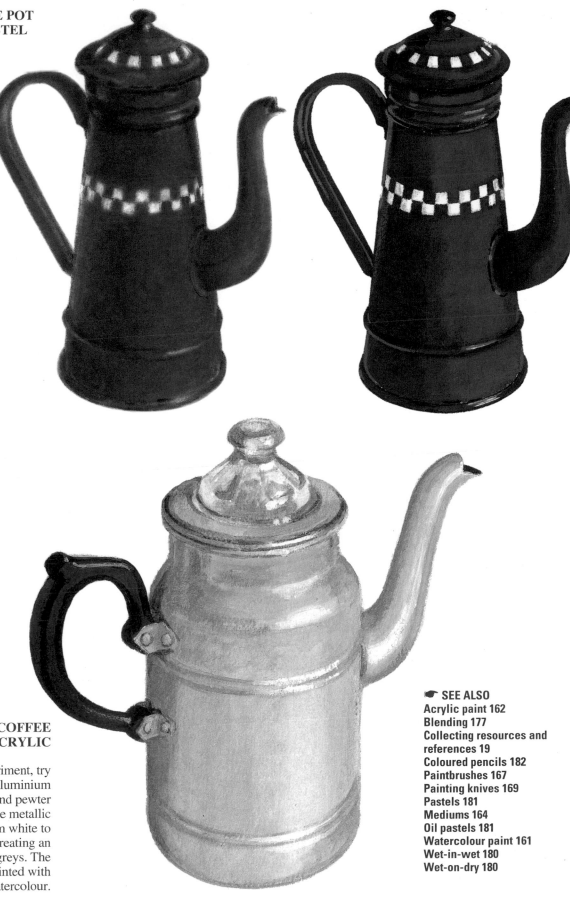

ENAMELLED COFFEE POT IN ACRYLIC AND PASTEL

Acrylic (far right)

The challenge here was to simulate the faded, semi-matt surface of old coloured enamel. This study was made with liquid acrylic paint – alizarin crimson, cadmium yellow, titanium white and raw umber. To achieve a gradation of colour and tone, blend the colours on the paper while the paint is wet. Add touches of thinned colour to create highlights and areas of chipped enamel.

Pastel (right)

A similar study was made with soft pastel. A soft-textured velour paper allows you to blend pastel into a smooth gradation of tone and colour. The pastels are laid thinly, allowing the white background to 'grin' through to create fresh luminous colours.

First draw the outline in soft graphite pencil or ink. When applying the colour, work from light to dark, using a stump to blend the pastel and a bristle brush to erase unwanted colour. Add the highlights last.

ALUMINIUM COFFEE POT IN ACRYLIC

By way of an experiment, try copying the surface of an aluminium coffee pot with silver and pewter acrylic paints. Mix the metallic paints with titanium white to produce the lighter tones, creating an infinite range of soft greys. The glass top is painted with watercolour.

☛ SEE ALSO
Acrylic paint 162
Blending 177
Collecting resources and references 19
Coloured pencils 182
Paintbrushes 167
Painting knives 169
Pastels 181
Mediums 164
Oil pastels 181
Watercolour paint 161
Wet-in-wet 180
Wet-on-dry 180

What shall I paint?
STILL LIFE
Basic composition
Painting with glazes
Highlights and reflections

The materials
Watercolour paint is the perfect medium for capturing the diffused colouring of the subject. This study was painted on 250gsm rough (coarse-surface) watercolour paper, taped but not stretched onto a drawing board. In addition, you will need a soft graphite pencil, round sable paintbrushes, an eraser for making corrections, and masking fluid to create the highlights.

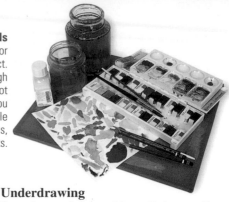

Fish on a plate

You can take the idea of painting a single object a step further by looking at the object in context. This requires you to observe a variety of textures, and introduces you to basic composition.

Fish on a plate make a simple yet fascinating still-life subject. The brittle glazed ceramic of the plate and the natural colouring and delicate scale patterns of the recently caught mackerel provide an opportunity to explore ways of using paint to express their contrasting qualities.

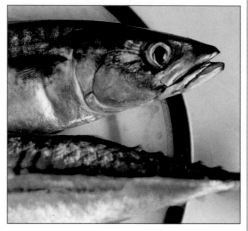

The lighting
A window to the right of the still-life table provides the main light source. Fish skin changes colour dramatically according to the direction of light, so you may need to try different arrangements to discover the most attractive viewpoint when setting up a composition of this kind.

Underdrawing
Start the work by making a light pencil drawing of your composition. Draw the elliptical shape of the plate in full – ellipses can be tricky to draw accurately, so don't be afraid to use an eraser to make corrections as necessary.

Next add the fish, noting their overall shape and proportion. You can erase the lines of the plate that would be hidden by the fish once you are satisfied with your drawing.

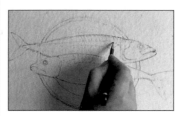

Drawing in pencil
Keep the underdrawing relatively simple.

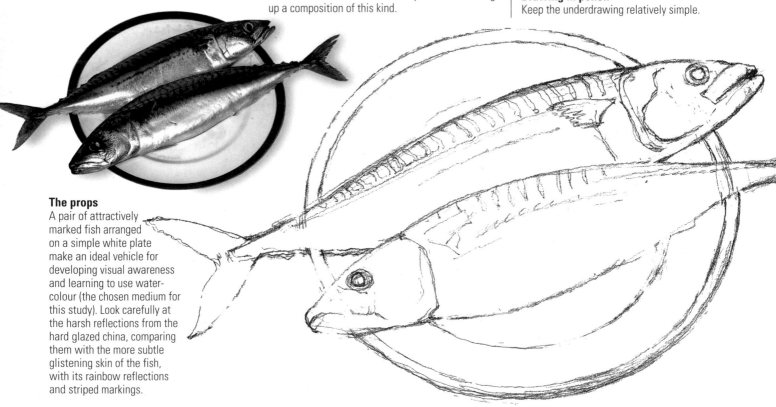

The props
A pair of attractively marked fish arranged on a simple white plate make an ideal vehicle for developing visual awareness and learning to use water-colour (the chosen medium for this study). Look carefully at the harsh reflections from the hard glazed china, comparing them with the more subtle glistening skin of the fish, with its rainbow reflections and striped markings.

Light and shadow
Note how light illuminates your still life, creating highlights on one side and throwing shadows on the other.

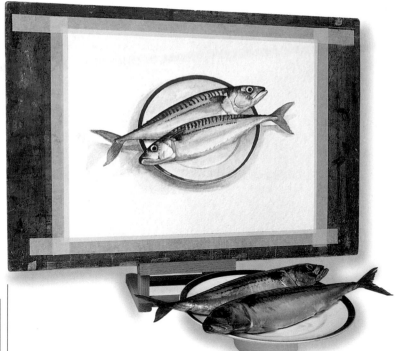

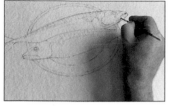

Masking out highlights
Identify the highlights on the plate and fish, and paint them onto the drawing with masking fluid.

Use the white of the paper to represent your strongest highlights. Paint the shape of each highlight with masking fluid which, when removed at a later stage, reveals the unpainted surface of the paper. Here, the highlights occur on various parts of the fish and also around the rim of the plate. Masking fluid dries fast, so work quickly and wash out your brush in soapy water before the fluid clogs the bristles.

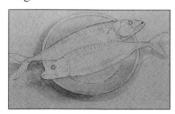

Painting the shadows
Mix tonal washes for the shadows and for modelling the form.

Start the painting itself, by wetting the areas of cast shadow around the plate, using clean water. With brushstrokes following the shapes made by the shadows, apply a light wash over the wetted area. Let the surface dry a little, then add darker washes to deepen and strengthen the tones. Also, add pale colour washes to model the hollow shape of the plate and to introduce shadows beneath the fish.

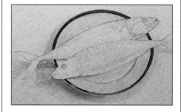

Painting the plate
Mix a suitable colour and carefully paint in the blue rim of the plate, taking note of the way reflected light gives it solidity and form.

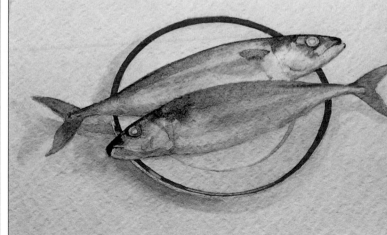

Using glazes to give shape to the fish
Apply translucent washes to describe the firm, rounded bodies of the fish.

Now begin to build up the form of the fish with overlapping washes of translucent colour. Note the subtle colour changes across the skin and mix suitable washes, testing them on a scrap of paper to check the strength of colour and tone. When dry, watercolours appear lighter than when they are first applied, so take this into consideration when mixing your colours. Lay the washes freely and let some blend together, wet-in-wet. If you need to modify the colouring, leave the wash to dry, then apply another colour over the top. Alternatively, lift off the paint while it is still wet by blotting with a soft paper tissue.

What shall I paint?
STILL LIFE
Fish on a plate

Now begin to add detail to the painting, emphasizing the form and character of the subject. Use a fine brush to define the shape of the fish, and to pick out features such as the eyes and gills.

Let the painting dry, then rub away the masking fluid applied at the beginning. Apply light washes to modify the shape and colour of the highlights, but leave the white paper to depict high-key reflections.

At this point, step back and take a good look at your painting to ensure you are maintaining an overall balance of tone and colour. Then make the necessary modifications with small touches of paint and coloured glazes, until you feel you have captured the essence of the still life.

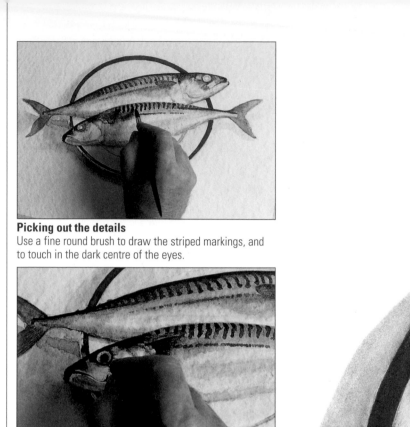

Picking out the details
Use a fine round brush to draw the striped markings, and to touch in the dark centre of the eyes.

Revealing the highlights
Once the paint is dry, use your fingertip or an eraser to rub away the masking fluid, revealing the white paper beneath.

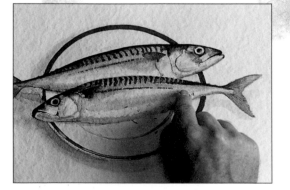

Fine detail
Add the finest details to a painting by drawing with a pointed brush.

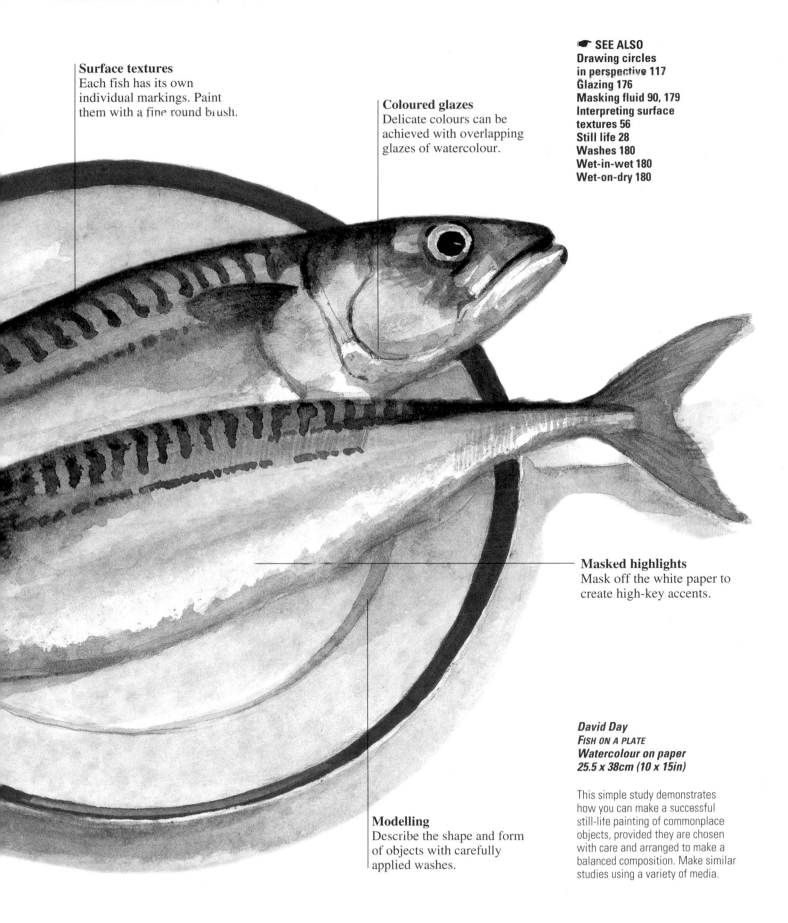

Surface textures
Each fish has its own
individual markings. Paint
them with a fine round brush.

Coloured glazes
Delicate colours can be
achieved with overlapping
glazes of watercolour.

☞ **SEE ALSO**
**Drawing circles
in perspective 117
Glazing 176
Masking fluid 90, 179
Interpreting surface
textures 56
Still life 28
Washes 180
Wet-in-wet 180
Wet-on-dry 180**

Masked highlights
Mask off the white paper to
create high-key accents.

David Day
FISH ON A PLATE
Watercolour on paper
25.5 x 38cm (10 x 15in)

This simple study demonstrates
how you can make a successful
still-life painting of commonplace
objects, provided they are chosen
with care and arranged to make a
balanced composition. Make similar
studies using a variety of media.

Modelling
Describe the shape and form
of objects with carefully
applied washes.

63

What shall I paint?
STILL LIFE
Composition
Balancing shape, tone and colour
Coloured ground

Painting a bowl of fruit

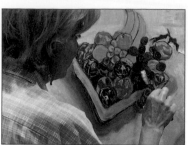

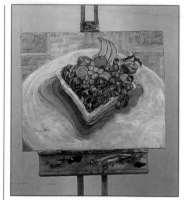

Fruit bowl
Jennie Dunn
Strong colours, uninhibited brushwork and bold outlines characterize Jennie Dunn's paintings. This simple still life relies on the careful orchestration of shape, tone and colour for its impact.

"Be quite free with your brushstrokes, and don't be afraid to let them show. You are not a housepainter, so try to create interesting textures and broken colour with your paint."

A selection of fruits is a relatively simple still-life subject – but, by introducing a variety of shapes, strong colours and tonal contrast into your composition, you are forced to think critically about the arrangement of these elements in your picture.

Individually, most fruits are similar in outline, but pile them one upon another and you become aware of the more interesting 'negative' shapes that are created by the spaces between and around the fruits. A careful assessment of the colours and tones is essential to make the best of these shapes and to create a strong composition.

WATER-MIXABLE OIL PAINTS

The featured painting was made with water-mixable oil paints. They behave much like conventional oil colours and produce similar results, but they are thinned with water instead of a solvent such as turpentine.

Colours used:
Alizarin crimson
Cadmium orange
Cadmium red deep
Cadmium yellow light
Cadmium yellow medium
Cerulean
Dioxazine purple
French ultramarine
Lemon yellow
Sap green
Titanium white
Viridian
Yellow ochre

Mediums
A range of mediums is available for altering the characteristics and working properties of the paint. For this painting, the artist used water as the diluent, plus a water-mixable painting medium when applying certain colours.

Brushes
When painting with water-mixable colours, it is advisable to use special synthetic brushes. For this painting the artist used Nos.2, 4 and 18 flats and Nos.2, 4 and 20 rounds. To preserve their shape, wash your brushes in warm soapy water and wrap the bristles in a paper towel.

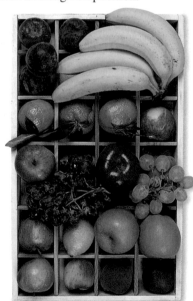

Complementary colours
When selecting the fruit for this painting, the artist intentionally chose colours that were complementary. When complementaries are juxtaposed, they intensify the eye's perception of colour, creating a more dynamic and vibrant picture. For more information on complementary colours, see *What are the basics?*

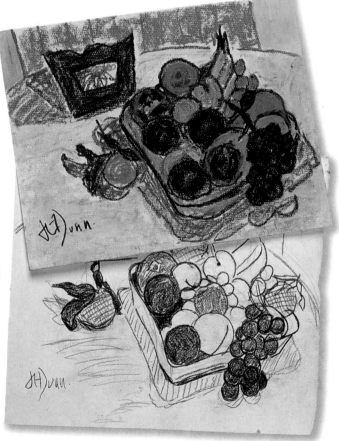

Preparatory drawings
Not every artist bothers to make preparatory sketches, but drawing gives you the opportunity to try out various arrangements of colour and tone. It is easier to evaluate the composition if your preparatory drawings are made on paper that has the same proportions as your canvas. Cut or tear the paper to match the canvas.

COLOURED GROUNDS

Coating a primed canvas or board with a neutral or coloured wash provides a surface upon which the artist can more accurately evaluate a range of colours and tones. In this case the ground colour is intended to form an integral part of the finished painting. A warm pink, mixed with just a touch of ultramarine, glows through to enliven the cool blues, greens and yellows and forms a perfect mid tone for warm reds and oranges.

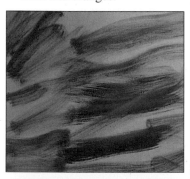

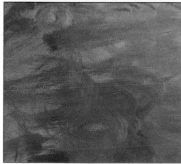

Applying a coloured ground
Scrub ground colour onto the canvas, using a wide flat paintbrush and a ball of damp paper towel. Provided you thin the paint with very little water, the ground will be dry enough to work on within a few minutes.

Underdrawing
Using a darker mix of the ground colour, draw the main elements of the composition in line only. Don't be afraid of making mistakes – while it is wet, water-mixable oil paint can be wiped off the surface very easily.

"You have to be aware of perspective, even when you are painting a simple study like this. In particular, the fruit bowl or dish must appear to be sitting firmly on the surface of the table."

Blocking in the tones
During the early stages of the painting, Jennie Dunn is less concerned with form than with balancing the tones. At this stage, she leaves narrow gaps between areas of colour, allowing the mid-tone ground to show through.

"I'm primarily concerned with achieving the right balance between tones and colours. Ideally, you should be able to stop painting at any stage and the picture will be balanced."

Introducing strong colours
When painting a subject that has strong colouring, your perception can become confused, making it quite difficult to differentiate tonal values. Narrow your eyes when looking at the still life, and you'll see the dark, light and mid tones more clearly.

"Now we can begin to see where the light is coming from. The various tones and a few key highlights indicate the light source."

Blocking in the stronger colours
Paint the overall shapes of the orange-coloured satsumas and the red and yellow patches on the nectarines and peach.

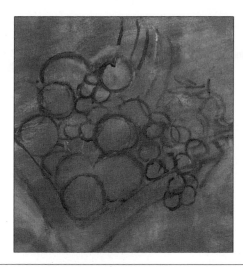

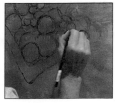

Modifying the composition
While making the underdrawing, the artist decided to simplify the picture by leaving out the extraneous picture frame and fruit she had included in her preliminary drawings.

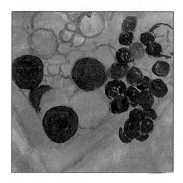

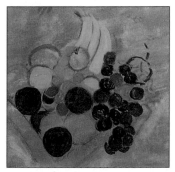

Darker tones
Start by blocking in the darkest shapes in order to suggest the plums and 'black' grapes. Note how the fruits in shadow have a different tonal value from those that catch the light.

Lighter tones
Now introduce the bananas and apricots. For the 'white' grapes, mix a cool base colour from cadmium yellow medium and cerulean, adding ultramarine and sap green to the grapes nestling in the shade.

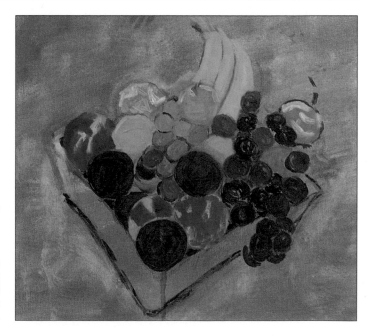

What shall I paint?
STILL LIFE
Painting a bowl of fruit

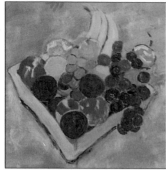

Painting the fruit bowl
Outline the bowl with deep ultramarine, then lightly brush pale Naples yellow along the sides of the bowl. Here the pink ground changes the colour to a warm grey. Define the inner edge of the bowl and deep shadows with sap green and purple.

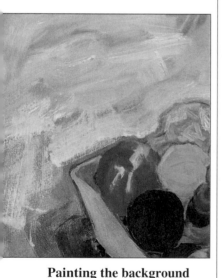

Painting the background
Using your largest flat brush, roughly block in the white tablecloth, scrubbing paint onto the canvas so that the warm ground shows through the brushstrokes.

Before you start to detail the focal point of the picture, paint in the background shapes and tones. These will help you to evaluate accurately the colours that are applied next.

BRINGING THE PAINTING TO LIFE

With the underpainting complete, the artist returns to the focal point of the picture, the bowl of fruit.

"This is where the fun begins. Don't hold back at this stage, thinking you are going to spoil your painting. Just go with the flow and enjoy it."

With deft strokes of paint, the picture is rapidly brought to life. Fruits begin to take on weight and solidity, and their surfaces glisten with reflected light.

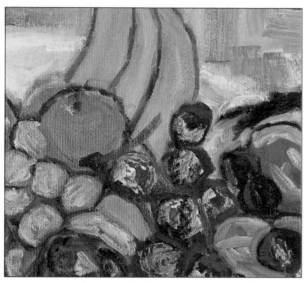

Defining shapes
To define shapes and unify the painting, Jennie Dunn paints distinct outlines, using colours that complement the colours of the fruit – soft purple around the bananas, and dark green for the warm-coloured nectarines, apricots and satsumas.

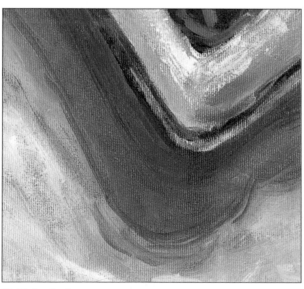

Multiple shadows
The combination of natural and artificial light throws multiple shadows alongside the fruit bowl. With their sweeping bands of cool pink blended with sap green, ultramarine and viridian, these shadows are an important feature of the painting.

Bananas
Paint the distinctive planes separately, using various tones of yellow mixed with sap green.

Satsumas
With a combination of cadmium red and yellow, keep the orange colour relatively low-key to ensure that fruits at the back of the bowl appear to recede. Apply pale-yellow highlights and dark-green leaves with a large paintbrush.

Apricots
Bring the simplest of fruits to life with vigorous brushstrokes. The base colour is cadmium yellow warmed with cadmium orange.

Nectarines
Dry-brush highlights over a mixture of crimson and cadmium red.

White grapes
Paint solid-looking grapes with complementary pink and yellow-green highlights, gradually blending into the blue-green shadows.

Peach
Having painted the yellow patches, stipple alizarin crimson and cadmium red onto the canvas to depict the velvety skin of a peach.

Plums
With bold brushstrokes, describe the form and rich colouring of the darkest fruits. Use pale blue and pink for the highlights, and define the darker areas with deep purple.

Black grapes
Scumbling pink and blue-grey onto the canvas creates a texture that resembles a natural bloom on the grape skins. Apply highlights with a painting knife, and enliven the spaces between with viridian.

Apple
A small patch of pale-green apple is the perfect complementary to the dark rich colours that surround it.

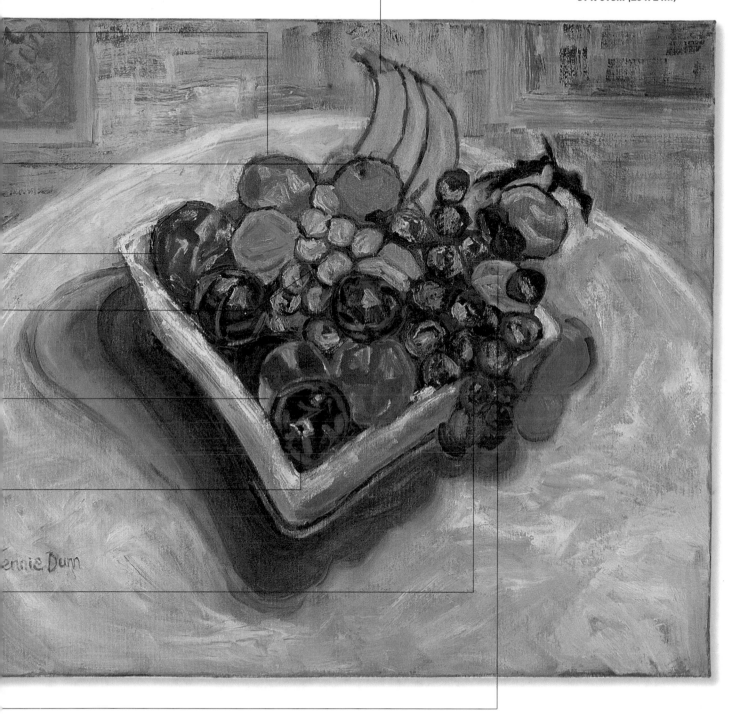

Jennie Dunn
FRUIT BOWL
Water-mixable oil on canvas
51 x 61cm (20 x 24in)

"I like to draw rounded shapes with a series of straight lines. Fruits are not entirely round anyway, and straight lines are more dynamic."

What shall I paint?
STILL LIFE
Absorbing feedback
Flexible approach to composition
Creating textures

Painting a vase of flowers

There is little doubt that making preparatory studies allows you to try out different compositions and absorb valuable information about a subject before you embark on a painting, but an artist must also be able to make sensitive and flexible responses to positive feedback as the work progresses. This is not an easy skill to develop, requiring the ability to recognize a good thing when it happens and the courage to change course, perhaps even to abandon your original concept, when something better presents itself.

Shirley Trevena has mastered this flexible and spontaneous approach to painting, taking pleasure in every fortuitous effect and texture an unpredictable medium like watercolour can offer.

"I am not inviting viewers to appreciate a beautiful arrangement of flowers. I hope they are enjoying the painting for itself."

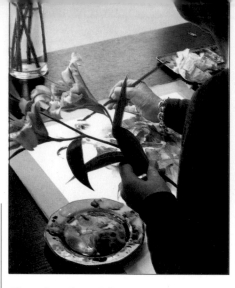

Don't approach this exercise with the idea that you are going to make an accurate botanical study. Instead, enjoy yourself as you try with colour and texture to convey an impression – your emotional response to a vase of flowers.

Choosing the subject

To avoid conflict within the painting, it is a good idea to select just one type of flower, and rely on the contrast between blooms, leaves and stems for visual interest. You will have your own ideas for suitable subjects, but an arrangement of lilies, irises or tulips offers such dramatic possibilities that these flowers invariably make rewarding subjects for painting.

The vase or container you choose for the flowers will make a considerable difference to the picture. The simple brass vase depicted in the featured painting is a perfect foil for the display of white lilies, but other types of flower might look better in a glass vase or a ceramic jug. You don't have to put flowers in water. Wrapping paper presents exciting opportunities for colour and pattern, too.

Lilies
The eye is drawn to the sculptural blooms of the lily, but for an artist, the shapes formed by the leaves and stem can be as important as the flowers.

Flexible approach to composition

To develop a loose, intuitive style, try not to be restricted by the shape and size of your paper. And as the work progresses, be prepared to develop the composition in ways that are suggested by the painting itself, such as a strong directional flow or a balance of forms.

For Shirley Trevena, the vase of flowers merely serves as the starting point for her composition.

"I work with one of the flowers in my hand. This allows me greater freedom of expression because, by taking information from the flower in my hand, I can paint a bloom from a slightly different angle, or insert a bud or a leaf in just the right spot."

PREPARATORY WORK

When following a more 'organic' approach to painting, there is no point in making a detailed underdrawing. But that doesn't preclude you from drawing the regular outline of a dish or jug if it helps you get started. Similarly, there is nothing to prevent you practising the techniques before you embark on a finished painting. The sketch painting opposite, for example, was made to try out a range of colours that the artist was considering for the main work.

Colours
For this painting, Shirley Trevena used the following artist-quality tube colours mixed on white plates.

Alizarin crimson
Burnt sienna
Cadmium lemon
Caput mortuum violet
French ultramarine
Green gold
Olive green
Payne's grey

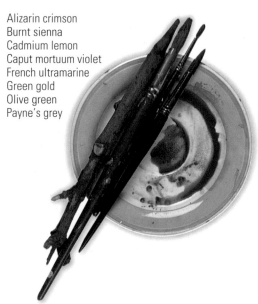

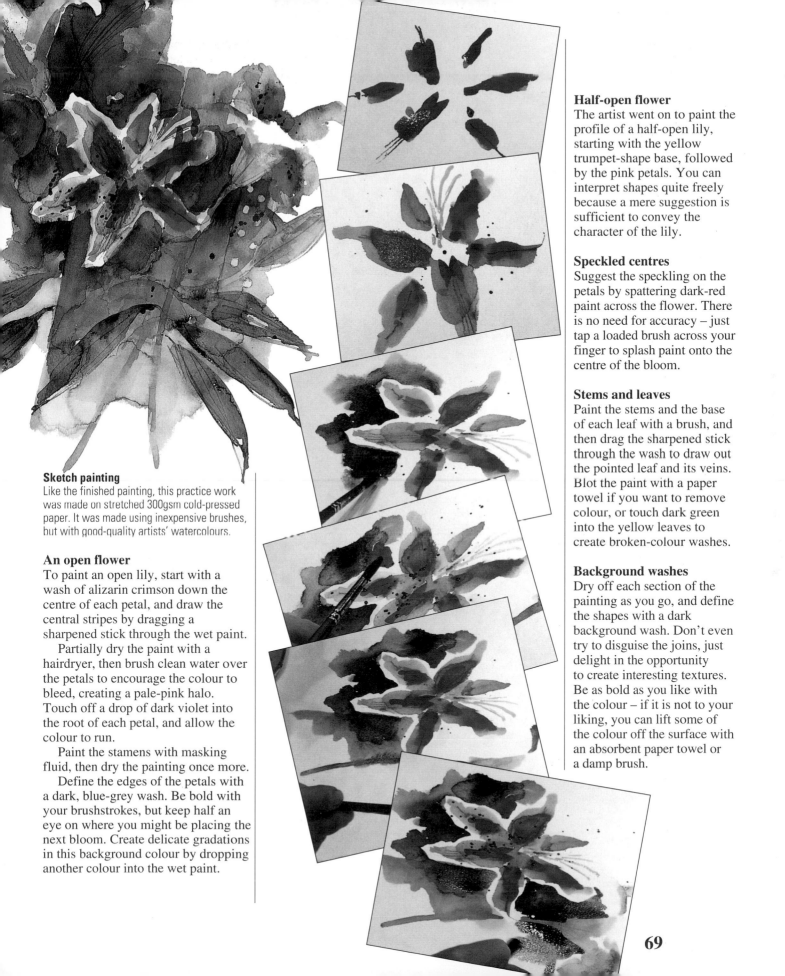

Sketch painting
Like the finished painting, this practice work was made on stretched 300gsm cold-pressed paper. It was made using inexpensive brushes, but with good-quality artists' watercolours.

An open flower
To paint an open lily, start with a wash of alizarin crimson down the centre of each petal, and draw the central stripes by dragging a sharpened stick through the wet paint.

Partially dry the paint with a hairdryer, then brush clean water over the petals to encourage the colour to bleed, creating a pale-pink halo. Touch off a drop of dark violet into the root of each petal, and allow the colour to run.

Paint the stamens with masking fluid, then dry the painting once more.

Define the edges of the petals with a dark, blue-grey wash. Be bold with your brushstrokes, but keep half an eye on where you might be placing the next bloom. Create delicate gradations in this background colour by dropping another colour into the wet paint.

Half-open flower
The artist went on to paint the profile of a half-open lily, starting with the yellow trumpet-shape base, followed by the pink petals. You can interpret shapes quite freely because a mere suggestion is sufficient to convey the character of the lily.

Speckled centres
Suggest the speckling on the petals by spattering dark-red paint across the flower. There is no need for accuracy – just tap a loaded brush across your finger to splash paint onto the centre of the bloom.

Stems and leaves
Paint the stems and the base of each leaf with a brush, and then drag the sharpened stick through the wash to draw out the pointed leaf and its veins. Blot the paint with a paper towel if you want to remove colour, or touch dark green into the yellow leaves to create broken-colour washes.

Background washes
Dry off each section of the painting as you go, and define the shapes with a dark background wash. Don't even try to disguise the joins, just delight in the opportunity to create interesting textures. Be as bold as you like with the colour – if it is not to your liking, you can lift some of the colour off the surface with an absorbent paper towel or a damp brush.

69

What shall I paint?
STILL LIFE
Painting a vase of flowers

THE FINISHED PAINTING

A traditional watercolourist would construct a painting systematically by applying the paler washes first, then overlay with progressively darker glazes of colour. It is also usual to work across the entire painting, rather than concentrate on small areas at a time. With this painting, the artist deliberately turns that approach on its head, in order to create a rich tapestry of colour and texture that is largely the result of chance.

"When I start painting I embark on a journey without knowing my destination. You should always be prepared to take a risk, because the unexpected accidents make for a more exciting painting. I am looking to incorporate those events that many watercolourists try to avoid. In fact, I try to re-create similar effects elsewhere in the painting, so that they become an integral and quite deliberate aspect of the work."

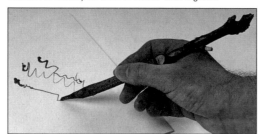

Don't be mean with your paint
Rich textural effects are only possible if you apply plenty of paint. For this reason, it pays to use tube colours and mix your washes on white plates or saucers. A paintbox of pan colours is useful, but only during the later stages of a painting when you might want to add small colourful touches or modify an area of colour with a glaze.

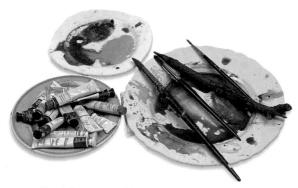

Special effects
In addition to conventional brushwork, Shirley Trevena achieves free-flowing lines with a sharpened stick.

Shirley Trevena
TALL VASE OF LILIES
(opposite)
Watercolour on paper
58 x 46cm (23 x 18in)

Although she paints a wide variety of subjects, from still life to figures, Shirley Trevena is perhaps best known for her exuberant flower paintings. Here, the lilies are bursting out of the painting, creating a thrust of energy that is counterbalanced by the dark weight of the vase. Flouting convention, the artist makes the stems visible.

Starting points
You want to get off to a good start, so select something that grabs your attention. From the beginning, the bold and colourful shape of the open flower (below) was seen as the focal point for this painting.

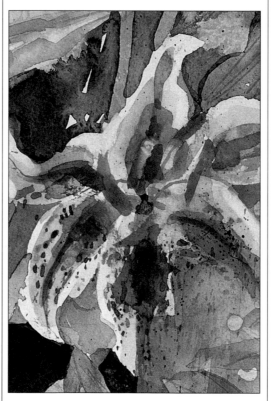

"I start painting whatever it was that drew me to the subject in the first place. In this case, it was the speckled 'Stargazer' in the centre of the picture. Having established my starting point, I work out from there, adding to the painting like joining the pieces of a jigsaw."

☛ SEE ALSO
Blooms and backruns 180
Glazing 176
Masking fluid 90, 179
Still life 28
Watercolour paint 161

Broken colour
If you touch a loaded brush into a wash that is still wet, the colours will merge, creating soft, irregular margins. To leave deliberate junctions between colours, allow one wash to dry before overlaying it with another.

Backruns
To create the delicate mottled edge of a backrun, drop paint or clean water from the tip of a brush onto a wash that has been allowed to dry out a little.

Masking off
It is difficult to reserve small areas of white paper when painting a background wash. Mask details like stamens with masking fluid, then paint over them and rub off the rubbery fluid when the paint has dried.

Spattering
Flicking paint from a brush creates the illusion of speckling on flower petals. Here the artist applied additional dots, using a sharpened stick.

Drawn lines
Leaf veining and other linear marks are made by drawing a sharpened stick through wet paint. You can create similar effects by dipping the stick into another colour before drawing the lines.

Drying the work
Using a hairdryer allows you to continue working on the picture. If you leave the paint to dry naturally, that will create richer textures.

Lifting colour
To remove colour, scrub the surface of the paper with a fairly stiff damp paintbrush, and blot the area dry with a paper towel.

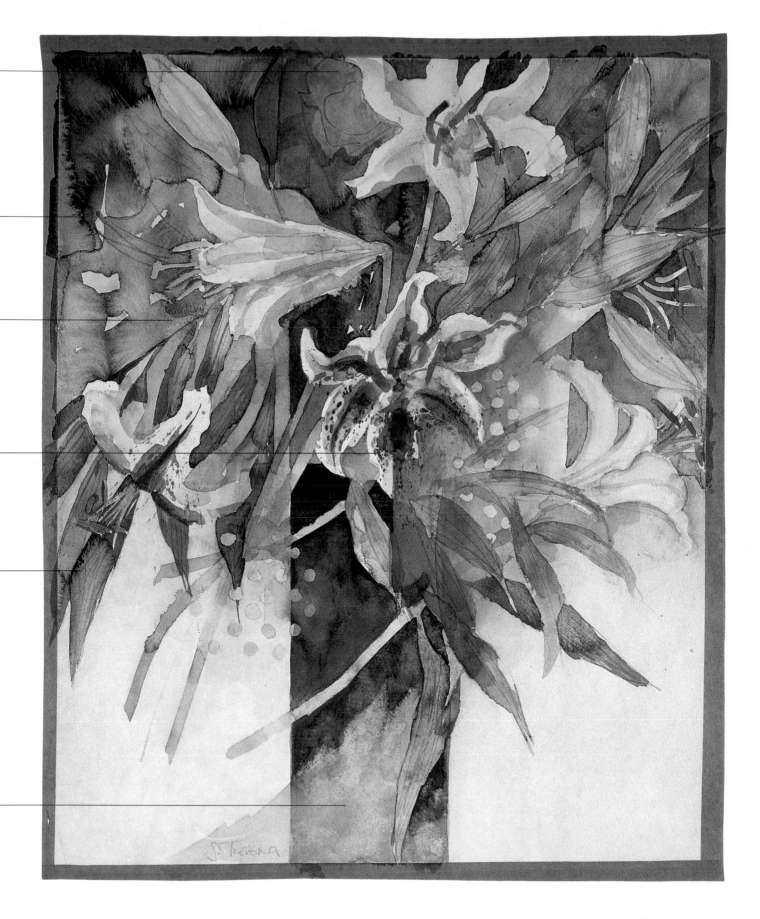

What shall I paint?
STILL LIFE
Composition
Introducing light
Painting with oils
Constructing a painting in detail

Painting a still-life group

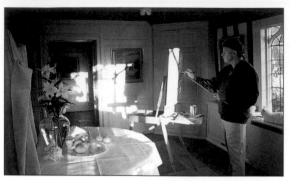

Anticipating the light

All paintings rely to some extent on the way natural or artificial light falls on the subject, but in this case the artist has decided to allow the light to dominate his picture. A choice like this brings its own challenges, requiring the artist to devote much of the day to working partly from memory, anticipating those brief periods of time when conditions are just right.

This still-life painting brings together the core of subjects we have seen earlier, but this time the artist has chosen to introduce another vital element – light. Timothy Easton is known for paintings composed with a strong geometric structure. Here he arranges a simple still life on a square canvas, placing the main group just off centre. A diagonal shaft of winter sunlight balances the composition and throws dramatic shadows across the table and backdrop, creating a grid-like pattern with the folds picked out by the intense light.

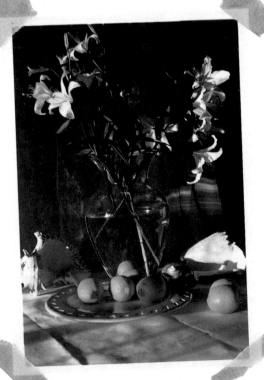

Painting with oils

Some people seem to find oil paint intimidating – something that they should work up to, having cut their teeth on another medium such as watercolour or acrylics. There is also a widely held view that it is impossible to paint in oils without creating such a mess that you need a special studio to work in. Neither assumption is correct. Being slow-drying, oil paint allows the beginner plenty of time for experimentation; and mistakes can be corrected by overpainting, or by scraping off the paint and starting again.

One drawback with any slow-drying paint is a tendency for colours to become 'muddy', simply because each new layer of paint stirs up the colours that have already been applied to the canvas. You can control this to some extent by starting with thin washes of diluted colour that are gradually overlaid with thicker paint as the painting develops. Also, it pays to keep your paintbrushes as clean as possible to avoid introducing colours inadvertently. Timothy Easton, who uses only the best-quality oil paints, takes extra care to keep his colours clean by premixing a range of shades from a relatively limited palette.

Various additives or mediums can be mixed with oil paint to modify its characteristics, but you can produce perfectly successful pictures using nothing but pure turpentine for thinning the paint and for washing out your brushes.

"Light is what interests me most as a painter. I like to work with very strong tonal contrasts and, in many cases, quite strong colours, too."

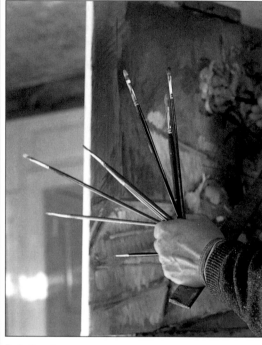

Paintbrushes

Timothy Easton likes to use a range of relatively small filberts for painting in oils, because it enables him to make a variety of strokes using a single brush. For very fine detail, he uses sable brushes.

"To keep my colours fresh and uncontaminated, I tend to reserve a separate brush for each group of colours. If necessary, I will work with seven or eight brushes at a time."

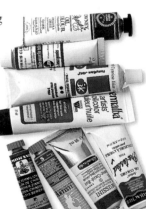

Basic palette of colours
Titanium white
Cadmium yellow deep
Cadmium yellow
Raw sienna
Indian yellow
Cadmium red
Geranium lake
Permanent red
Alizarin crimson
Cerulean
Cobalt blue

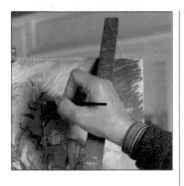

Improvized mahlstick
A traditional padded mahlstick is used for steadying the painting arm when executing precise work. When working at close quarters, improvize by resting any strip of wood against the frame of the stretched canvas.

Stretching canvases
Timothy Easton likes to paint on supports he makes from rolls of linen canvas. Using rolled canvas reduces the risk of creases that may not show until varnish is applied to the finished painting.

Mixing colours in advance
Because he is in the habit of working on a number of paintings, all at different stages of development, Timothy Easton usually has more colours on his palette than he needs for any individual picture. Consequently there is less space on the palette for mixing, and there's the inherent risk of colours becoming contaminated. As a precaution, he squeezes out the minimum amount of raw paint, but then mixes a range of hues and shades from each colour before starting work.

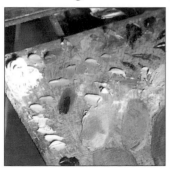

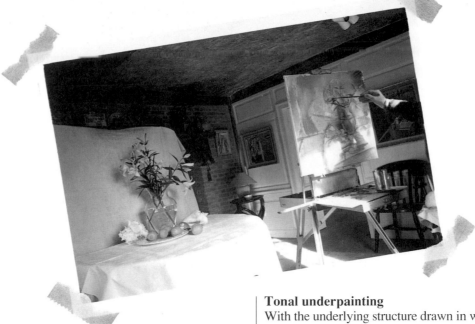

"Drawing is mark-making, painting is mark-making. All that is important is to find ways of translating what you see onto the canvas."

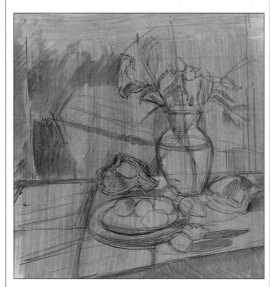

Initial brush drawing
Having primed and painted the canvas with a neutral olive-green ground, the artist begins to draw the subject to establish the basic composition. Even though he is applying diluted paint with a small sable brush, the work at this stage resembles a lively pencil drawing, with bold hatching used to indicate areas of shadow.

Tonal underpainting
With the underlying structure drawn in with line, the artist begins to block in a wider range of tones, using diluted blue-grey paint applied with bold diagonal brushstrokes.

During these initial stages, the artist can only approximate the depth of tone and degree of contrast that will be evident when the sunlight finally streams through the window to the left of the still-life table. Consequently, he concentrates on basic proportion and form, knowing that there may be considerable changes made to the colour at a later stage.

"Instead of painting the flowers and other objects on the table as they appear at this moment, I have to think ahead to what I anticipate they will look like a little later in the day. With this in mind, I am using a range of tones with very little contrast as a basis for the stronger shadows and highlights that I expect to see when the sun travels round."

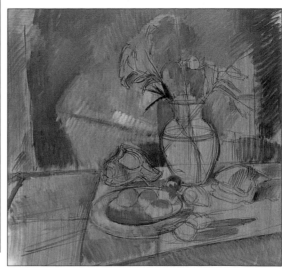

What shall I paint?
STILL LIFE
Painting a still-life group

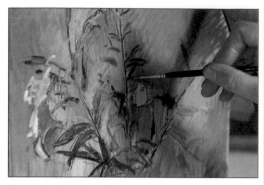

Introducing the lilies

The stems and leaves are drawn using broken lines and broad brushstrokes, and the position of each bloom is plotted with white and pale-yellow paint.

Whenever you paint flowers, be aware that buds eventually open into full blooms which, in turn, wilt as the flower dies. Since you can't arrest a flower's development, you have to decide what stage is best for your painting.

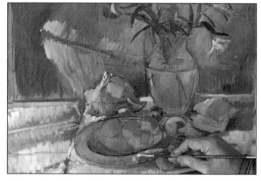

Flooding with light

Eventually the sunlight streams through the window, illuminating the still life as the artist anticipated. This gives him the chance to paint the high-key tones across the tablecloth and backdrop, and introduce highlights to the flat dish and shells. With the more intense light pervading the scene, now's the time to balance the tones across the painting.

Applying stronger colours

The sunlight brings the stronger colours to life, and the artist seizes the opportunity to block in the lemons, using cool grey-greens for the shadows, orange for the mid tones and various shades of yellow to depict reflected light and highlights. At the same time, he strengthens the shadows cast by the fruit and gives the shells body and form with pink highlights and warmer shades of blue-grey.

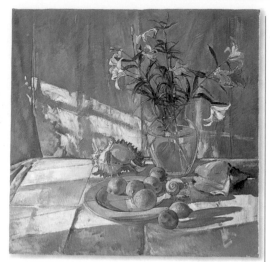

WORKING UP FORM AND DETAIL

With the main elements of the painting blocked in to his satisfaction, Timothy Easton starts to work up the details of the still-life group. The form of each lily is greatly enhanced, and carefully drawn highlights and shadows indicate the curve of individual leaves. More work goes into painting the water in the vase, introducing dark shadows, pink reflections and bright highlights, all of which serve to describe the rounded shape of the vase, the thickness of the glass and the surface of the water.

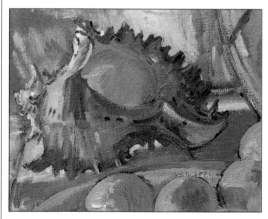

Detailing the shells
The shells, too, receive more attention. The hollow nature of the large shell is indicated with pink light glowing from inside. Darker tones are applied to make a stronger contrast with the bright light reflected from the table and backdrop.

Turning a painting upside down

If at any stage you feel that something is not quite right with your painting, turn it upside down. This invariably helps you to see the work afresh and makes you aware of problems with proportions, colour balance and tonal contrast.

Timothy Easton
REFLECTIONS AND SHADOWS
Oil on canvas
61 x 61cm (24 x 24in)

In its final stages, the painting begins to glow with light and colour, an illusion that is created by tonal contrast and the juxtaposition of warm and cool hues.
Colour is introduced to the shadows and areas of reflected light to imply the warm glow of evening sunlight. Although the glazing bars and raised folds are now clearly defined, Timothy Easton deliberately softens them with dry-brushed and scumbled colour to break up any hard edges and create an interesting surface texture. To balance the composition, he increases the area of shadow near the bottom of the picture and, at the same time, introduces reflected colour onto the white surface.
Colourful details bring the lilies into sharp focus, with a greater variety of tonal contrast among the leaves.
The form and surface texture of the fruits are sharply defined with fine brushwork and blending. The shallow dish is described with cast shadow and reflected light, and its rim is picked out with pale-pink and blue highlights.
All three shells are worked up with greater definition, their glinting pearlized surfaces reflecting warm shadows and specks of colour.

☛ **SEE ALSO**

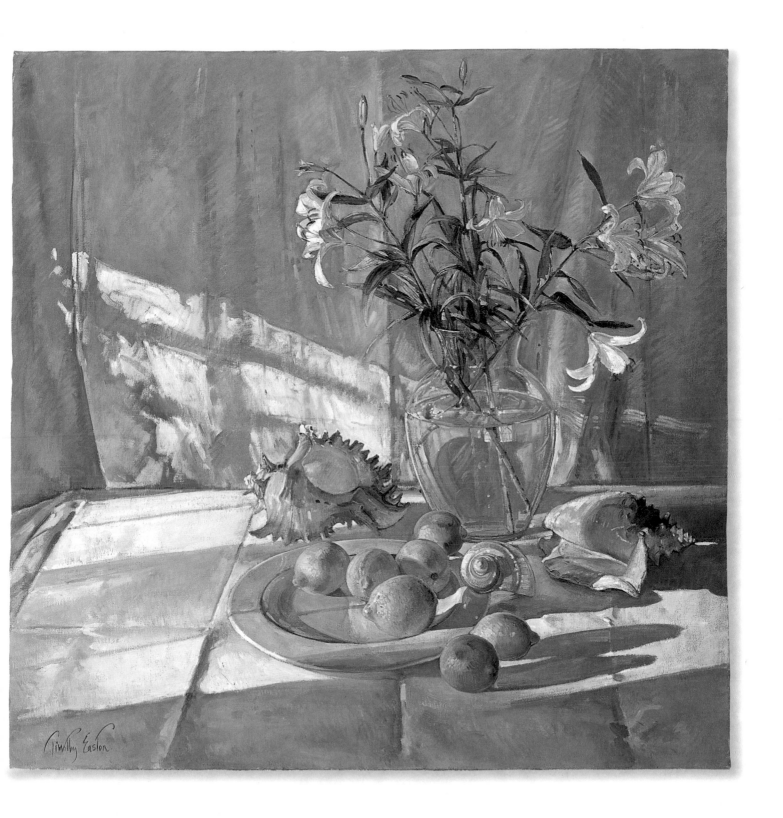

What shall I paint?
INTERIORS
Creating atmosphere
Simplifying a
complex subject
Scumbling
Glazing

Painting your room

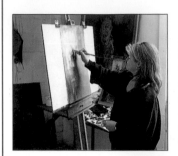

"I don't follow my drawings too closely. Painting is a different process from drawing. As the painting begins to develop, I sometimes find that what I liked about a drawing does not work as well when put down in paint."

Stepping back from the still-life table, an artist can take in a wider view of his or her surroundings, bringing pieces of furniture into the frame, and perhaps a window or the corner of the room. Some people would see it as just another still life on a larger scale, yet a room – someone's home or workspace – is more than an accumulation of inanimate objects. Every interior has a character that reflects the personality of the people who live or work there. Painting a room you know well gives you a better chance of conjuring up that atmosphere and conveying it to the onlooker.

The featured painting is a picture of a small intimate space, fused with rich earthy colours and strong daylight streaming through the window. A glass-topped table, a chest of drawers and a mahogany wall clock emerge from the shadows. This is the living room of the artist, Debra Manifold. Like most artists, she surrounds herself with a plethora of interesting objects and curios, but she has deliberately excluded most of these details in order to capture what she considers to be the essential character of the room.

"It's impossible to paint every object you see in a room. You have to simplify the clutter, and sometimes rearrange the furniture if you feel it's detracting from the painting."

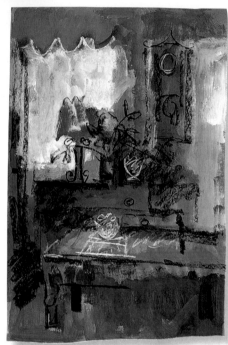

Tonal sketch

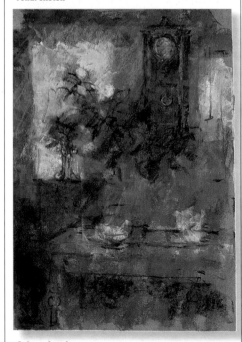

Colour sketch

Preparatory sketches

Before starting on the finished painting, Debra Manifold photographed her room from different angles. Having settled on a particular view, she made a tonal study, using pastel and acrylic paint on brown wrapping paper. She also made a coloured pastel sketch to get some idea of how she might interpret the effect of light on the room.

Everything you have learnt from painting still-life groups is relevant to painting an interior: form, shape, tone, light and shade all play their part. Basic perspective becomes even more important. You don't have to be precise with your calculations, but when making preparatory sketches and planning your composition, be aware of how the different surfaces – floor, walls, ceiling, table tops – relate to one another in space.

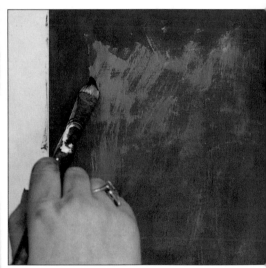

Scumbling colours
Debra Manifold creates rich overlays and subtle combinations by scumbling one colour over another. She scrubs the paint onto the surface, depositing very thin layers of colour. Scumbling is an easy technique to master because you can see the effect developing gradually.

"There are different ways to apply glazes with acrylics. You could overlay with wet translucent glazes, a bit like watercolour. I like to scumble my colours to create dry glazes that alter the colour beneath without obliterating it. The effect is similar to a pastel drawing, which is why it works so well with mixed media."

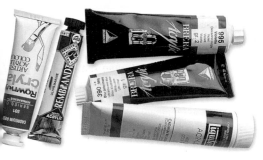

MATERIALS

The featured painting was made with acrylic paint overlaid with soft pastel. The support is Ingres board (pastel board), primed with gesso mixed with pumice. The primed board was coated with a rich ground colour – quinacridone violet – to establish a vibrant basis for the painting.

The artist's palette
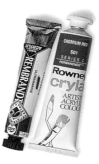

Cadmium red medium
French ultramarine
Hooker's green
Maroon
Mars orange
Olive green
Payne's grey
Quinacridone violet
Titanium white
Yellow ochre

"A lot of people worry about using acrylics because they dry so quickly – but for me, that's their strength. It means I can work lights over darks without them picking up the underlying colours. This suits my technique."

Keeping acrylics workable

Fast-drying acrylic paint is likely to develop a skin, sometimes before you have finished painting. One way to deal with the problem is to use a stay-wet palette that keeps the paint moist. Debra Manifold has a different approach. She simply squeezes out generous amounts of acrylic onto her palette – when a skin forms, the paint beneath remains workable, even on the following day.

Brushes

The artist prefers to use natural-bristle paintbrushes when working with acrylics, even though her vigorous painting style wears out her brushes at quite a rate. For this painting, she used two filberts – Nos.8 and 10.

UNDERPAINTING

Having made two sketches already, Debra Manifold is prepared to launch straight into the painting.

"I would find an underdrawing too restrictive. I think many people would enjoy the act of painting more if they abandoned the notion of making a careful drawing first."

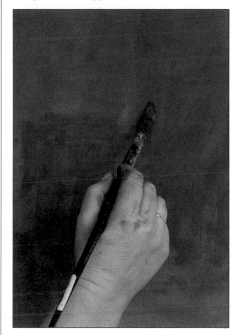

Blocking in the darker areas
The positions of the window surround, door opening and furniture are blocked in, using a darker tone of the violet ground colour. The artist scrubs neat paint onto the surface of the board.

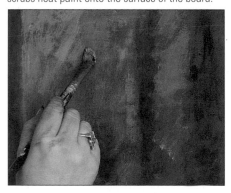

Laying complementaries
The real value of the strong violet ground becomes obvious when electric greens and blues are laid over it. This brings the painting to life.

"I like to apply these cool colours over the hot background. I want to get the feeling of a fairly dark room, but I still want the painting to be lively."

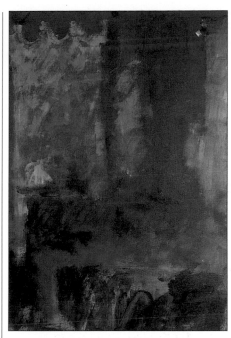

Positive and negative shapes
A lampshade, silhouetted against the window, is brushed in with blue-grey paint; the furniture and dark floor area are indicated with hatching.

"I am looking for negative and positive shapes – that is the shapes between and around objects as well as the shapes of the objects themselves."

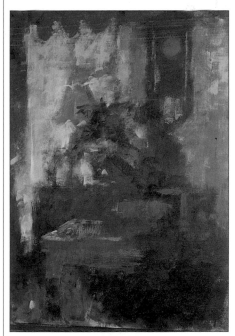

The finished underpainting
The details of the room are added quickly, with wall clock and table receding into shadow. Light from the window is intensified, and brushstrokes suggest reflections from polished surfaces.

What shall I paint?
INTERIORS
Painting your room

BRINGING LIGHT INTO THE ROOM

The way light spills into the room is vital to the painting.

"I am starting to diffuse the window surround, softening the edges to give the impression of strong light streaming in."

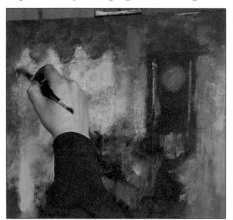

Scumbling over the window
The artist begins to scumble neat paint over the window itself. This enhances the contrast and breaks up the edges of the barely discernible windowframe.

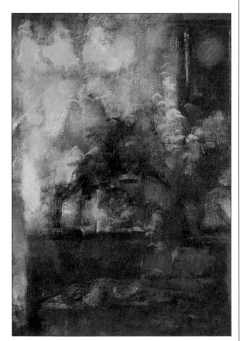

Scattering the light
Next, she uses a dry brush, barely loaded with paint, to scrub colour onto the walls and furniture in the vicinity of the window.

CHANGING THE COMPOSITION

The picture has reached a stage where Debra Manifold is forced to make a decision that will affect the composition of the painting.

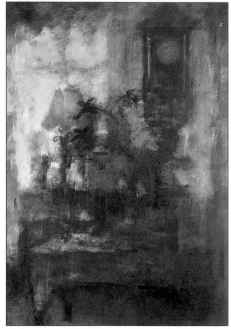

"I am trying to decide whether to move the plant that is right in the centre of the painting. There's a strong diagonal line or flow that leads the eye from the window, down through the lampshade and plant, towards the foreground. But there's nothing in the foreground to arrest the eye."

RETURNING TO THE UNDERPAINTING

Before tackling the foreground detail, the artist decides to glaze over the wall clock – which at the moment is too dominant.

"I am going to work on this area around the clock, to take it back almost to the underpainting stage. Then I can build it up again."

Overlaying with a wash of colour
With a wide brush, Debra Manifold paints a thin violet glaze over the right-hand side of the painting. Using diluted ground colour unifies this area of the picture but preserves the vitality of the other colours.

"If you find yourself struggling with one area of a painting, it's often a good idea to work on another section for a while, and see how that affects the area that's giving you the problem. Sometimes the solution becomes obvious."

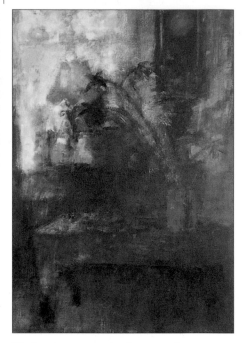

Moving the vase to the foreground
With a few brushstrokes, the artist finds the solution to the problem.

"I am going to move the vase onto the coffee table, so that the eye can come to rest there."

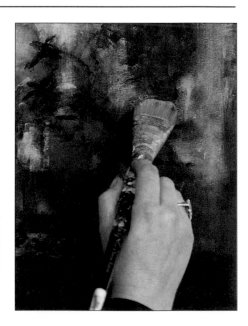

Debra Manifold
THE ARTIST'S ROOM
Acrylic and pastel on board
58.5 x 41cm (23 x 16in)

The final details are worked up with soft pastels. The doorway exudes cool light, but without detracting from the principal source of illumination. The same green light, scattered across the floor, balances the painting and throws the table legs into relief. As planned, the conflict between the background and foreground is resolved with the addition of a vase that now contains flowers. These bring touches of colour into what is otherwise a sombre area of the painting. Points of reflected light sparkle across the glass table top, where a freely drawn fruit bowl encourages the eye to linger.

"You can be working away for hours, then suddenly discover that all you need are a few details and the painting is finished."

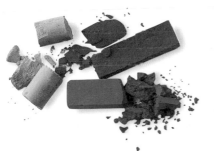

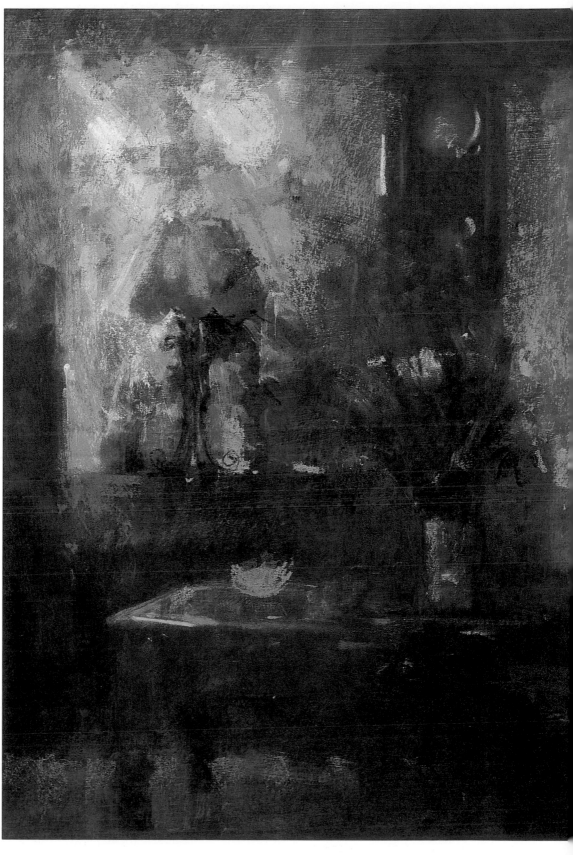

What shall I paint?
INTERIORS
Effects of light
Fat-over-lean
Light-over-dark
Layering colours

Painting against the light

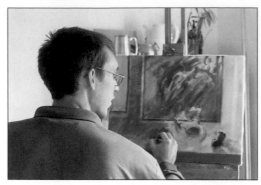

The artist
Colin Willey has become a specialist in *contre-jour* painting. At one time a landscape artist, he finds himself drawn to painting the elusive play of light on simple still-life subjects.

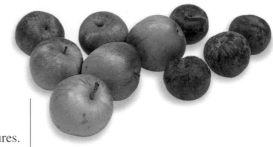

Painting subjects in front of a window – known as *contre-jour*, (literally 'against daylight') – is an activity that fascinates artists because, in one picture, they are able to combine traditions as diverse as interior painting, still life, portraiture and landscape. Above all, there is the challenge of dealing with the capricious nature of daylight.

"In this situation, the shadows and highlights change so dramatically, you have to work quickly to capture the light. In a sense, you have to seize the moment, then stick with it to avoid painting a picture that is full of contradictions."

Choosing your viewpoint
You don't have to be blessed with a stunning view to make exciting pictures. There are so many options and permutations in every location that you could paint the same subject over and over without exhausting the possibilities. When making one of the paintings featured here, the artist was seated so that the picture could encompass everything from the still life to the houses at the end of his garden. For the other painting, he positioned himself so that the objects were viewed against a dark background in order to make the most of reflections in the glass.

"There is so much to see in a set-up like this. There's light reflecting from the objects standing on the windowsill. Then there are the reflections of the same objects in the glass. Modulated colours are passed back and forth in a way that would never happen under a different form of lighting."

Setting out the props
The props for these paintings were selected for their simplicity and for the way they would reflect light and colour.

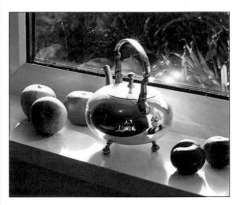

"It can be difficult to set up a still life without it looking contrived, which is why I sometimes paint whatever happens to be there."

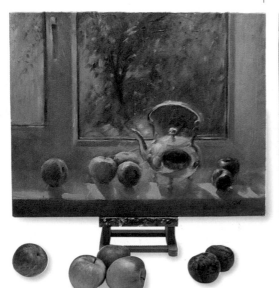

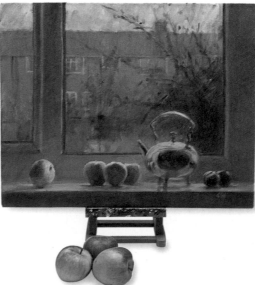

Transient light
Because daylight is so transient, Colin Willey has adopted the practice of working on two or more paintings at once. For this exercise, he has painted a still life that is flooded with bright sunlight. By the afternoon, the sun no longer streams through the window of his studio, so he began another painting of the same subject from a slightly different viewpoint.

MATERIALS

Oil paints

For both paintings, Colin Willey restricted himself to using just five colours – Venetian red, cadmium yellow, yellow ochre, French ultramarine and titanium white.

"I like to work with a limited palette because it means I have to mix my colours precisely. This reduces any tendency to paint the local colour of the subject. Using so few colours also has the effect of unifying the picture."

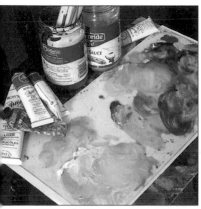

The palette
The artist mixes his paints on a sheet of glass laid over white paper. He uses turpentine as a thinner and for rinsing paintbrushes.

Brushes

These paintings were made, using a selection of rounds, flats and filberts. Working on coarse canvas is hard on paintbrushes, so Colin Willey is loath to spend too much on them.

"I use them up at such a rate that I think I would become too inhibited if I bought expensive brushes. In any case, I don't mind using cheap brushes so long as they do the job. If a brush makes the mark I want, that is all that matters to me."

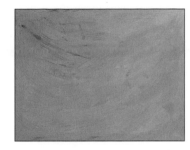

Applying coloured ground

In preparation, the artist stretched two canvases, using coarse cotton duck, then primed them with white acrylic paint. He then applied a coloured ground to obliterate the white primer.

"I invariably use one of three colours for my grounds – burnt sienna, burnt umber or, as here, yellow ochre. I sometimes work over old discarded paintings. I just turn them upside down and incorporate the existing brushmarks into the new painting."

Blocking in

Colin Willey likes to launch straight into a painting.

"I never make a separate preparatory drawing of the subject. I like to capture the moment directly on the canvas, so that the process of working everything out becomes part of the painting instead of it being a separate exercise. It can be hard work, but that for me is an advantage. When I am working on something that is difficult, it becomes totally absorbing and, after a while, I begin to see things in terms of paint and colour instead of actual objects. And that is good for the painting."

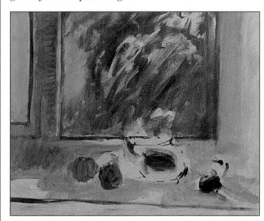

Drawing in the main elements
The main elements are drawn onto the canvas, using a dark mixture of ultramarine and red. The main areas of tone are blocked in with thinned paint. Scrubbing paint onto the canvas forces the colour into the coarse weave.

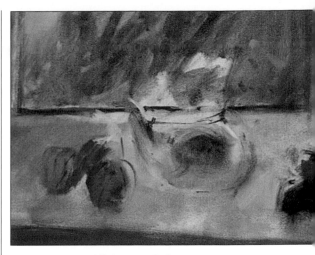

Fat-over-lean and light-over-dark
The featured oil paintings were constructed conventionally, observing the well-tried principle of painting 'fat-over-lean', which prevents the top layers cracking as the paint dries.

"I always begin by blocking in with thinned paint, gradually applying thicker paint as the work proceeds. At the same time, I prefer to work light-over-dark, because it helps me preserve a richness of colour and tone in the darker areas of the painting. It is easy to scrape off highlights and work up from the darks again, but I find working in reverse more difficult."

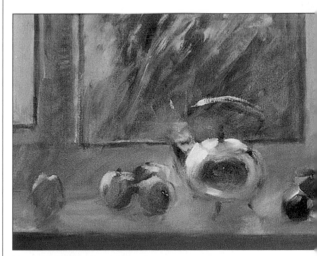

The finished underpainting
The main elements of the painting are now blocked in, and the composition is firmly established to the artist's satisfaction.

"By this stage you can usually tell whether the painting is going to work or not. Although it is very ill-defined at the moment, there is already something about the painting that makes me want to carry on."

81

What shall I paint?
INTERIORS
Painting against the light

WORKING ON THE STILL LIFE

Having established the tonal balance between the foreground and background, the artist went on to work up the still-life elements, using a variety of techniques.

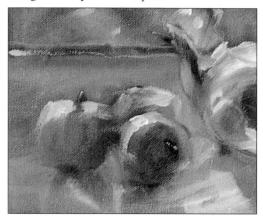

Creating layers of colour

Colin Willey spends almost as much time removing paint from the canvas as he does applying it. Having brushed colour onto the surface, he will often smudge it with his fingers or wipe the paint off again with a rag, leaving subtle overlays of transparent colour.

"I am not correcting mistakes when I remove paint in this way. This is an integral part of the painting process."

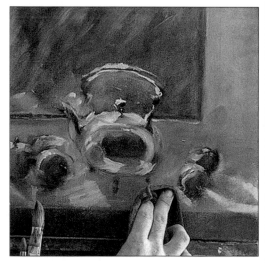

Using ground colour

Rubbing paint off the surface also exposes the warm ground colour. This technique is used successfully to suggest warm sunlight reflected onto the windowframe and sill.

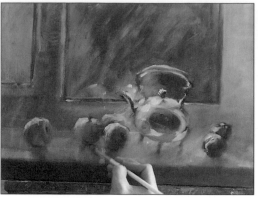

Painting shadows

Dry-brushing dark shadows under the fruit creates the illusion of solid objects resting on the windowsill.

"The colouring is quite subtle here, because it is a combination of shadow and reflected light. The colours I have used to paint the apples have been smudged and reapplied several times, so the canvas around that area is stained with the same colours. This gives the impression that the fruits are being reflected in the white surface."

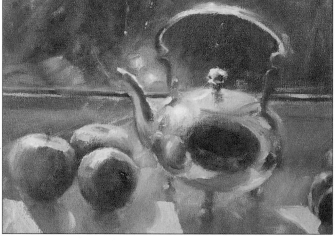

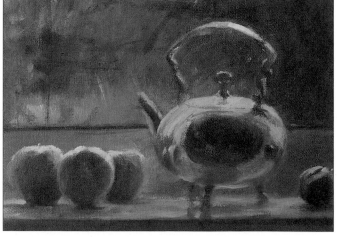

☛ **SEE ALSO**
Atmospheric perspective 106, 117
Dry brushing 177
Fat-over-lean 176
Painting three dimensions 50
Rooms and interiors 30
Scumbling 177

Contre-jour

The way that the light falls on the still-life group has a profound effect on the way the artist paints the subjects.

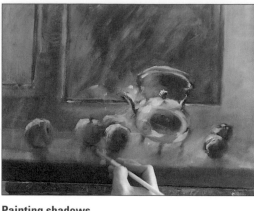

Strong sunlight

In one painting, strong sunlight is falling onto the highly reflective surface of the metal teapot. To create the impression of dazzling light, the artist smears paint and blurs the edges so that parts of the object disappear in the highlights.

Cool daylight

In the second painting, the sun has moved round, so there is not as much tonal contrast. The light is cooler, the reflections less intense, and the objects are more clearly defined.

Colin Willey
Silver teapot and summer fruits
Oil on canvas
41 x 51cm (16 x 20in)

The still life is the focal point of this painting. What you see through the window exists to create a relatively dark background, without which the foreground objects lack drama. The view outside is kept to a bare minimum. There is a patch of sunlit grass and foliage, dark branches, leaves, and barely discernible red berries. It is a flurry of brushstrokes that merely hints at a garden just beyond the glass.

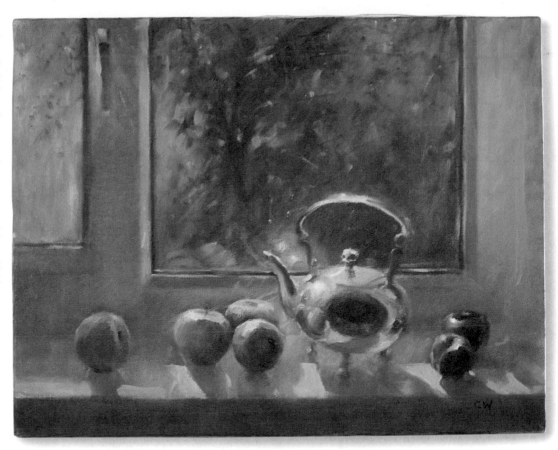

Colin Willey
Still life with view through the window
Oil on canvas
41 x 51cm (16 x 20in)

This picture is perhaps the trickier one to paint, because the artist has to contend not only with a detailed still life but also with the challenge of creating the illusion of depth normally associated with landscape painting. This he does by painting the distant buildings and middle distance with desaturated colours, all of a similar tone. By introducing darker tones into foreground foliage, he manages to bring the shrubs right up to the window.

"When I look at other painters' work, it often looks so easy. And, ideally, that is what you are trying to achieve – a finished image that looks as if it was achieved easily, even though it may have been a struggle."

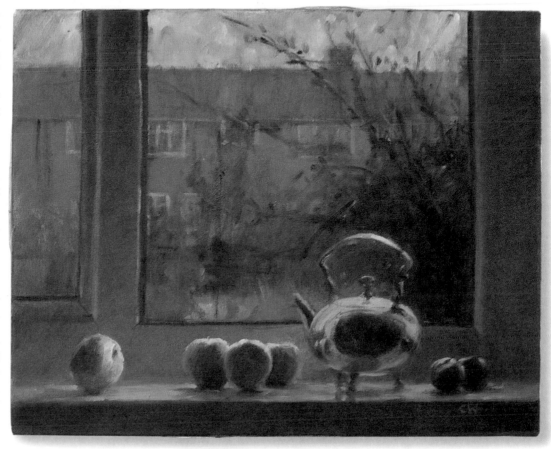

What shall I paint?
LANDSCAPE
Introduction to
landscape painting
Working with pastels

Painting a garden

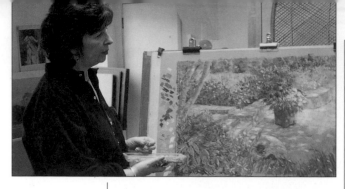

As a way of introducing themselves to landscape painting, many artists turn to working in their gardens. It provides a safe and convenient location with all the pleasures of working outdoors, but none of the disadvantages of unwelcome attention or being caught out by inclement weather. And if the light changes dramatically, you don't have to travel very far to resume working the next day.

Jackie Simmonds started painting gardens as an extension of her work on still lifes. It was a natural progression from pot plants and cut flowers to natural forms on a larger scale.

"I prefer the intimacy of a garden to the wide-open landscape. For me, a garden seems to offer a greater variety of shapes and colours."

Getting started

It couldn't be easier to move around within the confines of your own garden, looking for interesting subjects and viewpoints. Bear in mind that even familiar environments can vary in appearance, depending on the weather and time of day. And you don't have to be too literal. You can always omit a tatty shed if it is bothering you, or move an eyesore out of the way temporarily.

Jackie Simmonds likes to make preparatory sketches and colour notes on the spot, with perhaps a few photographic reference shots as a back-up.

Although not entirely satisfactory, you can work directly from photographs. This may be your only alternative if you want to paint during the winter, or if the garden is too far away from home to allow you to work from life.

Be prepared
Carry a sketchbook with you when visiting friends, so that you can jot down ideas for garden paintings.

WORKING WITH SOFT PASTELS

In many ways, pastel techniques have more in common with drawing than with painting. You need neither diluents nor mediums, and there's no need for a range of paintbrushes. However, just like other, more traditional painting methods, working with pastels relies on skilful mark-making and a developed sense of colour.

Despite being dry, pastel is a messy medium. Gently blow away loose particles as pastel builds up on the surface of the paper, and use fixative sparingly to seal the finished painting.

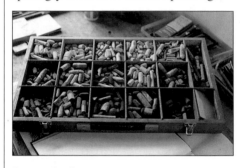

Range of colours
Pastel colours are not intermixable like paints. Consequently, pastels are made in an enormous range of subtly different colours. However, you need only about 30 to 50 colours to get started.

From your range of colours, choose those that closely match your subject and place them in a shallow tray. On average, you will need about 20 colours per painting.

In this case, the artist chose a range of dark, medium and light greens. Blues, greys, and purples were also selected for the trees; beige for the patio; and reds, yellows, oranges and white for the terracotta pots and flowers.

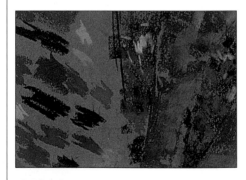

Choice of paper
The featured painting was made on a smooth neutral-coloured paper. The deep buff background serves as a warm complementary to the predominantly green hues of the painting, and is a useful mid tone for the stone walls and paving.

Composition

Well-designed gardens often contain the same elements that make for exciting two-dimensional compositions. Look for tensions created by curved and straight lines, repetition in the form of steps or posts, the contrast between hard and soft materials, and a variety of textures, tones and colours.

Jackie Simmonds has included all of these elements in the featured painting. She uses a predominantly warm area of stonework as a foil for sumptuous cool foliage and vibrant complementary colours. The shapes and areas of tone are carefully balanced, with the focal point – a terracotta pot full of flowers – placed to the right of centre.

"As you progress as a painter, there comes a point in time when you no longer see the subject for what it is. Instead, you see it as an arrangement of shapes – shapes that interlock like the pieces of a jigsaw puzzle."

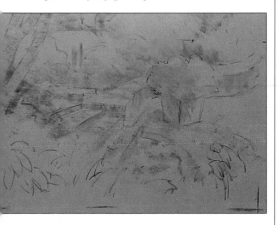

Underdrawing
Because it blends well with soft pastel, charcoal is ideal for making preliminary underdrawings. Graphite pencil is too greasy.

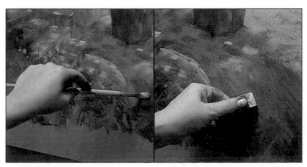

BASIC PASTEL-PAINTING TECHNIQUE

With practice, you can make a wide variety of descriptive marks and strokes, and you can learn to blend colours on the paper.

"It is quite helpful to get a feeling for the material before you start. Try out your selected colours in a sketchbook, experimenting with different linear marks, crosshatching and blending."

Use the side of a pastel stick to make broad strokes, and draw fine lines with the point. It is important to vary the direction of your strokes, in order to avoid a 'rainy-day' effect.

Use firm pressure if you want full-strength colour; a lighter touch produces a thinner, more transparent coating of colour.

Achieving colour balance
Using the charcoal drawing as a guide, the foliage is blocked in with dark-green and blue pastels. Similar colours applied to different parts of a painting create balance and harmony.

Developing the foliage
Observe closely how light changes local colour. Sunlight adds a warmer yellow to the foliage, but broad leaves turned towards the sky may take on a bluish tinge.

Creating depth
Abstract textures are sufficient to suggest foliage in the distance – but paint leaves and stems in the foreground individually, to help reinforce the impression of depth in a painting. Pale shades applied over darker tones and deep colours separate areas of foliage from the background.

Correcting mistakes
If necessary, you can remove pastel with a bristle brush and then use an eraser to get back to the original paper background. Alternatively, remove an area of pastel by scraping with a knife blade

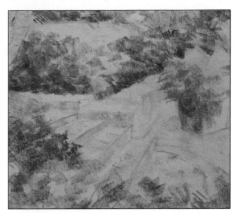

Achieving colour balance

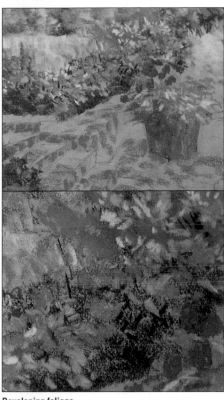

Developing foliage

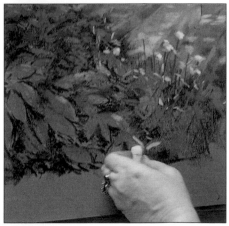

Creating depth

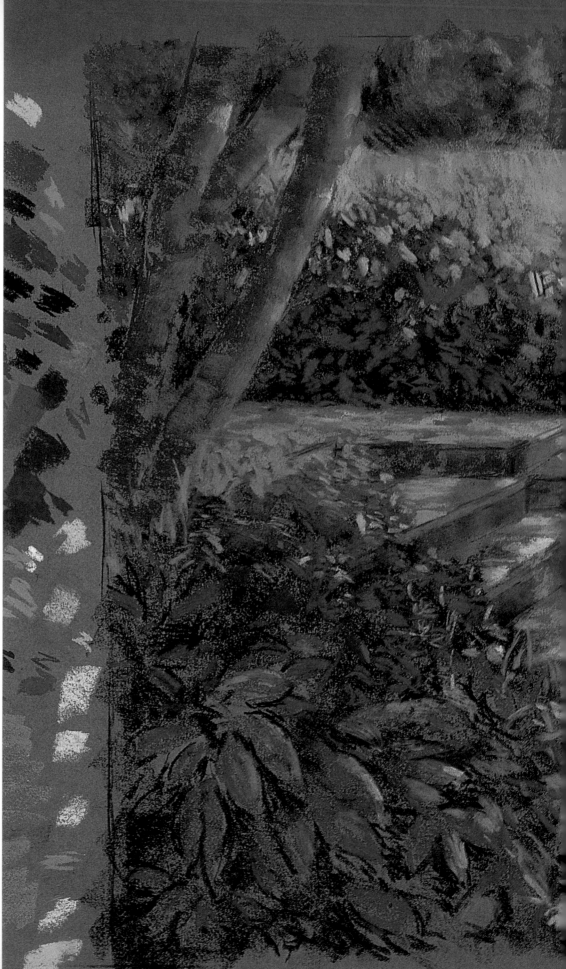

Accents of colour

Accents of bright colour add
sparkle to a painting.
Gradually working towards
the high-key tones, the artist
creates the effect of dappled
sunlight across the patio.
Small touches of red, orange
and white suggest flower
heads amongst the blues and
greens of the foliage.

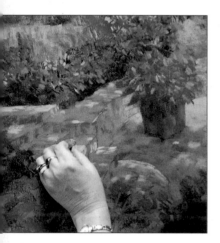

Jackie Simmonds
SHADY PATIO
Soft pastel on paper
46 x 61cm (18 x 24in)

As the work nears completion, step
back to look at the composition as
a whole, and check that the picture is
balanced in colour, tone and shape.
To put the finishing touches to this
painting, the artist worked up the
foreground detail by feeding in darker
tones to clarify the shapes of the
leaves, added lighter tones to the
areas of dappled sunlight and applied
charcoal to indicate the edges of the
random-shaped paving slabs.

86

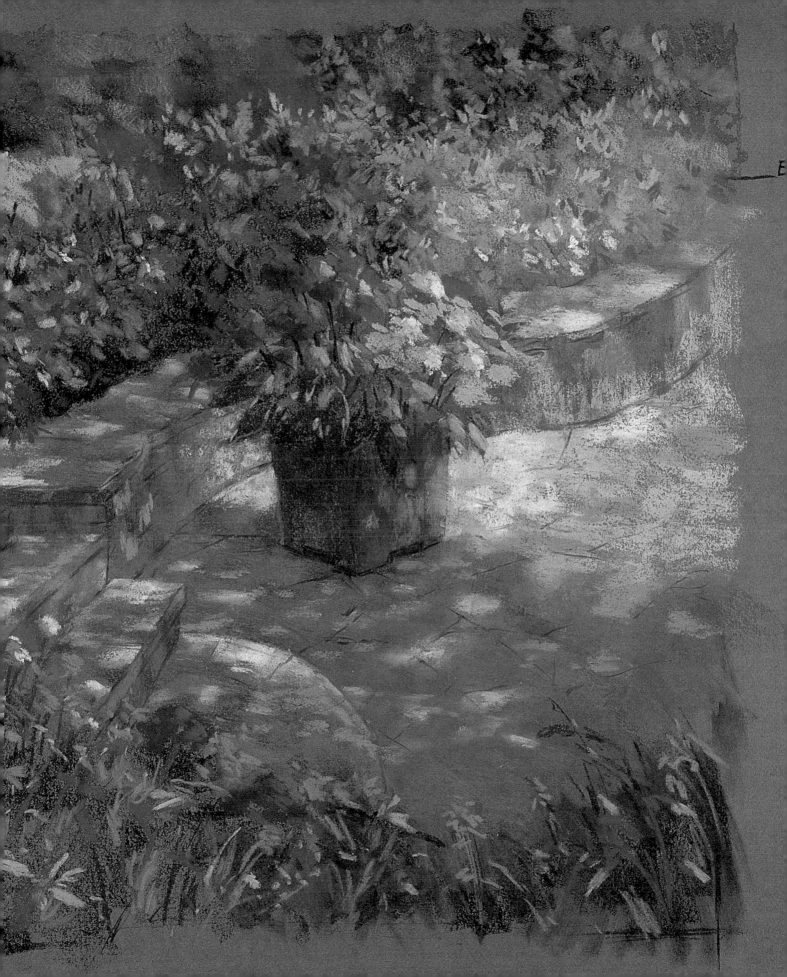

What shall I paint?
LANDSCAPE
Open landscape
Depth and distance
Traditional watercolours

Painting a landscape

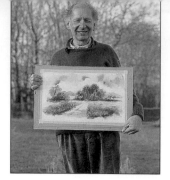

A wealth of possibilities

Sketchbook studies are no more than starting points – points of reference from which any number of compositions could evolve. Not only can you vary the scale and position of the various elements contained in a sketch, but you can alter the light, suggest different weather conditions, change the time of day, or even substitute summer for winter.

Not surprisingly, watercolour has enormous appeal for landscape painters. In practical terms, it is perhaps the ideal medium for working on location – but more importantly, it's possible to create subtle atmospheric effects with an immediacy that is difficult to match using other comparable media.

There are two distinct phases to John Lidzey's landscape paintings. First, he works directly from nature, making colour notes and relatively detailed sketch paintings. For him, there's no better way of experiencing the many qualities of the living landscape and translating them onto paper. Back in the studio, he uses his sketchbook observations to create finished paintings on a larger scale.

"Some of my sketches have inspired as many as three or four completed paintings."

Working in the studio provides a greater degree of control. You have more time to work on your composition, and the freedom to experiment with techniques and materials.

Paints and materials

John Lidzey keeps his watercolour paints and brushes in two reproduction nineteenth-century wooden boxes. Now well used and somewhat battered, they have been his constant companions for over thirty years. When working on location, he uses a simple portable paintbox.

Like most artists who have been painting landscapes for a number of years, John Lidzey picks his watercolours from a standard palette that he knows will give him the range of colours and effects he is after. For the featured landscape painting, he chose aureolin, cadmium yellow pale, yellow ochre, French ultramarine, monestial blue, indigo, Payne's grey, cadmium scarlet, carmine, and burnt umber. He also used white gouache to mix opaque body colour.

He paints with round Kolinsky sables – Nos.2, 4, 6, 8 and 12. He also uses an 18mm squirrel-hair mop for broad washes, and cotton wool for lifting out colour and for removing dried paint.

The paper used for the samples and the studio painting is 300gsm smooth (hot-pressed) watercolour paper, wetted then stretched on a drawing board.

Tips for watercolourists

When looking for suitable subjects to paint, don't be too readily seduced by overly dramatic or picturesque views. They don't always make the best subjects – and it's your painting that should be beautiful, not the view.

On occasion, allow the paint to 'do its own thing'. Let one colour run into another, and create unpredictable textures by dropping clean water into areas of concentrated colour.

Avoid too many sharp edges – they look out of place in a landscape.

Attention to scale
There has to be a difference in scale between the foreground, middle distance and background. But don't be overly concerned with foreground detail. It's enough to suggest plants – you are not painting a botanical study.

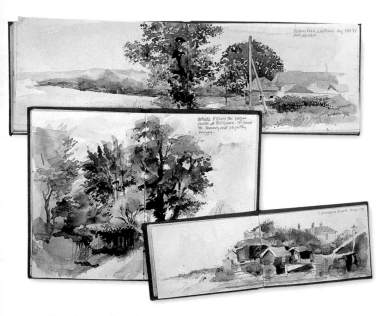

Sketches made on location
John Lidzey's field studies are more than simple sketches. Some of them are so detailed they are almost finished paintings, but even these are merely the basis for larger works that he creates in his studio.

MAKING THE FINISHED PAINTING

Despite an apparent freshness and spontaneity, traditional watercolours require an element of planning or forethought. Colour is built up with translucent washes laid dark over light; and since it's a process that is difficult to reverse, watercolourists adopt a systematic approach. More importantly, white highlights are created by leaving areas of paper unpainted – something the artist has to consider at an early stage.

Laying the first washes
Initially, pale washes are laid over a simple pencil drawing. The principal areas of the composition, including the sky, are blocked in with diluted yellow ochre. Aureolin – a golden yellow – is laid over the meadow in the foreground.

Building up the sky and middle distance
The sky is then built up with washes of French ultramarine mixed with monestial blue. To add variety, pale yellow is dropped from a brush to break up some areas of the blue sky. To create the impression of billowing cumulus clouds, cotton wool is used to mop up some of the colour while the washes are still wet, revealing white paper and some of the original pale-yellow wash.

   Pale carmine is washed over the mountains. The meadow is neutralized with a hint of monestial blue, and the track is laid in with a weak wash of yellow ochre.

   The mid-ground trees are now defined with mixes made of aureolin, cadmium yellow pale, yellow ochre, monestial blue and carmine. Yellows and blues suggest foliage, and the pale carmine red brings the warmth associated with woody growth.

Applying masking fluid
Once the initial washes are dry, the artist draws grasses in the foreground and a gate at the end of the track, using a dip pen and masking fluid.

Painting the tree line and undergrowth
At this point, the foliage is strengthened with deeper tones and stronger colours, creating depth and shadow. The main trunks and branches are painted with Payne's grey, then the smaller branches are drawn with a dip pen charged with watercolour.

   Several loose washes of colour are laid for the undergrowth beneath the trees. These washes are made using various strengths of indigo, cadmium yellow pale and aureolin, mixed with small amounts of Payne's grey, to create neutralized greens.

   When these washes are dry, a slightly opaque yellow ochre is laid in patches over the greens of the undergrowth, to suggest mixed foliage that is turning autumn gold.

The gate at the end of the track
To complete this stage, the masking fluid is removed to reveal the gate. The stark white paper is toned down with a pale wash, then French ultramarine is brushed across the gate to imply cast shadow.

Painting characterful skies
Give your skies plenty of character. Paint them freely, using lots of water and washes of different colour. The background to this page was created by painting warm colours, wet-in-wet, alongside a deep-blue wash. Colour was lifted to indicate clouds, using the technique described for the finished painting.

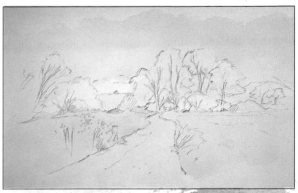

Applying the first washes
Using his sketchbook studies as reference, John Lidzey makes a simple pencil drawing to help him fix the positions of the main features. Then he applies the first pale-yellow washes across the sky and foreground.

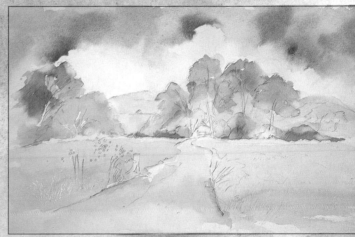

The sky and middle distance
Clouds are blotted from a blue sky; foliage is indicated with broad washes.

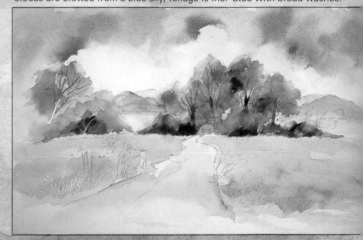

Tree line and undergrowth
Trunks and branches are drawn in with watercolour. Strong tones suggest deep shadows beneath the trees and undergrowth.

What shall I paint?
LANDSCAPE
Painting a landscape

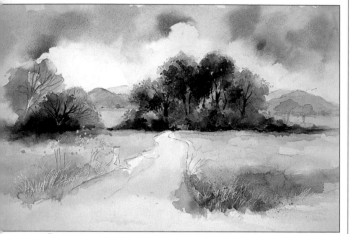

Removing masking fluid
Pale grass stems are revealed against dark washes in the foreground.

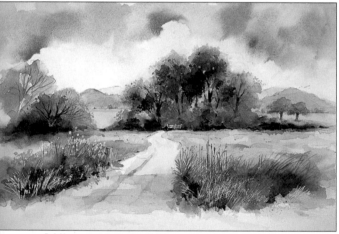

Adding weeds and wild flowers
Shadows are deepened, then weeds and flower heads introduced.

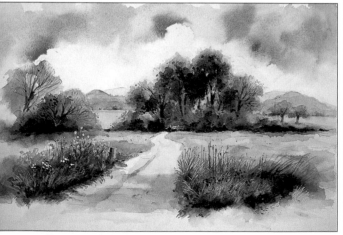

Foreground shadows
The correct tonal balance adds depth to the picture.

WORKING UP THE FOREGROUND

The foreground in shadow helps to balance the composition. The finished painting is divided horizontally into bands of contrasting tone – the bright sky, the dark groups of trees, a sunlit meadow, and the foreground in shadow. This is a device often used by painters to draw the viewer into the picture; it is an invitation to step into the sunnier parts of the scene.

Revealing grass stems and flower heads
Loose washes of colour are laid across the foreground to lower the tonal values and give a feeling of shade. When the washes are dry, the artist removes the masking fluid, applied during an earlier stage in the painting, by rubbing it with a fingertip. By revealing the pale underlying colour, the grass stems and flower heads stand out clearly against the dark background washes.

The distant trees and meadow
Before proceeding with foreground detail, the artist paints the merest hint of a tree line at the base of the mountains, and adds two small trees to the right of the main group. Very little detail is required at this distance, and it is important to use pale desaturated colour to make the trees recede. Loose washes of cool green are laid across the distant meadows, with just a few horizontal lines of a darker colour to suggest uneven ground.

Painting weeds and flowers
Freely applied brushstrokes add interest to the foreground. Warm yellows and brown give an impression of tall weeds and dried grasses, and the flower heads revealed by removing masking fluid are coloured with cadmium yellow.

Additional flowers provide accents of bright colour to complement the dark weeds and foreground scrub. These flower heads are painted randomly with red and white gouache – opaque paint that has exceptional covering power.

Don't make arrangements of flower heads too regular. Clump them together in groups, and vary their shapes and sizes.

Foreground shadow
The shadow that runs across the track is deliberately light in tone. Any darker, and it would begin to compete with the tone of the trees in the middle distance and destroy the illusion of depth.

The colour is built up in stages by applying three pale washes of French ultramarine mixed with yellow ochre. This allows the artist to judge the weight of the tone precisely.

Don't paint shadows with hard edges, unless you want to create an impression of strong sunlight. And avoid using black paint to darken your shadows – deep blues or purples have a similar effect, but without creating a dead, inky blackness.

Masking fluid
This is a rubbery solution that prevents colour soaking into the paper. It is used primarily to mask off fine details and highlights that would be difficult to paint in later with opaque body colour.

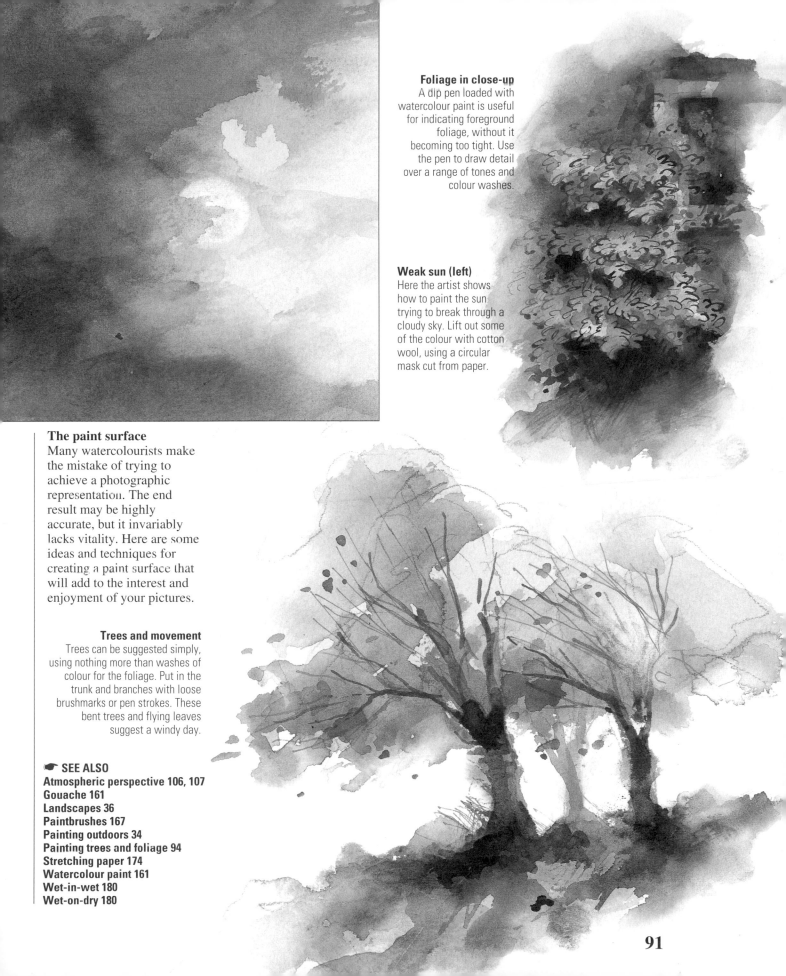

Foliage in close-up
A dip pen loaded with watercolour paint is useful for indicating foreground foliage, without it becoming too tight. Use the pen to draw detail over a range of tones and colour washes.

Weak sun (left)
Here the artist shows how to paint the sun trying to break through a cloudy sky. Lift out some of the colour with cotton wool, using a circular mask cut from paper.

The paint surface
Many watercolourists make the mistake of trying to achieve a photographic representation. The end result may be highly accurate, but it invariably lacks vitality. Here are some ideas and techniques for creating a paint surface that will add to the interest and enjoyment of your pictures.

Trees and movement
Trees can be suggested simply, using nothing more than washes of colour for the foliage. Put in the trunk and branches with loose brushmarks or pen strokes. These bent trees and flying leaves suggest a windy day.

☞ SEE ALSO

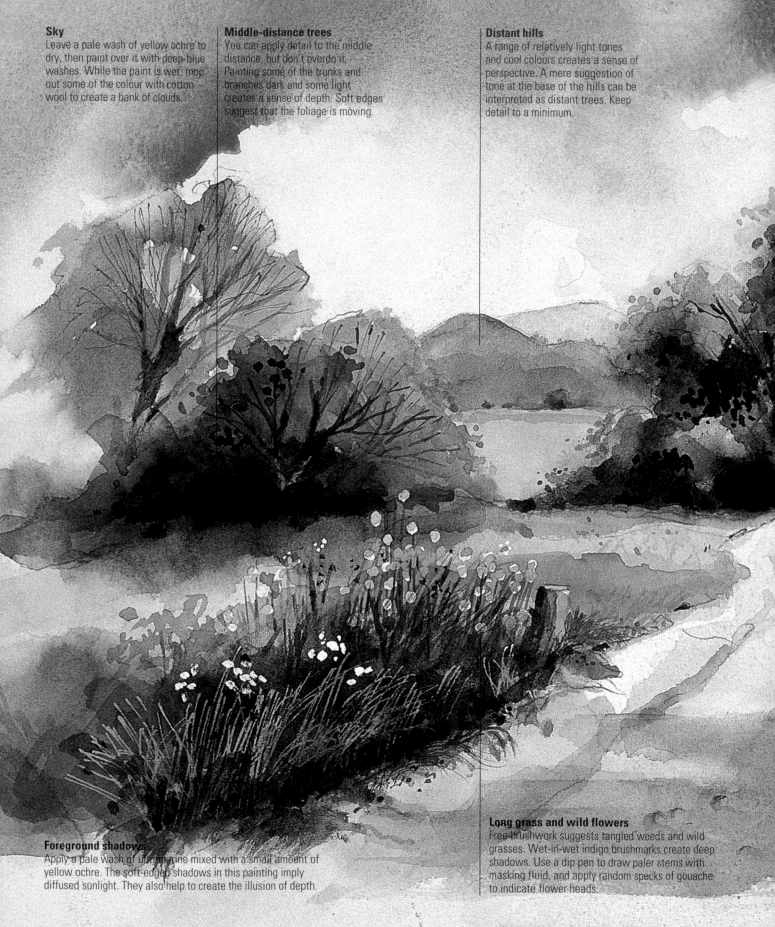

Sky
Leave a pale wash of yellow ochre to dry, then paint over it with deep-blue washes. While the paint is wet, mop out some of the colour with cotton wool to create a bank of clouds.

Middle-distance trees
You can apply detail to the middle distance, but don't overdo it. Painting some of the trunks and branches dark and some light creates a sense of depth. Soft edges suggest that the foliage is moving.

Distant hills
A range of relatively light tones and cool colours creates a sense of perspective. A mere suggestion of tone at the base of the hills can be interpreted as distant trees. Keep detail to a minimum.

Foreground shadows
Apply a pale wash of ultramarine mixed with a small amount of yellow ochre. The soft-edged shadows in this painting imply diffused sunlight. They also help to create the illusion of depth.

Long grass and wild flowers
Free brushwork suggests tangled weeds and wild grasses. Wet-in-wet indigo brushmarks create deep shadows. Use a dip pen to draw paler stems with masking fluid, and apply random specks of gouache to indicate flower heads.

92

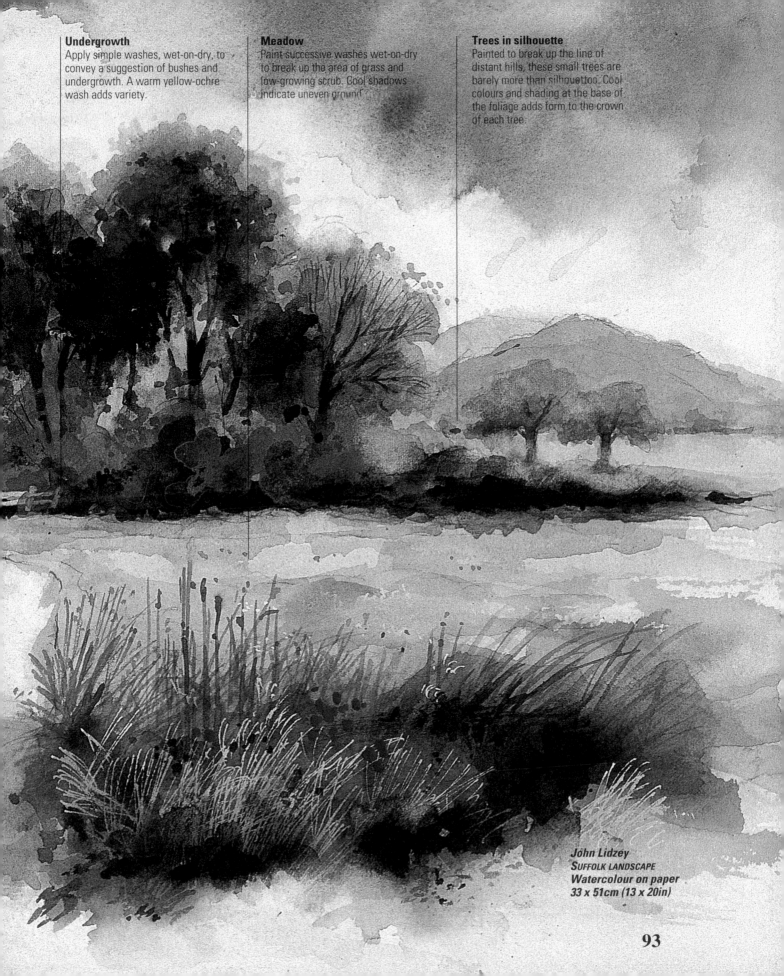

Undergrowth
Apply simple washes, wet-on-dry, to convey a suggestion of bushes and undergrowth. A warm yellow-ochre wash adds variety.

Meadow
Paint successive washes wet-on-dry to break up the area of grass and low-growing scrub. Cool shadows indicate uneven ground.

Trees in silhouette
Painted to break up the line of distant hills, these small trees are barely more than silhouettes. Cool colours and shading at the base of the foliage adds form to the crown of each tree.

John Lidzey
SUFFOLK LANDSCAPE
Watercolour on paper
33 x 51cm (13 x 20in)

93

What shall I paint?
LANDSCAPE
Tree shapes and textures
Creating depth
Seasonal changes

Painting trees and foliage

In landscape painting, trees and foliage are often represented by little more than abstract brushmarks, but it is helpful to be acquainted with individual species in order to make those marks convincing. Not only do species differ in their shape, but many change their appearance with the seasons and, in so doing, confer a very different atmosphere on the painting.

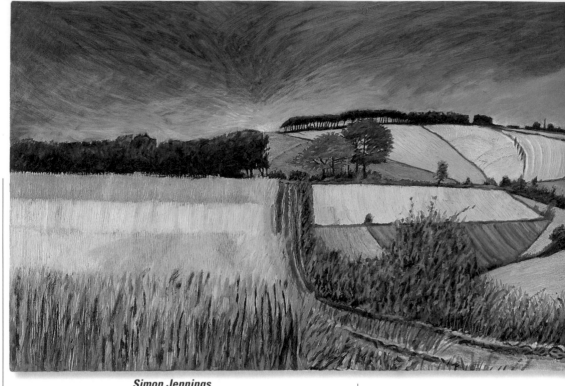

Simon Jennings
TREES IN A LANDSCAPE
Oil on canvas 51 x 76cm (20 x 30in)

Atmospheric perspective

Create a sense of depth in your pictures by painting foreground trees with strong colours and well-defined details. Treat those in the distance more like silhouettes, using lighter tones to make them recede. Soft-edge forms, painted wet-in-wet with watercolour, also create an illusion of distant trees.

Textured effects (opposite)

Having painted the trunk and branches, dry-brush the clumps of foliage that hang from a silver birch.

Stippling oil paint or watercolour – using the tip of a flat brush or fan blender – produces the layered foliage of a typical fir tree.

Create a subtle dappled effect by stippling with a natural sponge dipped in paint. As each layer dries, apply another colour or tone, then brush in the trunk.

Paint the distinctive foliage of a tall pine by using a painting knife to apply thick acrylic paint. Add texture with the edge of the blade.

Paint the overall shape of the tree's canopy with a broad wash, then scribble in the branches, using a pointed stick.

Paint the bare branches of a pollard by drawing a pointed stick through wet paint.

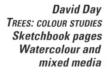

David Day
TREES: COLOUR STUDIES
Sketchbook pages
Watercolour and mixed media

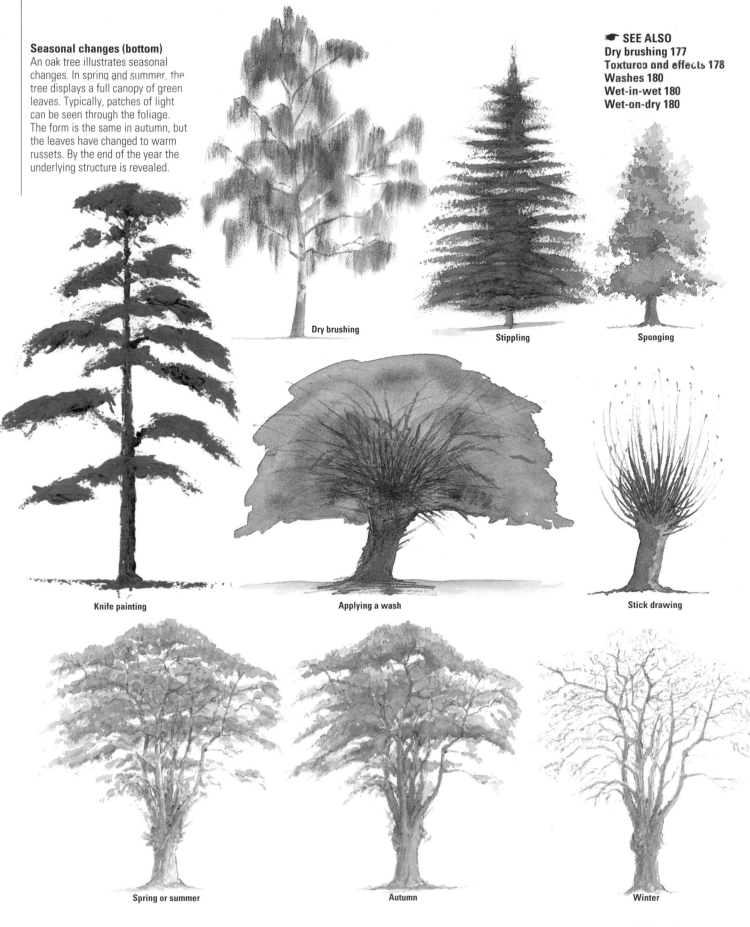

Seasonal changes (bottom)
An oak tree illustrates seasonal changes. In spring and summer, the tree displays a full canopy of green leaves. Typically, patches of light can be seen through the foliage. The form is the same in autumn, but the leaves have changed to warm russets. By the end of the year the underlying structure is revealed.

☞ SEE ALSO
Dry brushing 177
Textures and effects 178
Washes 180
Wet-in-wet 180
Wet-on-dry 180

Dry brushing

Stippling

Sponging

Knife painting

Applying a wash

Stick drawing

Spring or summer

Autumn

Winter

What shall I paint?
LANDSCAPE
Painting outdoors
Fields and foliage
Creating depth

Landscape
on location

This stretch of countryside is at least five
miles wide, and stretches another ten miles
to the horizon. It is a patchwork of fields
and woods on rolling hills set in a valley
that melds into a range of hills visible in
the distance. There is the occasional farm
building, and the foreground and middle
distance are bisected by rows of trees.
The viewpoint chosen by the artist provides
exceptional width and depth, and looks down
onto the scene from a high vantage point. Known as an 'open
landscape', it would appear at first sight to be a daunting mosaic
of shapes and undulations, with many hues and colours beneath
a deep-blue sky. The first challenge is to decide what to focus on,
and how to begin the painting.

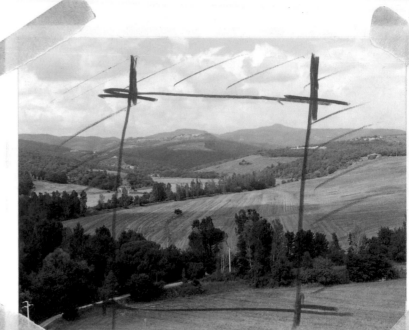

MONTALTO ~ SIENNA

Starting points
Preliminary sketches and visual
notes help you to 'get your eye in' and to
familiarise yourself with the colours and
shapes in a landscape. One automatically
thinks of painting landscapes in the
horizontal 'landscape' format. In this case,
the artist made preparatory sketches in
this format, but
executed the final
painting in an upright
'portrait' format.

Preparatory sketches
The artist was drawn,
in particular, to the stripes
in the recently mown
fields and to the shapes
of the distant hills against
the sky. The work began
with colour sketches in
a wide-format landscape
sketchbook. The colours
were taken directly from
the tubes, as required. For
broad areas such as the
sky, for example, the paint
was squeezed onto the
page and blended with
the fingers.

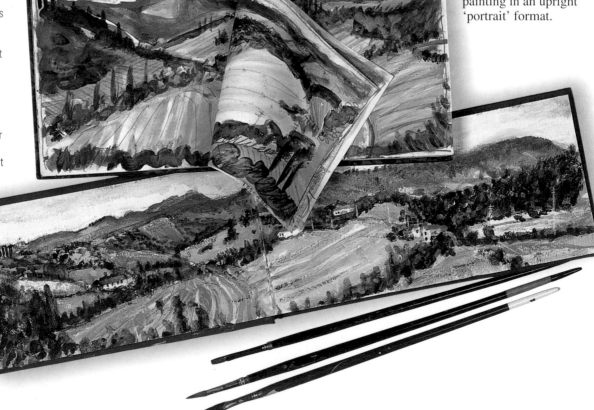

Selecting colours and setting out the palette

You can set out a palette in whatever order you wish but, as there were many shades of green in this landscape, the artist laid out the ready-mixed colours in line on the left, because these were to be picked up and used 'straight from the tube'. The earth colours, yellows and blues were laid out on the right as these were more likely to be mixed. Water is the only diluent needed for acrylics – but keep two jars on the go, one for thinning paint and the other for washing out your brushes.

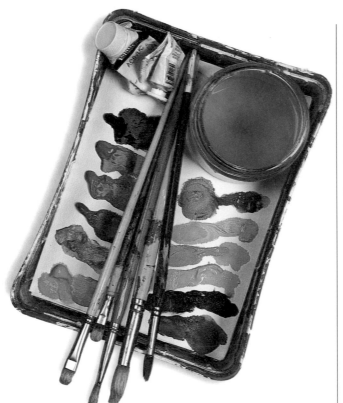

KEEPING ACRYLICS MOIST

Acrylic paints are notoriously fast-drying. This has many advantages when working outdoors on location, but in hot, dry weather the colours can skin over in minutes and set solid before you have had time to use them up. Consequently, it pays to squeeze out small amounts of paint and use a 'stay-wet' palette. You can buy a ready-made palette or make one from a shallow plastic tray. Line the bottom of the tray with an old dishcloth or layers of newspaper generously dampened with water. On top of this, lay a sheet of greaseproof paper or a damp sheet of thick white cartridge paper. Squeeze your colours out onto this paper as you would with a conventional palette. If you seal the tray with clingfilm when you take a break, the paint will stay workable for hours, if not days. Another solution is to make a stay-wet palette from a shallow food-storage box with a snap-on, airtight lid.

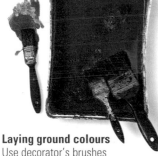

Laying ground colours
Use decorator's brushes to lay ground colours.

Laying a toned ground

Artists have traditionally primed their canvases with a base colour. The chosen ground colour affects the surface and appearance of the finished painting.

In this painting, the toned ground serves two purposes. Firstly, it works as a primer to seal and stretch the paper – a purely practical function. However, it also acts as a ground colour that is integral to the painting. Here, a mixture of cadmium red and permanent rose is laid onto the paper. Being a 'hot' colour, it reflects the warm climate of the location and is complementary to the predominantly cool colours in the landscape. As the painting builds up, the ground shows through here and there, lifting the other colours and creating a vibrant surface. Lay a fairly thin wash, evenly but quickly, with a decorator's paintbrush.

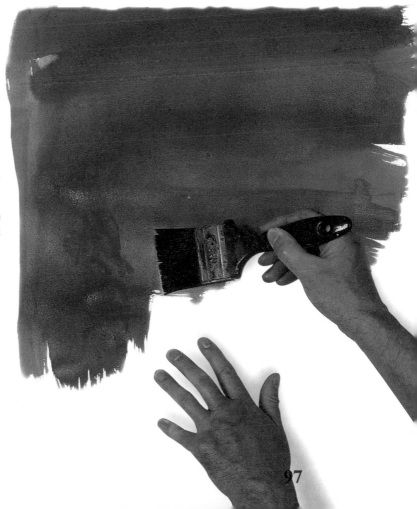

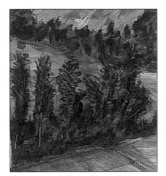

Creating a vibrant surface
The 'hot' ground colour shows through the painted surface.

What shall I paint?
LANDSCAPE
Landscape on location

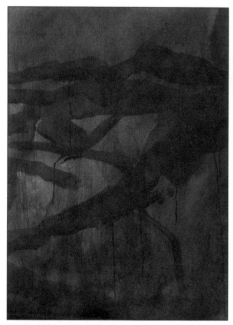

Blocking in broad strokes
Using tones of the original ground colour, broad strokes are blocked in quickly to get a feel for the overall composition.

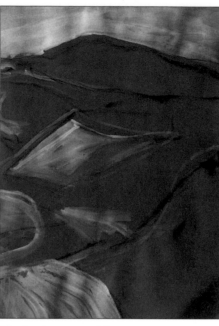

Plotting the composition
The main elements of the composition are sketched in with charcoal, using paint to define shapes and focal points.

EXPERT ADVICE

There is no prescribed formula for making a painting. All artists have distinctive styles and tackle the job in their own way. For many painters, especially beginners, the main difficulty seems to be in getting started, and the first stages depicted here are often the most difficult and disheartening. The best advice is to seek out a subject that will hold your attention for several hours – in this case, an arresting view – then keep at it, concentrating on the crucial elements and adding essential detail until the picture begins to emerge, almost by itself. Only then does the real enjoyment begin.

Here is some invaluable advice on how to approach landscape painting from a world-famous artist:

" *When you go out to paint, try to forget what objects you have in front of you, a tree, a field… Merely think here is a little square of blue, here an oblong of pink, here a streak of yellow, and paint it just as it looks to you, the exact colour and shape, until it gives you your own naive impression of the scene.*"
CLAUDE MONET (1840–1926)

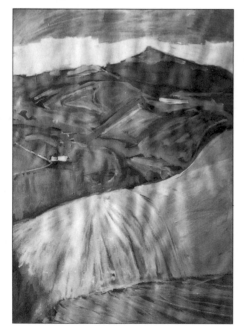

Building up the surface
Colour, tone and surface detail are gradually introduced and refined as the work continues.

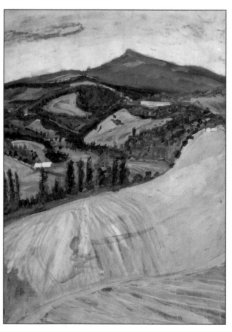

Creating depth
Having sketched in the sky, the artist concentrates on creating depth and space with deeper tones and strong colour.

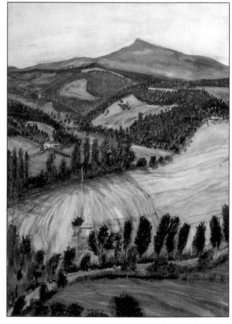

Foreground detail
The foreground comes to life with the clearly defined trees, foliage and the all-important ground textures.

Simon Jennings
VIEW FROM MONTALTO
Acrylic on paper
100 x 79cm (40 x 31in)

☞ SEE ALSO
Acrylic paint 162
Painting outdoors 34
Painting trees and foliage 94
Papers 173
Primers and grounds 165

WHEN IS A PAINTING FINISHED?

Every painting has a knack of telling you when to leave it alone. Many a picture has been stripped of its essential life and initial spontaneity by being overworked. When you reach a point where you feel satisfied that you have done your best within the given constraints, then leave the painting alone for a while – perhaps for hours or even a couple of days – and then come back to it with a fresh eye. At that stage, you will be better able to judge whether the painting has reached a satisfactory conclusion. If not, you can either return to the location or make further modifications and improvements in the studio.

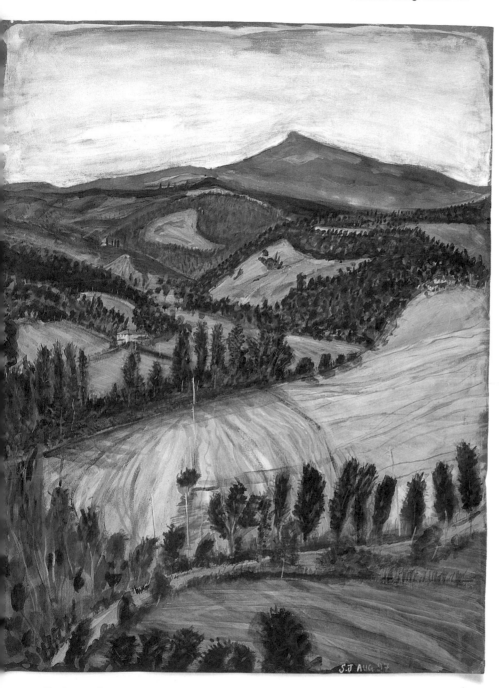

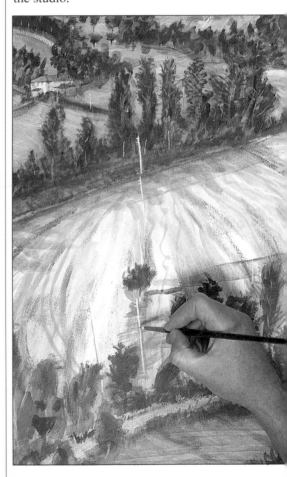

Finishing touches
Back in the studio, you can include additional details, such as telegraph poles and fence posts, using a fine paintbrush. These details reinforce the illusion of depth and add textural interest to the painting.

Six hours later
This landscape is the result of about six hours' work. The sequence opposite shows key points in the development of the picture, but the creation of any painting is rarely a straightforward linear process. The various stages show how the artist first established a foundation and then built a loose framework for the picture. From then on, it was a matter of constant modification within this framework until the painting arrived at this point.

What shall I paint?
LANDSCAPE
The effect of skies and
weather on landscape painting
Experimenting with media

Painting skies and weather

For every landscape painter, the elements provide an endless supply of inspiring and often surprising source material. How you incorporate it is vital to the outcome of a painting. As a rule, if the land mass is complicated and highly detailed, then keep the sky simple. Changing the emphasis gives you the freedom to include dramatic cloud formations and atmospheric skies.

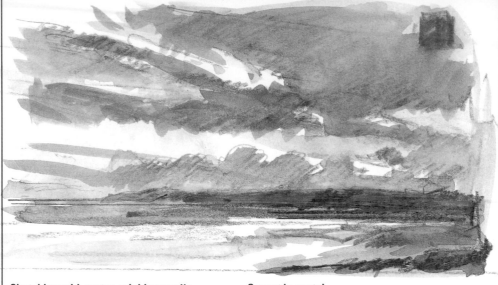

Sketching with water-soluble pencils
Quick impressions sketched in monochrome (above) play a vital role in exploring tonal relationships and mood. Brushing clean water over water-soluble pencil turns a line drawing into a watercolour. As soon as the washes dry, you can strengthen the tones with darker hatching.

Sunset in pastel
You have to work quickly when painting sunsets. Soft pastels (below) are ideal, because they are so expressive and no time is wasted mixing colours. For this sketch painting, colours are blended on smooth pastel paper, and a strip of land is reduced to a simple silhouette.

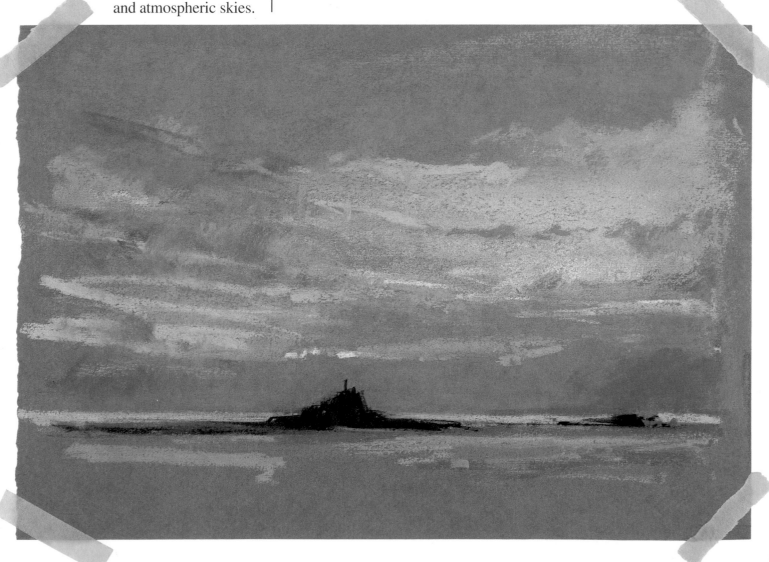

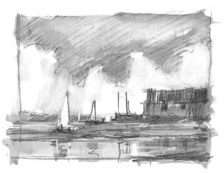

Sketching outdoors

Draw and paint outdoors as often as you can – there's no substitute for direct, first-hand experience. You can't rely on the light and weather – but, with luck, you will be able to work for a couple of hours before conditions change too dramatically. Place the horizon in the lower half of your sketch if you want the sky to dominate.

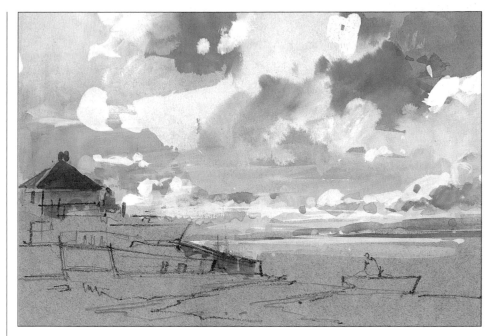

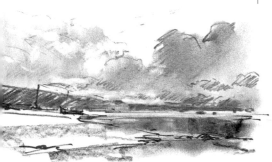

Fair-weather clouds in gouache

Gouache is a versatile medium for painting skies (above). Diluted with water, it can be used like watercolour; opaque body colour acts more like oil paint. Evoking a balmy summer's day, these towering cumulus clouds are painted with broad brushstrokes over a tinted-paper background. The rules of perspective apply to the sky as well as the landscape.

Sunrise in watercolour

Early-morning skies are usually more subtle in colouring than those at the close of the day. Watercolour (right) lends itself to these soft atmospheric effects. Here, washes of cadmium orange and cerulean blue, laid wet-in-wet, create the required softness of a dawn sky. Touches of opaque body colour suggest the sun is about to break through. It always helps to balance a painting if you can pick up certain sky colours in the landscape. Reflections in water provide the ideal opportunity.

Ray Balkwill
SKY STUDIES
Various media on paper
Average size:
14 x 19cm (5½ x 7½in)

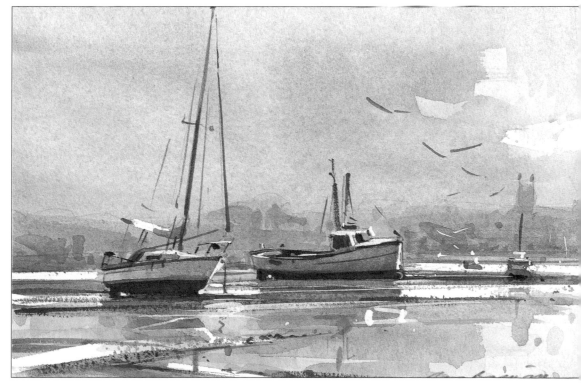

101

What shall I paint?
LANDSCAPE
Painting skies and weather

Mist and fog in watercolour
When mist and fog descend upon a landscape, colours are starved of intensity, and forms become ill-defined, with little variation in tone. Watercolour is perfect for conveying these effects, provided you keep detail to an absolute minimum. Here, a light mist rises from a body of water at dawn (right). Pale winter sunshine tries to burn off dense mist or fog painted wet-in-wet (bottom right).

High-summer sky in watercolour
Using soft paper tissue, the artist blotted clouds from a cobalt-blue sky (below). Alizarin crimson adds warmth to clouds on the horizon.

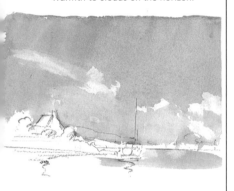

Stormy weather in pastel
Distant hills shrouded by a dark brooding sky suggest approaching rain (opposite top). The downpour on the hillside is created by smudging the pastel with a fingertip.

Snow scene in watercolour
Leave areas of white paper to depict drifting snow (opposite bottom), and paint in the shadows with cool blues and purples. Create flying snow-flakes by spattering white gouache across a heavy, snow-laden sky.

Wind in gouache
Windy weather is difficult to convey in any medium. You usually have to rely on devices such as trees bent in the wind or a flurry of leaves. In the sketch painting (opposite, far right), horizontal strokes made with a dry brush help convey a sense of movement in clouds that scud across an energetic sky. Also, birds can be seen battling with the strong wind.

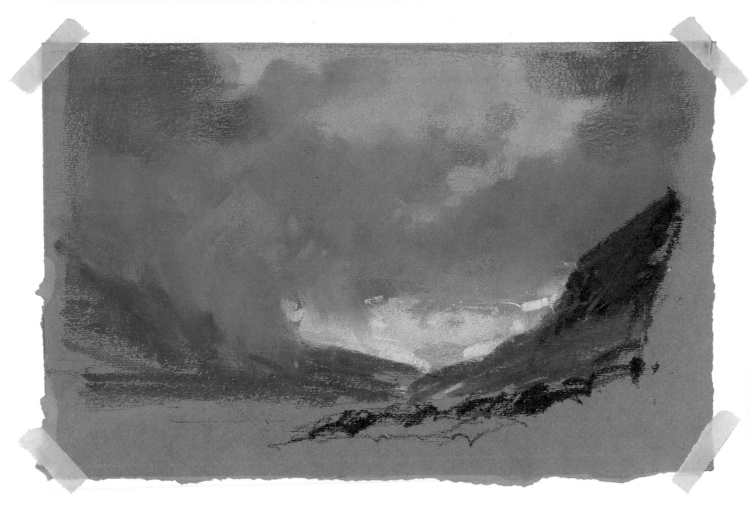

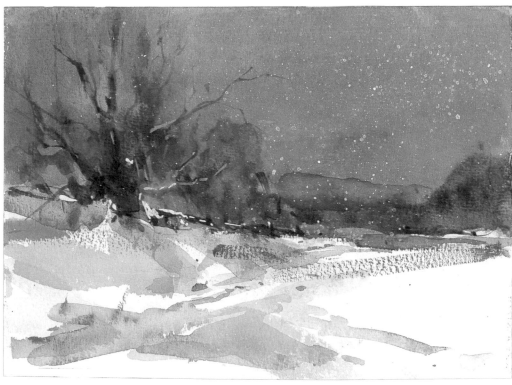

Ray Balkwill
STUDIES OF WEATHER CONDITIONS
Various media on paper
Average size:
14 x 19cm (5½ x 7½in)

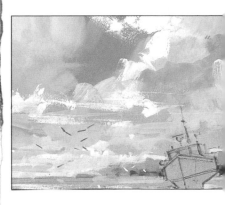

☛ **SEE ALSO**
Body colour 161
Dry brushing 177
Perspective 116
Wet-in-wet 180

What shall I paint?
LANDSCAPE
Dealing with the elements
Light and reflections
Perspective
Returning to the studio

The changing landscape

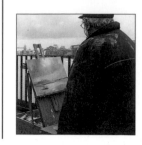

"Light changes all the time. When painting, I may stay with the original light or amend it as time goes by, and even change it again back in the studio. The knack comes with experience, but you have to be flexible and open-minded to get a result."

Landscape painters have to deal with the realities of working outdoors, which inevitably means coping with changeable light and weather. As we have seen, some artists make rapid sketches to capture the moment. Others might start another painting when there's a radical change in conditions. And then there are artists who accept the inevitable, and are prepared to allow their paintings to change and adapt along with the elements.

David Griffin, an experienced marine painter, has learnt how to deal with the changing landscape – and with working in public.

"On one occasion, I was being watched closely by two tattooed youths, each drinking from a can of lager. I found the experience most disconcerting, but kept on painting and tried to ignore them. After about ten minutes, one of them approached me – but not with the usual sneering question 'How much do you expect to get for that?' Instead, he asked 'How do you come to terms with the problems of changing light, tide and lengthening shadows?' At the time I was really surprised, as this is one of the fundamental challenges of landscape painting. The simple answer is 'Carry on regardless!' – and when it feels like an uphill struggle, just remember you are not the first to feel that way."

The finished painting
This picture was painted during a period of unsettled weather, when the artist was forced to deal with an ever-changing sky and the fleeting shadows and reflections that come with it.

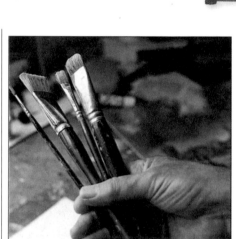

PAINTS, BRUSHES AND SUPPORT

When painting outdoors, David Griffin usually works on stretched canvas, but on this occasion he used a lightweight canvas board (primed cotton canvas mounted on thick cardboard), measuring 30 x 40cm (12 x 16in). He uses three or four brushes only – a No.10 or 12 flat bristle brush, a couple of medium-size filberts, and a rigger.

The overall impression of the featured painting is one of subtlety – it is tonal rather than colourful. To create the brooding atmosphere of an impending storm, the artist used a limited palette of good-quality oil colours (right).

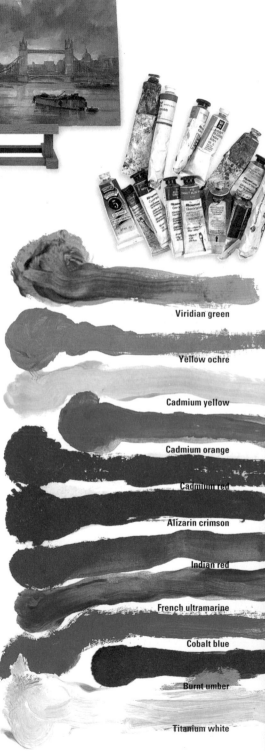

Viridian green

Yellow ochre

Cadmium yellow

Cadmium orange

Cadmium red

Alizarin crimson

Indian red

French ultramarine

Cobalt blue

Burnt umber

Titanium white

LAYING THE GROUND

"I like a warm painting. It's very inviting to have a bit of warmth – like a nice open fire!"

Having set up his easel, David Griffin's first step is to lay a warm ground to cover the stark white board, using whatever colours come to hand.

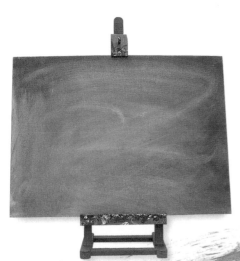

Applying a coloured ground
Heavily diluted with turpentine, the paint is scrubbed on, using a large flat brush.

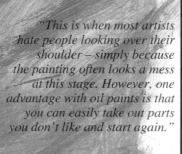

The coloured ground
The ground for this painting is a bold mix of cadmium yellow and cadmium orange.

BROAD STROKES

Blocking in the sky and water with bold washes of colour conveys an impression of the prevailing weather and general direction of light.

With the one large brush, thinned paint is mixed and blended on the board to represent a stormy sky and sunlight reflecting off the surface of the water.

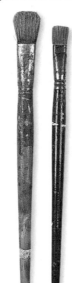

Broad-stroke brushes
Use large brushes when laying the ground, and for blocking in. A No.12 flat is the only brush you need for blending paint on the board.

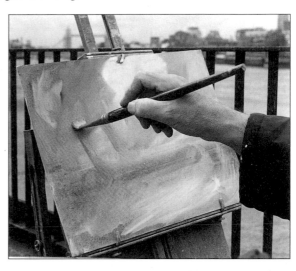

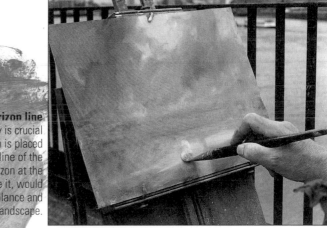

Fixing the horizon line
Because the turbulent sky is crucial to this painting, the horizon is placed well below the centre line of the picture. To place the horizon at the centre, or even above it, would dramatically alter the balance and emphasis of the landscape.

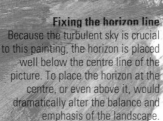

"This is when most artists hate people looking over their shoulder – simply because the painting often looks a mess at this stage. However, one advantage with oil paints is that you can easily take out parts you don't like and start again."

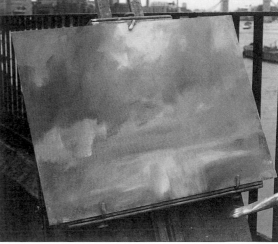

What shall I paint?
LANDSCAPE
The changing landscape

ADJUSTING THE COMPOSITION

As a painting evolves, the artist is free to rearrange the elements in order to improve the composition and dynamics of the picture.

"What can I put in to make the painting more interesting – a boat, a buoy, some figures on the deck? Here, I moved a jetty into the picture. In reality it is way out to the left, but the composition is stronger for its inclusion."

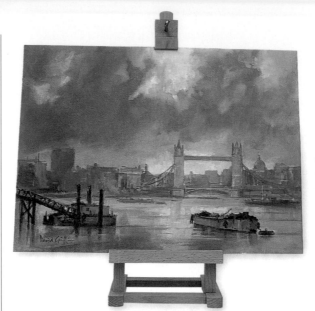

Telling details
The moored barge balances the composition and draws the eye into the picture. A buoy is introduced to add interest to the foreground.

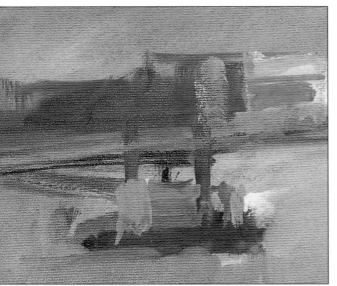

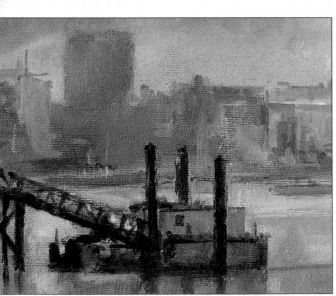

Creating depth (left)
Sharper details in the foreground and the reflections beneath the jetty add depth to the picture.

ATMOSPHERIC PERSPECTIVE

Water vapour and dust particles suspended in the air tend to obscure our view of distant objects. Introducing what is known as atmospheric perspective reinforces the illusion of depth.

Using relatively dark tones and warm colours in the foreground pushes the sketchy skyline back into the distance.

Darker reflections beneath the barge and jetty serve a similar purpose, and also keep them from looking as if they are floating in space.

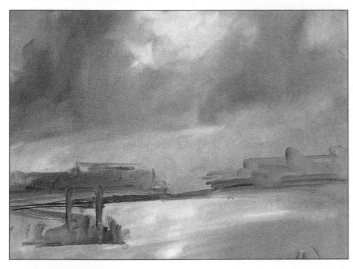

☞ **SEE ALSO**
Capturing water 110
Painting skies and weather 100
Painting space, depth and distance 116
Primers and grounds 165
Water and seascapes 38

After about two hours' work, the artist has conjured up an atmospheric landscape that accurately captures the mood of the river on that particular day. However, he invariably continues a painting back in his studio, where he can work without the constraints of trying to portray the actual scene in front of him.

"Before I set off home, I sometimes take a photograph of the scene I have been painting – but I seldom use it except occasionally as reference for the details of something in the foreground. I find that having looked intently at a landscape for a couple of hours, the image is imprinted firmly in my head."

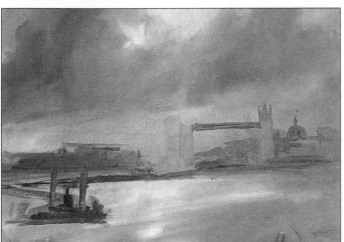

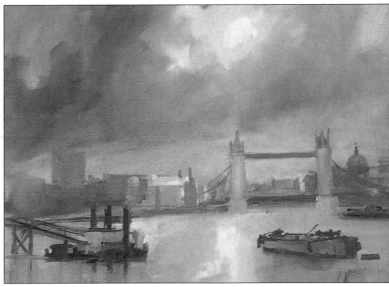

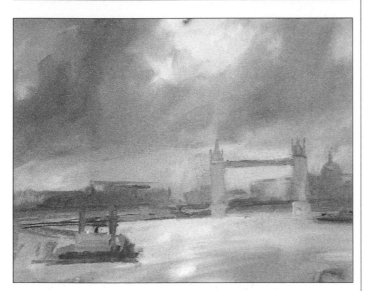

"I sometimes blend paint with my fingers. I find it more convenient than using brushes. Kids love making mud pies and getting dirty – I suppose finger painting must be an extension of childhood."

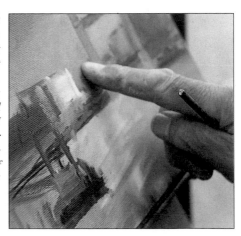

107

What shall I paint?
LANDSCAPE
The changing landscape

BACK IN THE STUDIO

When he gets home, David Griffin usually
mounts his paintings temporarily in a frame.
He admits there is an element of brief satisfaction
in gazing at a newly painted picture, but there is
also a practical point to the frame.

When you are painting seascapes and river
scenes on location, it can be difficult to get all the
horizontals and verticals aligned with the edges
of the board. Using the frame as a visual guide,
you can correct any mistakes with a fine brush or
the point of a knife.

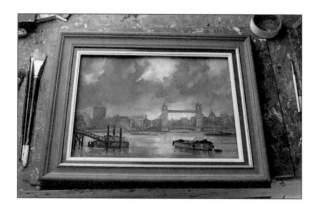

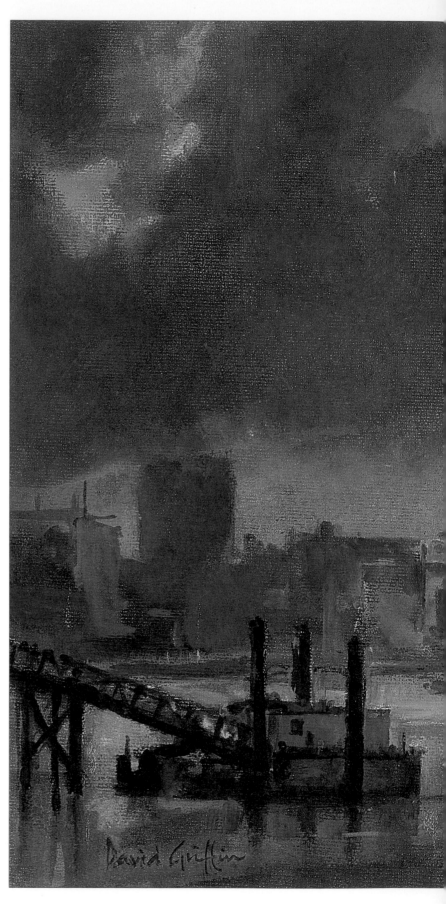

David Griffin
STORM BREWING
Oil on board
30 x 40cm (12 x 16in)

Looking at the finished painting, you can see the
additional work done in the studio. There is
considerably more variation in colour and contrast
in the sky, with bright accents of light piercing
the clouds. Similar colours and tones are
reflected in the water.
Distant buildings have been picked out with colour.
And much greater detail has been included in the
foreground – with spots of intense colour that
attract the eye, and sparkling highlights scratched
into the water with the edge of a blade.

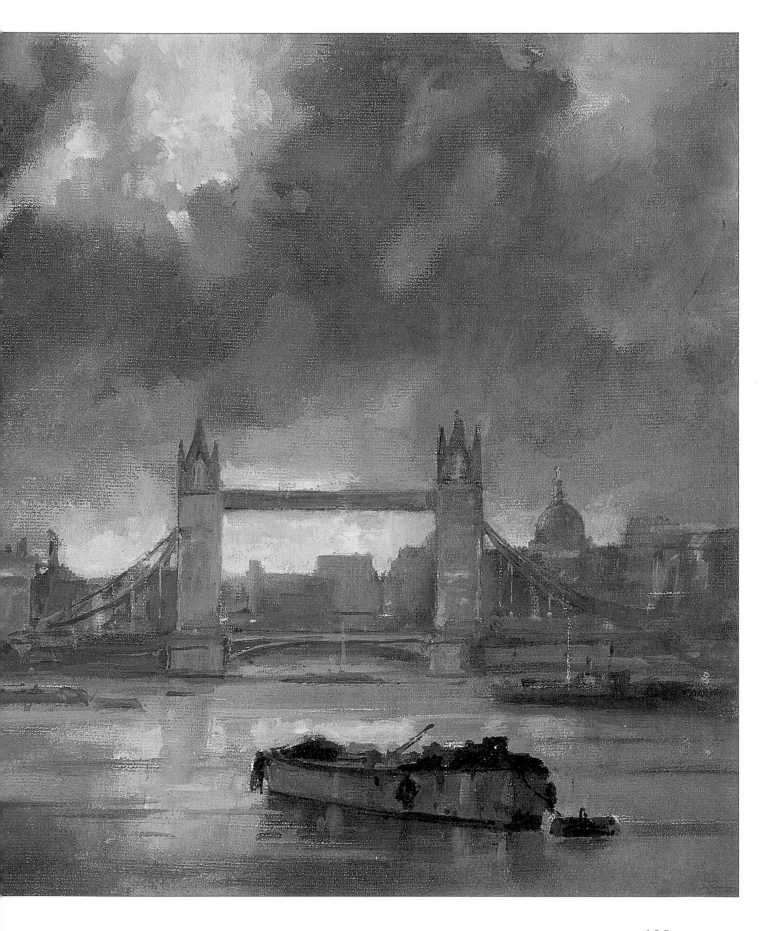

What shall I paint?
LANDSCAPE
Capturing movement
Water and reflection

Capturing water

Within the context of landscape painting, we tend to think of water as a calm element seen in a river, lake or harbour scene. However, although water is often associated with a vision of tranquillity, that is not always the case. In addition to conventional composition and techniques for painting water, David Jackson introduces some alternative ideas for capturing the energy and excitement of water, rain, mist and spray.

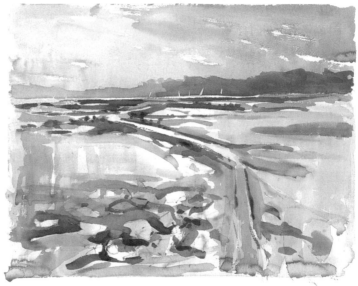

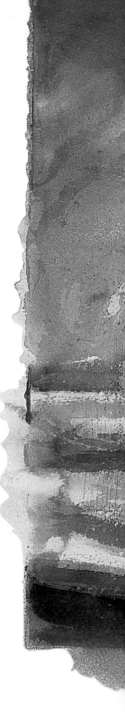

Alternative techniques
Conventional brush techniques are seen in David Jackson's view over watery mud flats (centre). In his study of the Venice Lagoon (bottom), he introduced gesso paste to add texture and then painted over with watercolour to impart a misty, atmospheric perspective.
In the top painting, he made use of a stiff brush (like the ones used for combing in hair conditioner) to create etched linear indents; and scratched the surface of the painting with a sharp blade to create the effect of a late-spring cloudburst over an exceedingly watery lake.

David Jackson
COLOUR STUDIES
Watercolour on paper
40 x 50cm (16 x 20in)

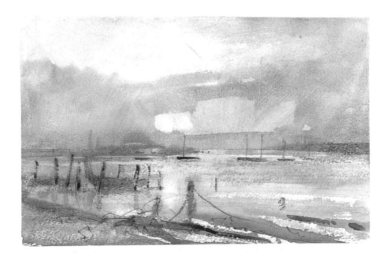

110

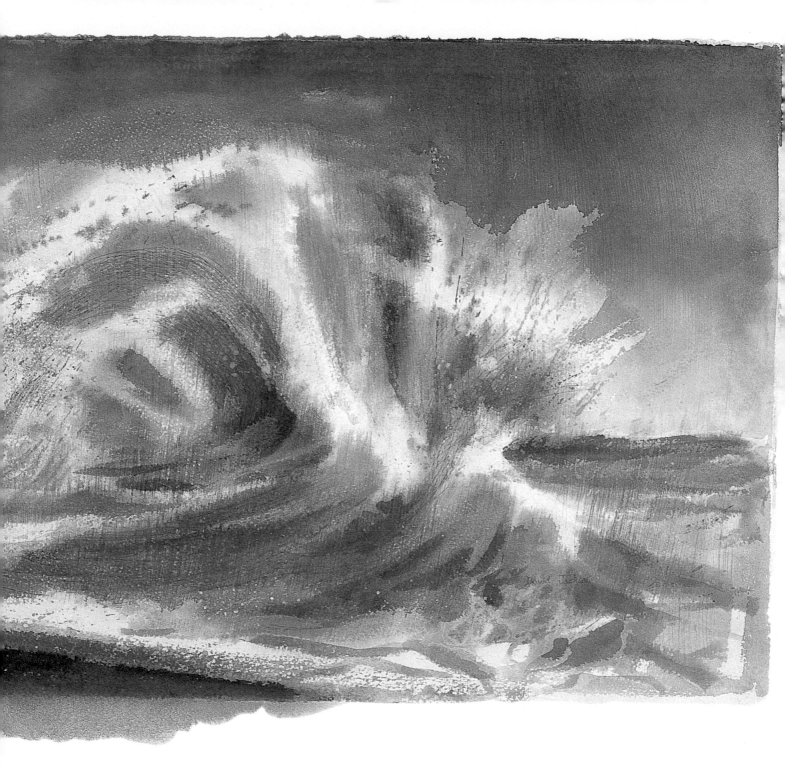

David Jackson
BLUE BREAKER
Watercolour on paper
54 x 71cm (21 x 28in)

Movement and energy
Fluid, liquid paint is applied vigorously and generously to dampened paper, wet-in-wet. In places, the white of the paper is left showing through to represent foam and spray. Colour is lifted out with sponge and rag, and then reapplied to build up the opacity of the ocean surface. Paint is splattered and thrown, and the surface scored with a hard-point hairbrush – so that the paint sinks into the grooves, creating a linear directional effect of an exploding wave in a boiling rain-dashed ocean.

☛ SEE ALSO
Painting outdoors 34
Painting skies and
weather 100
Textures and effects 178
The changing landscape 104
Water and seascapes 38
Wet-in-wet 180

111

Painting a townscape

Making buildings the focal point of a landscape introduces the possibility of a greater variety of colour and texture. Whether it be modern steel and glass or the mellow patina of crumbling render and battered woodwork, there is much to paint and enjoy.

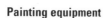

Painting equipment
In addition to a standard square-tipped flat paintbrush, Kay Ohsten employs a variety of less conventional equipment, including a sharpened stick and a calligraphy pen.

A personal approach
Watercolourists usually start by painting the sky, then work systematically from background to foreground, gradually overlaying pale washes with darker and richer colours. For the artist Kay Ohsten, conventional methods are too inhibiting. She prefers to work in reverse, because she feels it helps to inject more depth into her pictures. Her vigorous painting style encompasses a range of techniques, from drawing with a pointed stick to holding the paper under running water. Spontaneity is the key word, which is why she is unable to recall the colours she uses for a particular painting.

"Without thinking, I let my brush dance in and out of the palette."

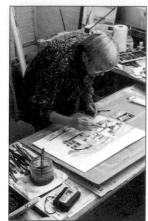

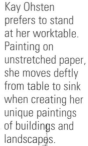

The artist at work
Kay Ohsten prefers to stand at her worktable. Painting on unstretched paper, she moves deftly from table to sink when creating her unique paintings of buildings and landscapes.

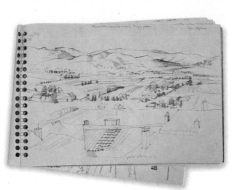

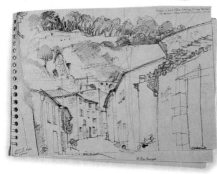

Underdrawing
The first stage of the painting is a moderately detailed pencil drawing. Although it includes very little architectural detail, there is sufficient information to enable the artist to begin painting with confidence.

Sketching on location
Kay Ohsten makes drawings on the spot, which include detailed notes on colour, texture and tone. She also takes one or two reference photographs, then starts work in earnest at home while her memory is still fresh.

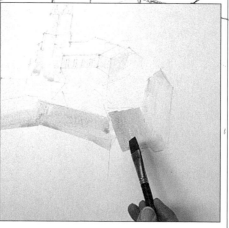

First brushstrokes
Using a broad flat brush, the artist blocks in the sides of the buildings that are in direct sunlight. She applies a pale parchment yellow to the walls and light terracotta to the roofs.

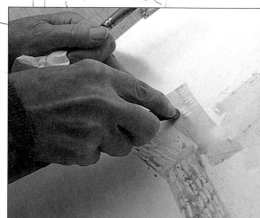

Removing colour with a palette knife
Before the washes have had a chance to dry, the artist begins to remove colour by drawing the rounded tip of a palette knife through the paint. Short strokes represent highlights on the pantiles.

PAINTING FOREGROUND TEXTURES

Before the painting gets very far, Kay Ohsten introduces colours and textures into the foreground to capture the nature of the weathered surfaces.

"I love painting buildings that are crumbling, because the rougher I paint, the more mistakes I make, and the more accidents I have, the more authentic the buildings look."

Pale mauve, red and umber brushstrokes warm up the roof tiles; and other colours are splattered across the paper to meld with the wet paint. Additional texture is created using the edge of a pastel stick and by blotting the surface with absorbent paper.

Working into the shadows

Dark shadows define the shapes of the buildings. Broken colour is flooded into these areas, with the occasional touch of a warmer shade to give the impression of sunlight reflected from the buildings across the street.

Once the washes dry, windows are added with a single brushstroke.

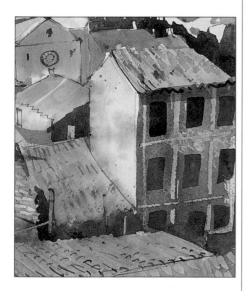

"Even though they are simplified, you have to be aware of perspective when painting rows of windows. If the scale is wrong or you paint them at the wrong angle, they won't be convincing."

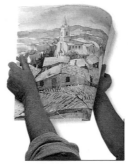

Unstretched paper
It is impractical to work on stretched paper if you are going to hold the painting under the tap to make the colour flow across the surface. A tough 300gsm paper will flatten out if it is left under weights overnight.

PAINTING THE DISTANT LANDSCAPE

In the distance is a fertile valley that stretches away to a range of mountains. Fields and vineyards are described with freely applied brushstrokes, leaving small patches of white paper that add sparkle to the landscape and give a vague impression of distant buildings.

Darker-green foliage immediately behind the buildings throws the strongly lit walls into relief. Tall cypress trees are indicated with the edge of a flat brush, and dark lines that crisscross the landscape are applied with a pen loaded with diluted watercolour paint.

Having brushed in the blue-grey mountains, Kay Ohsten tilts the paper to encourage the colour to run towards the skyline, then back again to avoid leaving a dark edge.

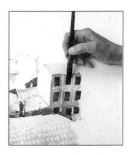

Bonnieux, Provence *Kay Ohsten*

Brushmark library

Kay Ohsten likes to use a single flat paint-brush with which she is able to make a wide variety of marks.

To make broad strokes, she uses the full width of the brush. Nipping the tip of the brush between finger and thumb creates narrow strokes.

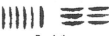

Full-width brush

Using the edge of the same brush makes linear marks; the dryer the paint, the narrower the strokes.

Brush edge

Placing the brush tip on the paper makes rows of identical marks.

Brush tip

Printing with the edge of the brush makes attractive tapered brushstrokes.

Printing with the edge

Pressing the side of the brush against the paper leaves broken colour.

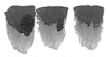

Pressing with the side

Flicking the brush spatters paint across the paper. If you spatter onto wet paint, the colour disperses. Tip the paper to control the run.

Flicking and spattering

113

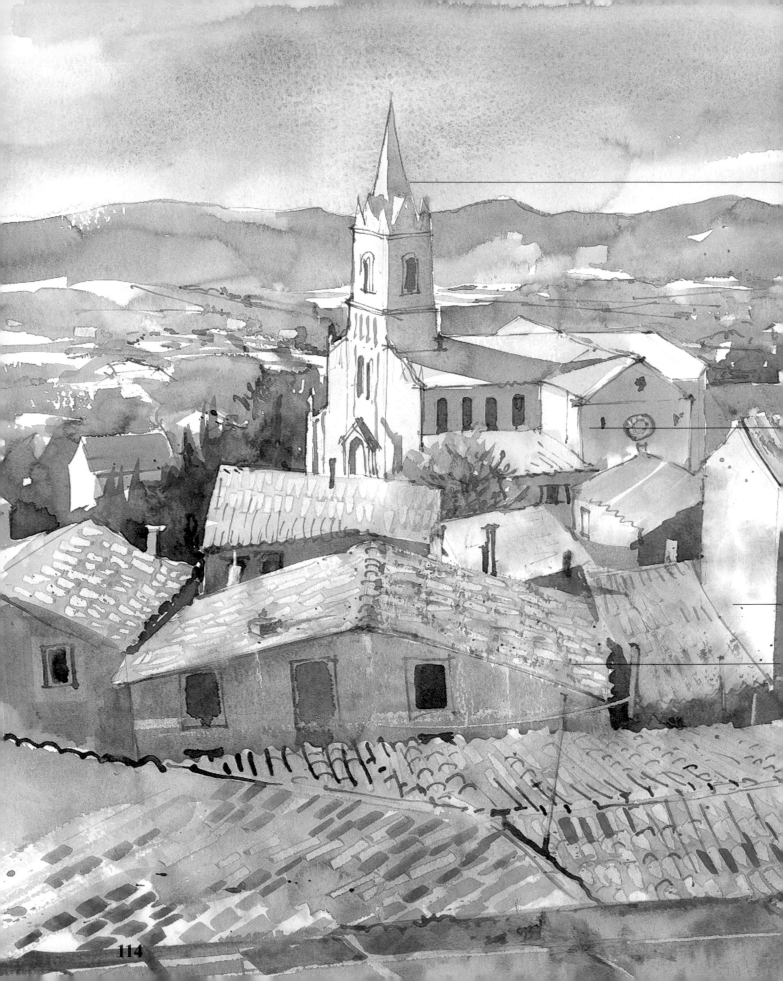

Kay Ohsten
Bonnieux, Provence
Watercolour on paper
42 x 46cm (16 x 18in)

The overall impression is one of looking down onto a jumble of rooftops that beat back the sultry heat of late-afternoon sunlight.

Perspective

As a subject, townscapes require at least a basic appreciation of perspective, but an exciting painterly surface is more delightful to the eye than a carefully measured drawing.

Painting shadows

Cool-grey shadows create the impression of strong sunlight. Broad areas are blocked in with a flat brush; linear marks are made with a pen.

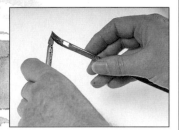

Load a calligraphy pen with watercolour

Linework

Make broad expressive lines with a sharpened stick dipped in watercolour. For finer work, use a calligraphy pen loaded with thinned paint.

Pastel and Conté

Create textures by drawing with the tip of pastel and Conté sticks.

Spattering

Flicking paint onto a painting creates random textures.

Scraping with a palette knife

Scraping the tip of a palette knife through wet paint squeezes the colour out of the paper. To make very pale marks, lift the paint soon after applying the wash. Waiting longer allows time for the paint to stain the paper.

Blotting

Lift paint off the surface by blotting with absorbent paper. Blot out stripes, using tissue paper wrapped round a ruler.

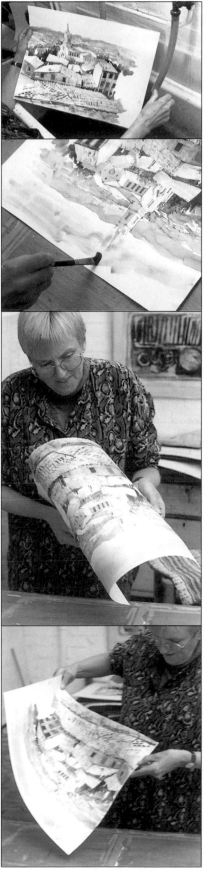

☞ SEE ALSO
Atmospheric perspective 106, 117
Buildings and townscapes 32
Paintbrushes 167
Painting a vase of flowers 68
Painting outdoors 34
Painting skies and weather 100
Painting space, depth and distance 116
Watercolour paint 161

Painting on damp paper

One advantage of working with unstretched paper is that you are free to manipulate the colour with copious amounts of water. Provided the paint is dry, you can hold your painting under running water without fear of the colours running.

Creating an orange glow

An overall tone of orange-yellow creates an impression of warm sunlight. Wet the bottom half of the painting by holding it under a running tap, allowing surplus water to run off into the sink. Spatter the wet paper with dilute cadmium orange and yellow, then tilt the paper back and forth to move the colour around on the surface. Blot excess water with a paper towel.

Painting the sky

Turning the painting upside down, you can adopt a similar method to paint the sky. Having wet the paper, paint a blue wash around hills and buildings, then tilt and bend the paper to direct the colour exactly where you want it. This also prevents the paint pooling and leaving obvious ridges. If you want to create clouds, blot them out of the blue sky, using an absorbent paper tissue.

115

What shall I paint?
LANDSCAPE
Picture plane
Horizon line
Vanishing points
Foreshortening

Painting space, depth and distance

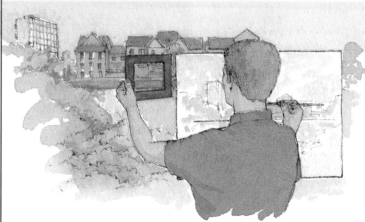

Perspective is an optical illusion whereby objects appear to diminish in size as they recede into the distance. It is possible to reproduce this illusion in a drawing or painting, using a system of lines and reference points for plotting the real three-dimensional image onto a two-dimensional surface. Although perspective drawing can be precisely measured and constructed, you only need to apply the basic principles when painting and sketching.

Picture plane
Your drawing or painting is a representation of a view as it might appear when projected onto an imaginary clear screen in front of you – this is similar to looking at the same subject through a window-pane. This surface, known as the picture plane, is taken to be at right angles to your centre of vision.

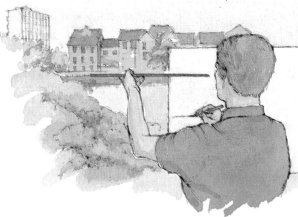

Using a viewfinder
Some artists use a cut-out cardboard window to establish their viewpoint, and to help assess perspective in relation to the picture plane.

Horizon line
When you look straight ahead, neither looking up nor down, your eyelevel falls on the horizon line (**HL**). This is the primary line of reference in perspective construction and is always at eyelevel no matter what height you are looking from. In a seascape the horizon line is visible, but in most situations it is obscured by high ground or buildings.

Vanishing points
In perspective views, all lines at right angles to the picture plane and parallel to the ground appear to converge on the horizon line. These points of convergence are called vanishing points (**VP**). Usually, one or two vanishing points are used, depending on the angle of the subject being observed in relation to the picture plane. Sometimes a third vanishing point is introduced above or below the horizon line. In practice, vanishing points may fall outside your picture area.

Establishing the horizon line
To establish the horizon line from any working position, hold a ruler horizontally in front of your eyes, so you see only the edge. Make a mental note of the line the ruler makes across the scene in front of you. Mark this line across your drawing to represent the horizon.

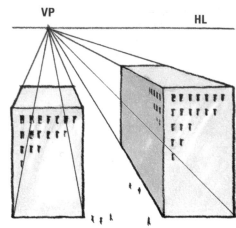

Single-point perspective
Subjects seen head on – with one face parallel to the picture plane – can be constructed, within limits, using a single vanishing point.

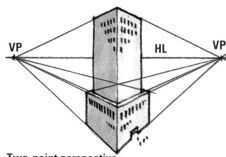

Two-point perspective
This method, also known as angular perspective, uses two vanishing points for constructing three-dimensional objects set at an angle to the picture plane. It provides a more natural view than single-point perspective.

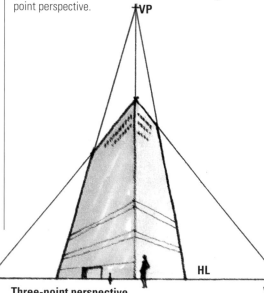

Three-point perspective
This is used to give a sense of realism to subjects viewed from above or below. Unless the vanishing points are widely spaced, the view is distorted.

Foreshortening

When an object is seen in perspective, receding towards the vanishing point, it appears shorter than it is in reality. This is known as foreshortening. This diminishing in size is progressive, so that a row of windows of equal size and spacing, for example, will appear to get smaller, and the spaces between them narrower, as they recede.

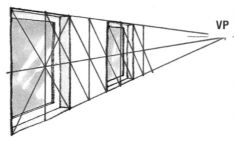

Accurate foreshortening

One way to achieve this illusion is to draw the subject, say a window, in perspective, then draw in the diagonals. Draw a line through the centre of the cross to the vanishing point, then draw a vertical line through the same centre, dividing the window into four quarters. Now draw a diagonal through one quarter and extend the line to cross the lower receding line. Draw in a vertical where these lines cross. Mark the diagonal as before and continue in this way towards the vanishing point.

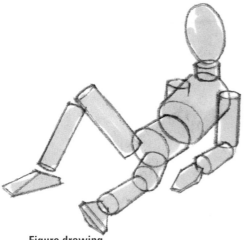

Figure drawing

Foreshortening is relevant to everything you draw or paint. When drawing figures, for example, foreshortening affects the proportions of the limbs and torso. As an aid, think of these elements as cylinders in perspective.

☞ SEE ALSO
Landscape on location 96
Painting a landscape 88
Painting a townscape 112
The changing landscape 104

Drawing circles in perspective

A circle touches all four sides of a square. When seen in perspective, the square is foreshortened and the circle becomes an ellipse.

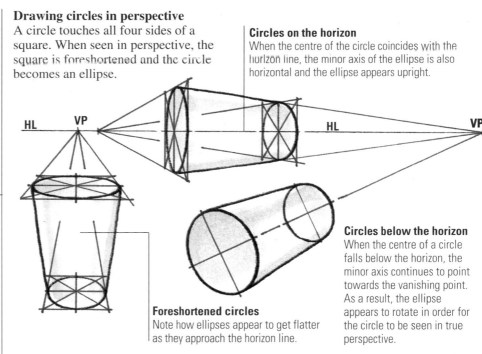

Circles on the horizon

When the centre of the circle coincides with the horizon line, the minor axis of the ellipse is also horizontal and the ellipse appears upright.

Circles below the horizon

When the centre of a circle falls below the horizon, the minor axis continues to point towards the vanishing point. As a result, the ellipse appears to rotate in order for the circle to be seen in true perspective.

Foreshortened circles

Note how ellipses appear to get flatter as they approach the horizon line.

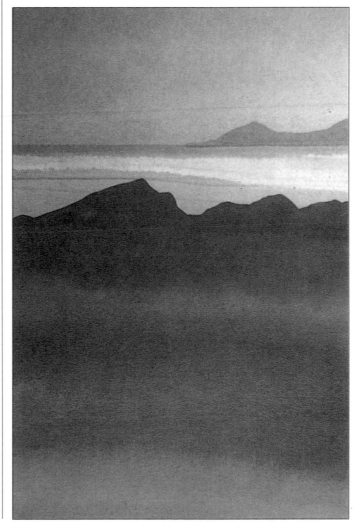

Atmospheric perspective

Dust and water vapour suspended in the atmosphere partly obscure our view of distant objects. As they recede into the distance, details become less distinct, tones become lighter and colours appear to get cooler, moving towards shades of blue. Simulating these effects with paint helps create the illusion of depth and distance.

Robert Tilling
ROCKS, LOW TIDE
Watercolour
on paper
65 x 50cm (26 x 20in)

117

What shall I paint?
LANDSCAPES
Painting single figures
Painting groups

Putting life into a painting

Painted cityscapes and interiors bereft of people appear eerily deserted. John Yardley, known for his ability to inject vitality into these subjects, shows us how to bring a painting to life by including simple well-conceived figures.

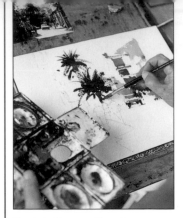

Working position
It is often best to paint standing up, especially when working outside. When seated, you look across the paper at an acute angle, which can give a distorted view of perspective and proportion.

Proportion and scale
If a figure is wrong, even by a small margin, it can spoil what is potentially a good painting. In particular, it is easy to forget that if people and animals aren't in scale the whole picture will look out of balance. The heart of the problem lies in the fact that the eye is capable of perceiving very subtle differences.

"Artists often make their figures appear stiff and wooden, almost like clothes pegs. If you paint a figure with the legs just a fraction too far apart, it no longer reads convincingly."

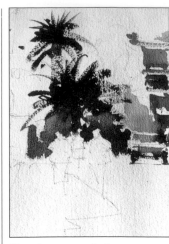

Planning your painting
When painting in watercolour, the artist adopts the conventional method of working from background to foreground, leaving white space in which to paint the figures.

All at eye level
Regardless of their scale, the heads of all figures standing on the same area of flat ground will be more or less at eye level. This assumes that you, the painter, are also standing on the same surface. If you are seated, then the heads of the figures closest to you will appear higher than the rest.

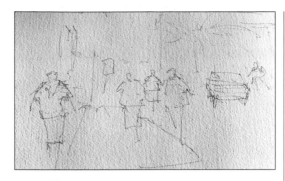

"There is only so much you can say about painting – painting is a doing thing."

John Yardley always starts by drawing in pencil (see left) to indicate where he wants to place the figures. They constitute an integral part of the composition, not merely afterthoughts inserted at random.

The background is painted first to establish broad areas of tone and colour, leaving patches of white paper where the artist intends to introduce local colour, perhaps to suggest a dress or a man's coat.

Figures are painted freely to suggest movement, precluding detail that would spoil the illusion. A broad area of shadow anchors the group of figures to the ground.

"The secret to successful watercolour painting is knowing how much water to use. This only comes with experience, but once you get a feel for the right combination of water and colour, you have control over the medium."

☞ SEE ALSO
Figures and portraits 40
Human proportions 137
Painting a landscape 88
Painting outdoors 34
Perspective 116
Watercolour paint 161
Wildlife painting 43

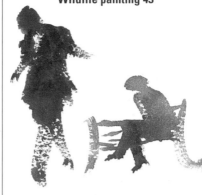

Economy of means

Figures should look credible, even when painted simply – but don't concentrate on unnecessary detail. For example, the brain tells the viewer that people have legs that end with feet, so there is no need to paint the shoes.

The most basic effects can be used to imply movement and direction. A small white 'V' left at the neckline will indicate that a figure is coming towards you. Paint it in with solid colour and the figure appears to be walking away.

Cast shadows suggest that figures are standing on solid ground, but they too need to obey the rules of perspective.

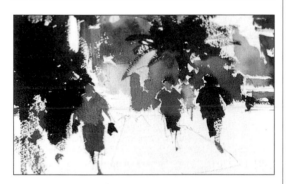

Brushes

The artist is in the habit of using two No.10 round sables. One is a new brush, which takes a point well and is ideal for painting detail. The other brush is older and slightly worn, but is perfect for broad washes.

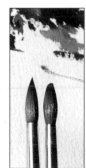

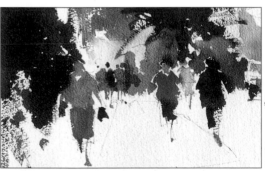

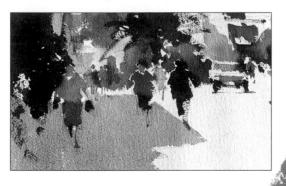

John Yardley
FIGURE STUDIES (above)
STREET SCENE, SORRENTO (opposite)
Watercolour on paper
51 x 76cm (20 x 30in)

What shall I paint?
FACES & FIGURES
Composing a portrait
Getting a likeness
Optical mixing

Painting a face

There's no question that portraiture can be somewhat daunting, even for experienced artists. It can be difficult to concentrate on the mechanics of drawing and painting when, at the back of your mind, you are wondering what your sitter is going to think of your efforts. The image we have of ourselves is often quite different from how others see us. Consequently, attempting to create a faithful portrait that neither offends nor flatters may well be a delicate balancing act.

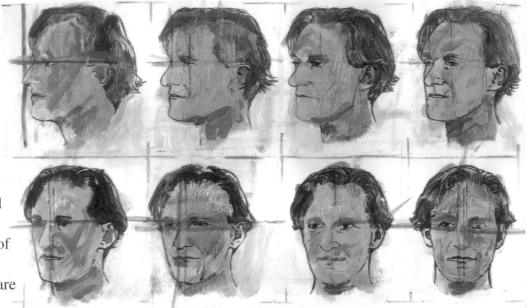

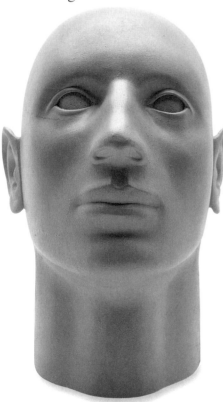

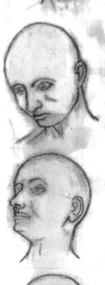

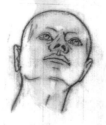

Posing your model
Before you settle on a pose, try out various views, from full face to three-quarter view and profile. Tilting the head up or down offers even more possibilities.

CHOOSING YOUR MODEL

One way to avoid embarrassment is to paint a self-portrait. You can then be totally objective, and work for as long as you like without fear of tiring your model! If you don't want to paint a full-face portrait, set up a pair of mirrors in such a way that you can see yourself from different angles.

Other obvious candidates are your friends and members of your family, who usually prove to be willing participants. Painting people you know intimately should help you bring out their true character, provided you can discipline yourself to look beyond your own preconceptions.

Whatever the relationship with your sitter, you are more likely to approach the task with enthusiasm if you genuinely feel that person will make an interesting subject to paint.

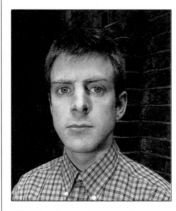 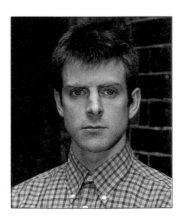

Working from photographs
There is no substitute for painting from life, but there's something to be said for taking a few photographs of your sitter at the beginning of a session and again at the end. Photos can be helpful if you want to work on the painting between sittings, or if your model is very young and likely to tire quickly. However, be aware that a camera lens can produce a very distorted image, particularly when shooting close-ups with a wide-angle lens (above left).

COMPOSING A PORTRAIT

The featured painting is a conventional head-and-shoulders portrait against a plain background that emphasizes the contours of the face and throws the features into stark contrast. The artist has selected a three-quarter view, which makes it easier to see the features in three dimensions.

Lighting will affect your subject. A face under even illumination can appear almost flat, whereas a strong sidelight throws the features into relief.

You could show more of your sitter, and include a setting that helps to convey the model's lifestyle or interests, but if your objective is to achieve a recognizable likeness, it pays to keep it simple.

Help your model to feel comfortable and relaxed – don't expect anyone to hold a smile or other exaggerated expression for any length of time. Be encouraging, and involve your sitter in the process by allowing him or her to see and comment on your work during the breaks.

Agree on what your sitter should wear. It does not have to be anything elaborate, but the addition of jewellery, a scarf or necktie, or even a hat, may contribute something to the painting. As the work progresses, feel free to alter the colour and texture of the sitter's attire if you feel it would improve the painting.

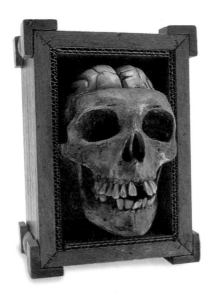

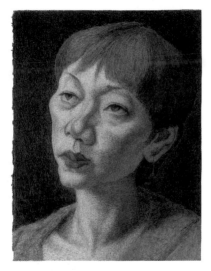

Portrait of Joyce *Nick Hyams*
A strongly lit three-quarter view makes the features stand out against the dark background.

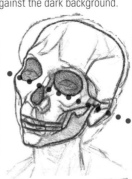

Basic proportions
A line through the bottoms of the eye sockets divides the human skull in half. When painting someone with a full head of hair, the line runs through the centre of the eyes.

MAKING A PRELIMINARY DRAWING

We all have the capacity to recognize individuals and can tell when a portrait actually looks like someone we know. As an art tutor, Nick Hyams encourages students to harness this instinctive power of observation when drawing or painting a likeness of another human being.

Before you commit yourself to paint, it is worth making a preliminary drawing of your subject. Drawing concentrates the mind and gives you an opportunity to observe your sitter closely.

Even a basic understanding of how the body is constructed enables an artist to draw and paint with confidence, and it is the underlying bone structure that gives us the most important clues to work with.

The eyes are set deep within roughly circular sockets in the skull (you can detect them beneath the layers of skin and muscle). The cheek bones just below the sockets are invariably prominent features, as is the curve of the lower jawbone. Even when it is covered with hair, the size and shape of the cranial dome is vital to the overall proportion of the sitter's head.

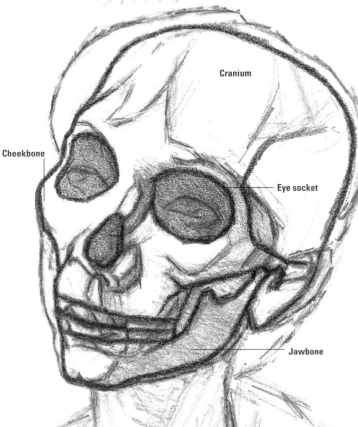

Cranium

Cheekbone

Eye socket

Jawbone

Achieving a likeness
A person's skull contributes in large measure to their appearance. Our model has high cheekbones, relatively large well-defined eye sockets, and a delicate chin. These characteristics, together with her full lips, slightly almond-shape eyes and distinctive nose, distinguish Joyce from every other individual.

121

What shall I paint?
FACES & FIGURES
Painting a face

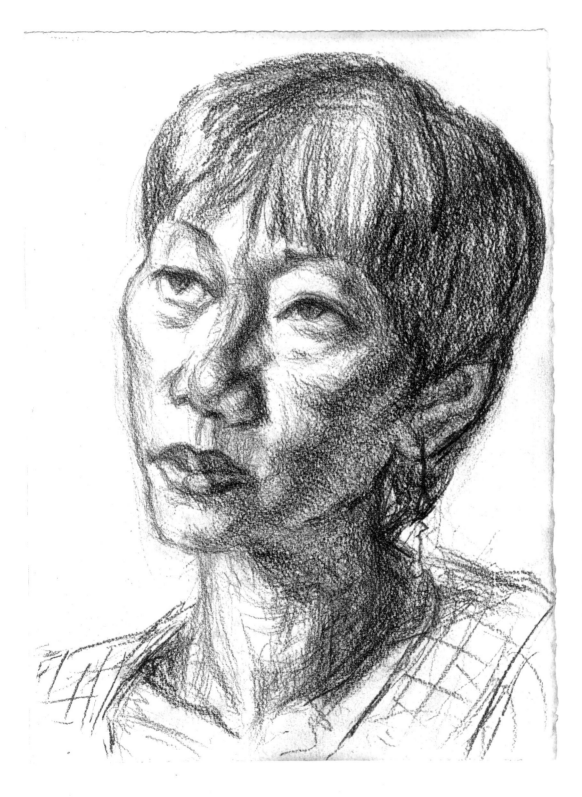

Portraiture is never easy, but Nick Hyams advocates a method of painting that allows you to correct the inevitable mistakes without having to throw away all the valuable work you have put into a portrait.

The featured painting is the result of a number of sessions, spread over an extended period. Although the drawing was made from life, the finished portrait was painted from memory.

The advantage that a painted portrait has over a photograph is that the artist is free to make subtle changes of emphasis in order to draw attention to a person's unique characteristics. Compare the finished painting with the carbon-pencil study on the left, and you can see how Nick Hyams has deliberately emphasized the sitter's cheekbones and pointed chin.

"Almost instinctively, I will select certain features that characterize the model. I am trying to arrive at something that says more about the sitter without it becoming a caricature."

Preliminary drawing
Carbon pencil on paper
38.5 x 28cm (15¼ x 11in)

UNDERDRAWING AND GROUND

The finished work began with a simple pencil drawing that was used as a guide to the painting. The whole surface was then covered with a wash of raw sienna, applied with a 50mm (2in) brush.

"*I like to start with a coloured ground. It imparts harmony to a painting. It also gives you a warm background so that you are not having to deal with the stark white paper, which can be very distracting.*"

Don't attempt to create a flat wash, just apply the paint in any direction, even mixing in a second colour if you want a bit more variation. The ground fixes the pencil underdrawing, so there is no fear of it smudging.

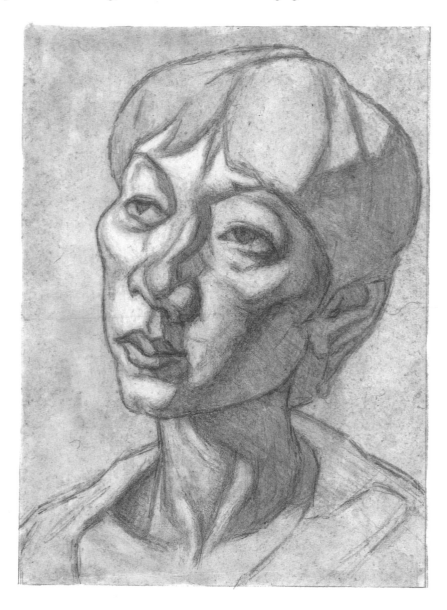

Underpainting

Using the coloured ground for your halftones, develop an underpainting to work out the basic tonal values. For this painting, various mixtures of raw umber, cadmium lemon and white were used to roughly paint in the darker areas and highlights with washes of colour.

Having blocked in the basic lights and darks, paint a dark wash across the background so that you can check the relative tonal values of the face before you proceed with colour.

MATERIALS

Paints

If you are new to painting portraits, and especially if you are intending to use acrylic paints, it is a good idea to confine yourself to a limited palette consisting primarily of 'earth' colours. Until you become more experienced, painting a portrait with bright colours can make your sitter look like a painted doll.

The featured portrait was painted using the following colours:

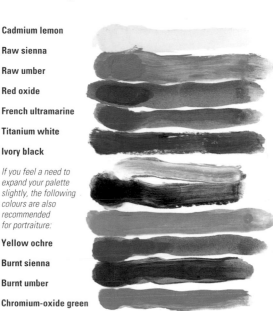

Cadmium lemon

Raw sienna

Raw umber

Red oxide

French ultramarine

Titanium white

Ivory black

If you feel a need to expand your palette slightly, the following colours are also recommended for portraiture:

Yellow ochre

Burnt sienna

Burnt umber

Chromium-oxide green

Medium

A gloss medium was used to increase the transparency of the acrylic paint and improve the flow.

Brushes

Synthetic brushes are ideal for acrylics. Their bristles are strong and springy, and are relatively easy to clean. Nick Hyams uses round brushes in a range of sizes.

"*Personally, I use round brushes because I prefer the marks they make. I might start with a No.8 or 10 in order to work freely, but I will switch to something like a No.4 as the painting gets closer to what I am trying to achieve.*"

Paper

This painting is made on 100 per cent cotton, 300gsm hot-pressed paper. Having a smooth surface, the paper does not impose a texture on the painting.

What shall I paint?
FACES & FIGURES
Painting a face

☞ **SEE ALSO**
Acrylic paints 162
Mediums 164
Mixing colours 158, 177
Painting a friend 128
Scumbling 177

Nick Hyams
JOYCE
Acrylic on paper
38 x 28cm (15 x 11in)

MODELLING WITH COLOUR

Some artists adopt a bold approach, attacking the canvas with gusto. Such paintings are often alive with energy and amply reward the risks taken by the artist. However, what appears to be carefree abandon is often the result of years of experience and experimentation.

You have a better chance of success, especially with acrylics, if you approach your work systematically. Nick Hyams' technique, which relies on simple combinations of colour, enables you to keep the process under control.

As you work up the painting, keep stepping back to evaluate the effect of the modelling and to check the overall tonal balance. If one part appears too dark, just add a few specks of a paler tone to modify it. If the highlights are too bright, knock them back with dots of darker colour.

Optical mixing
This process utilizes optical mixing, whereby small specks of pure colour laid side by side merge together when viewed from a distance, suggesting a different and more subtle colouring.

The hair
Don't lose sight of the underlying shape of the head when you are painting hair. Linear brushstrokes are more expressive than dots, and scumbling with a dry brush adds texture.

Painting the eyes
Note how the circular iris is partly hidden beneath the eyelid, which also casts a shadow across the eyeball. The spherical shape of the eyeball is suggested with modelling of the upper and lower lids. Here, specks of red oxide, cadmium lemon and white paint have been used to depict the 'whites' of the eyes. Make sure that both eyes are looking in the same direction. Many a portrait has been spoilt by giving the sitter a squint.

Working up the details
Line is an artistic convention. In reality, there are only edges where a curved surface is seen as a horizon or where one surface meets with another. Draw these margins as broken lines, using dots of colour that merge and blend to create the shape you want. The darkest areas of drawing in this painting are made with specks of raw umber and black.

Background
What appears to be a plain background from a distance, shimmers with tiny blue-grey, brown and black brushstrokes.

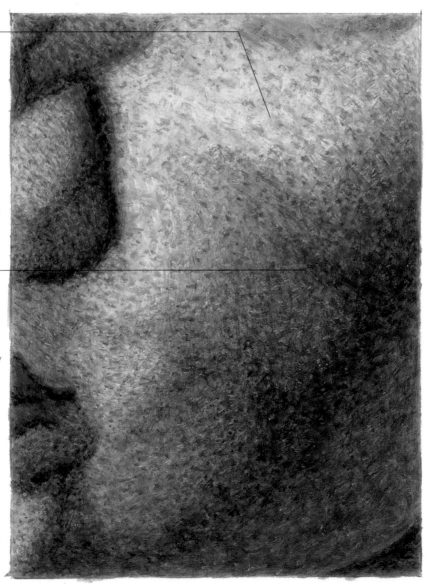

Highlights
The lightest areas are painted with cadmium lemon and white. These highlights are warmed with specks of red oxide which, when grouped together, begin to model the form.

Shadows
The same three colours are used in the shaded areas, where the underlying raw umber makes for a cooler colouring generally. Deepen the shadows with specks of darker and cooler colours until you achieve the required depth of tone.

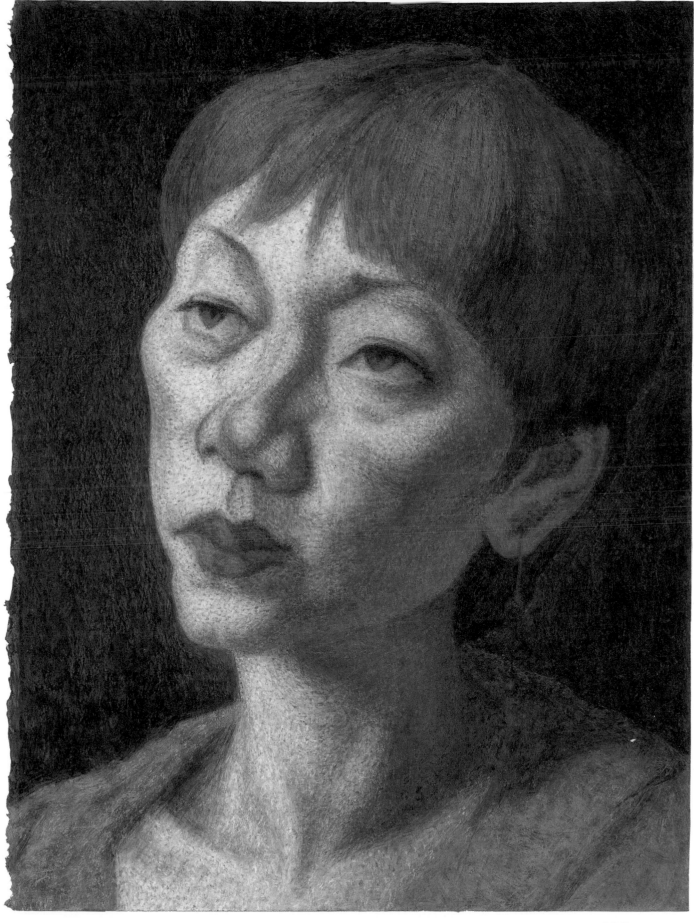

What shall I paint?
FACES & FIGURES
Close observation of
facial features

Working on the features

When using words to identify an individual, we tend to rely on descriptions of their distinguishing features – thin lips, long nose, big ears, and so on. Similarly, in painting, an accurate depiction of facial features goes a long way towards obtaining a recognizable likeness. This is what most portraitists are striving to achieve, and what most sitters want to hang on the wall.

Before painting a full portrait, get to know your model's unique facial characteristics by making preliminary sketches, not forgetting to relate them to the overall proportions of the face and head. Use the opportunity to make tonal studies and colour notes.

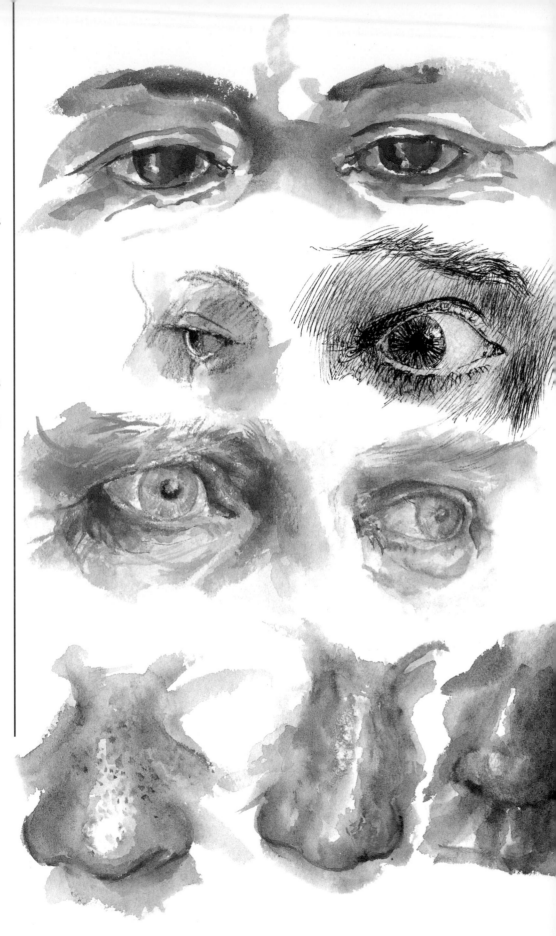

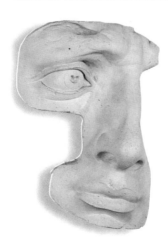

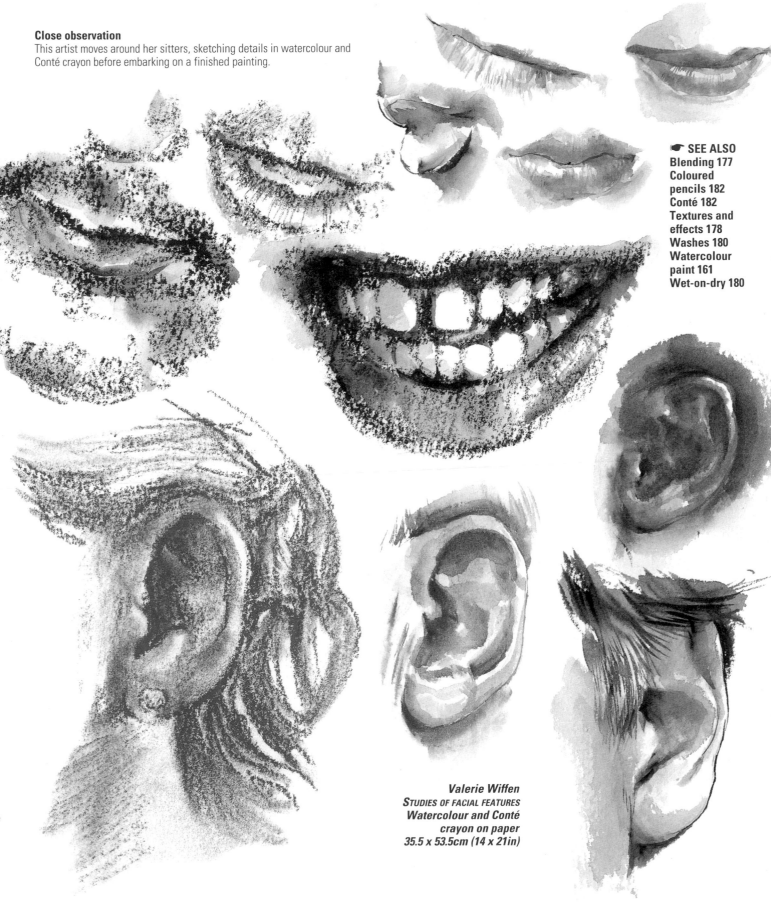

Close observation
This artist moves around her sitters, sketching details in watercolour and Conté crayon before embarking on a finished painting.

☞ SEE ALSO
Blending 177
Coloured pencils 182
Conté 182
Textures and effects 178
Washes 180
Watercolour paint 161
Wet-on-dry 180

Valerie Wiffen
STUDIES OF FACIAL FEATURES
Watercolour and Conté crayon on paper
35.5 x 53.5cm (14 x 21in)

Painting a friend

This is an example of portraiture made with panache and energy. It's a style no complete beginner could hope to emulate, but it is a goal to which many artists aspire. Watching Ken Paine at work is an invigorating experience, because he is a firm believer in throwing caution to the wind.

"Be bold. It's only a painting. It's never going to be life-threatening."

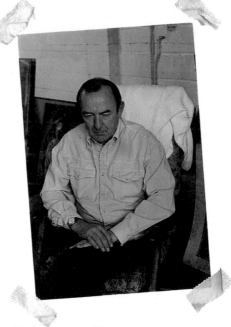

Posing your model
When you pose your model, think about how you can use 'body language' to convey different aspects of the sitter's personality. It is easy to imagine how taking up a forceful aggressive stance would give a completely different impression from, say, lounging in an armchair. But human beings can pick up more subtle messages. A model staring straight out of the canvas could be interpreted as challenging or engaging, whereas downcast eyes may be seen as passive or melancholy. With a little direction from the artist, this model took up a natural contemplative pose.

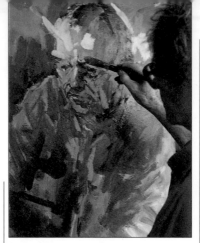

Painting more than superficial appearance
As we have seen previously, an artist will sometimes exaggerate facial characteristics in order to convey the true likeness of the sitter. Taking it a step further, a perceptive painter can express more than superficial appearance.

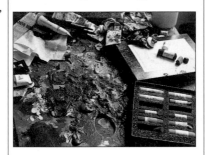

MATERIALS

This is a painting made with acrylic paint and soft pastels, a rich combination that allows for a huge variety of bold and expressive marks. There is very little time spent waiting for paint to dry – so the artist can switch from paint to pastel and back again, as the mood takes him.

The support is a good-quality mounting board coated with gesso, which is then sprinkled with powdered pumice. This provides a finely textured surface that accepts both materials equally well.

When working with mixed media, Ken Paine uses one, or possibly two, large filberts for the underpainting, which is subsequently overlaid with layer upon layer of pastel strokes.

"When I am painting a portrait, I don't set out to flatter the sitter. I am more concerned with how I feel about him or her on the day, because that helps me make appropriate marks – energetic marks, gentle marks, and so on. Unless you know the person, it may not be a totally accurate assessment, but it's what comes over that counts."

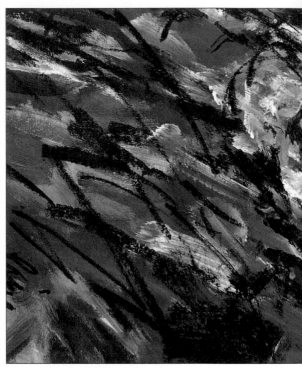

Mark making
Expressive marks, made with brush and pastel stick, are the artist's direct response to the subject of the painting.

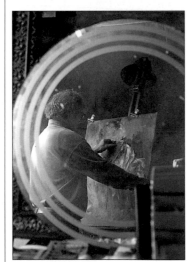

Mirror image
Use a mirror to look at your portrait from a different viewpoint. This will help you evaluate the painting in terms of composition and tonal balance. It also enables you to see the canvas from a distance – useful if you work in a small studio.

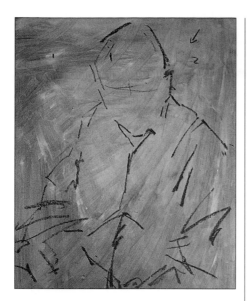

UNDERDRAWING

In order to pin down the main elements of the composition, the artist begins by drawing with pastel. From the beginning, the lines of the torso direct the onlooker towards the focal point of the picture, the sitter's head. Placing the focal point slightly off centre creates well-balanced shapes on each side of the figure and makes for a more dynamic composition.

"When you are drawing, try to feel the form as if you were a sculptor. Don't worry about the details for the moment – just work on the overall picture, checking that the proportions are reasonably accurate."

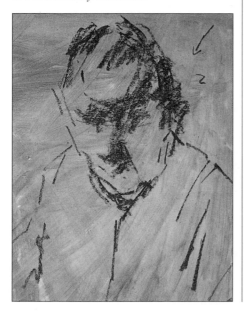

UNDERPAINTING

Within minutes of starting the portrait, Ken Paine picks up a brush and starts modelling the form with light and shade. He blocks in the darker tones, using a wet brush to manipulate the pastel, and paints the highlights with white acrylic.

"When I look at a person, I don't see their body or their features: I see shapes – shapes within shapes and shapes between shapes. And if I paint those shapes well, I will get a good likeness of that person."

The artist brings in warm and cool accents, using a mixture of yellow ochre and raw sienna for the flesh tones, and a cool green for the areas in shadow. Flashes of scarlet, warm black and deep yellow are used to chisel out the features. Painting a dark background shows up the side of the face and shoulder.

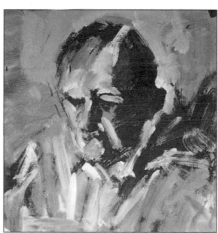
Blocking in the tones

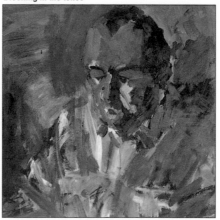
Adding warm and cool accents

CREATING A PAINTERLY SURFACE

Having established the basic form, the artist becomes engrossed in the struggle to get the sitter's likeness down on canvas. Using cool greys and ochres, he draws in the halftones; brings the face to life with deft strokes of black and red pastel; and then introduces the strong highlights with the side of a pastel stick.

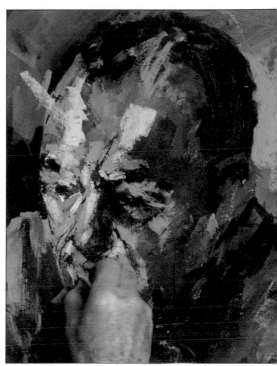

Bringing the face to life
Ken Paine draws the features with bold pastel strokes, but he doesn't hesitate to take up a paintbrush and rework the portrait when it isn't quite going his way.

"A painting goes through many different stages. You must be prepared to build it up then break it down again. It's not easy, but it is an essential part of the process."

Eventually, the painting reaches a point which the artist feels is a firm foundation for the final stages.

"These are the underlying colours that will show through the all-important marks I shall be making to finish the portrait. If you proceed with that process before the painting is ready, the portrait will be lifeless, but if you persist with the basic modelling until you are happy with it, then you can really enjoy the next stage."

129

What shall I paint?
FACES & FIGURES
Painting a friend

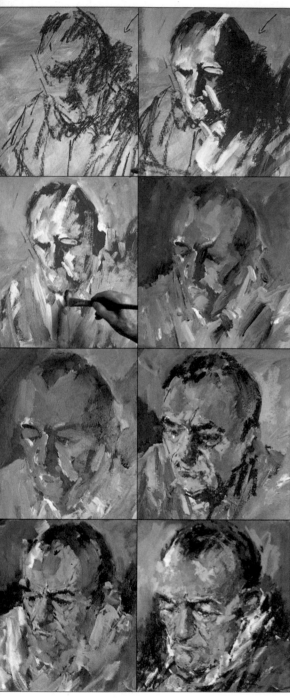

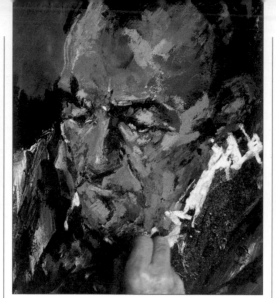

Ken Paine
ANDY
Acrylic and pastel
on mounting board
84 x 58cm (33 x 23in)

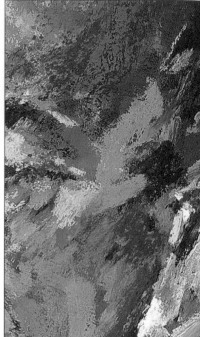

FINISHING TOUCHES

Returning to pastels once more, the artist puts the finishing touches to the portrait. Even when he is concentrating on detail, Ken Paine continues to work freely; he applies broad strokes, using the side of a stick, then makes delicate marks and lines by drawing with the point and edge.

"This is what art is about, making marks and lines that are exciting and full of rhythm."

BALANCING THE PAINTING

The portrait is all but complete, but now the artist must decide how to convey the bulk of the figure without distracting from the focal point of the portrait. This he achieves with bold brushstrokes and vigorous lines that break down the edges of the torso and direct the viewer's attention towards the highly detailed features. The final balance is made by blocking in the background colours, using dark and light areas to throw the sitter's head into relief.

A complete illusion
Close up, the finished painting could be compared with the work of an abstract painter, yet step back and all those expressive marks coalesce into a compelling and convincing portrait of the artist's friend, Andy.

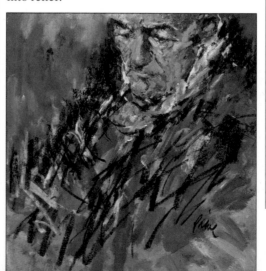

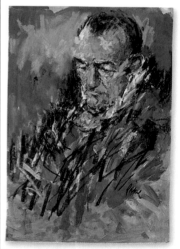

☞ SEE ALSO
Acrylic paint 162
Experimenting with poses 136
Figures and portraits 40
Painting a face 120
Pastels 181

"I am trying to produce an interesting painterly surface. It is important to realize that you are creating a painting, you are not making a copy of what you can see in front of you. Just as a jazz musician might improvise on a theme, so I am taking certain liberties with the portrait. It's what we call artist's licence."

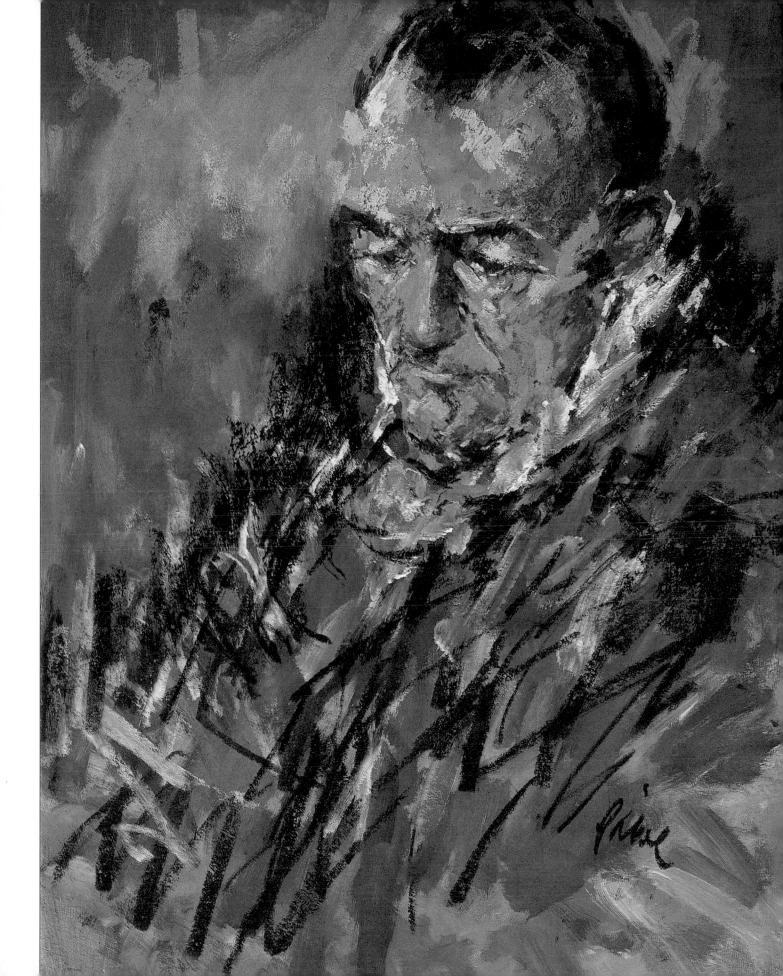

What shall I paint?
FACES & FIGURES
Full-figure portraiture

Painting a person

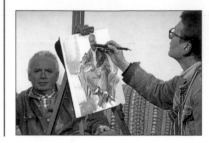

Choosing your viewpoint
In a small studio, standing over a seated model may produce an awkward bird's-eye view – in which case, you may be better off seated at the same level as your sitter. However, standing at your easel gives you greater freedom of movement, and you can step back from time to time to look at your work from a distance.

☞ SEE ALSO
Foreshortening 117
Gouache 161
Interpreting surface textures 56
Painting a face 120
Painting hands and feet 144
Stay-wet palettes 97, 170
Washes 180
Working on the features 126

A portrait can encompass more than the head and shoulders. With this exercise, we set out to paint a full figure, clothed and set against a simple background. It is perhaps more important to create an impression of a solid well-proportioned human being than it is to achieve a recognizable likeness of the model. As the artist, Val Wiffen, is quick to point out, there is often too much emphasis placed on the features, when at this scale posture and meaningful gestures are equally important for conveying character and personality.

"Don't be too concerned if you don't achieve an obvious likeness, because your painting may still be a very good representation."

FIRST STEPS

Making a sketch plan
Val Wiffen dispenses with a detailed underdrawing, opting instead to make a sketch plan, using a sepia water-soluble coloured pencil and wash to plot the main elements of the composition.

"I like to put down a few lines, sort of landmarks that will guide me through the early stages of painting. I can check the proportions of the figure and at the same time resolve the composition, which in this case is a play on triangles within a square format."

To strengthen the image on the paper, the artist takes a brush loaded with clean water and draws it across the linework, dissolving the pencil and creating washes of colour.

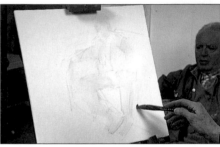
Tonal washes are created by brushing water over the initial water-soluble pencil drawing

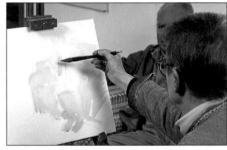
Tempera blocks are a solid form of gouache

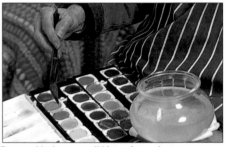
The first washes are laid in with tempera-block colour

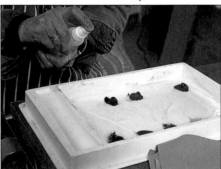
Keeping gouache moist
The artist uses a stay-wet palette when working with tubes of gouache. She keeps the paint moist by misting it occasionally with water from a small plant spray.

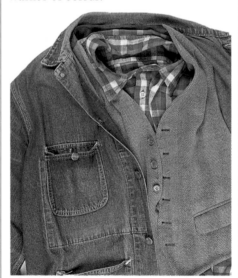
Dressing your model
Encourage your sitter to choose clothes he or she is used to wearing – something that expresses the sitter's personality. This will help to reinforce the sense of likeness in your painting. The simplest textiles are often the most difficult to paint. Distinct patterns, such as stripes or checks, will follow the contours of the body and make it easier to depict the model in three dimensions.

Materials and equipment
This painting was made on 410gsm watercolour paper, using gouache and tempera-block colour applied with a single weasel-hair brush.

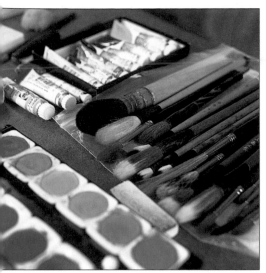

PAINTS AND PAINTBRUSHES

Paints

Gouache is a versatile medium. It can be laid as transparent washes, much like watercolour; but when applied in a thicker consistency, gouache has good covering power, which gives an artist the option to alter or correct a painting without the colours becoming muddy. When dry, the surface of the paint has an opalescent glow, similar in some ways to soft pastel. Unlike watercolour, which stains the paper, gouache merely sits on the surface and can be washed off with a damp sponge, leaving very little trace of colour behind.

For the early stages of the featured painting, the artist used tempera blocks (gouache in solid form) to render colour washes. As the work progressed, she reverted to conventional gouache paint supplied in tubes.

Paintbrushes

Val Wiffen's personal preference is for Chinese-made brushes, with which she can make a wide variety of marks. For figure painting, she advocates using at least one brush that comes to a fine point and a large mop for applying broad washes. For a small-scale work like this, she can make do with a single brush that fulfils both purposes, a large weasel-hair brush (equivalent to a No.14 round).

"It is worth spending time experimenting with your brushes to see what marks you can make. I use the pointed tip of the brush for detail, and the side for making broad strokes."

THE PICTURE DEVELOPS

Positive and negative shapes

With the next stage, the artist gets to grips with drawing and working on the tonal values of the composition. Applying tempera washes, she blocks in the positive shapes, which constitute the focal point of the picture, and also the negative shapes created by spaces and areas of colour that surround the figure.

"If I am having trouble painting the negative shapes, it means the figure drawing requires some adjustment."

Solidity and form

With the pose firmly established, the artist begins to home in on specific shapes and colours. She introduces stronger and richer colours to render folds in the clothing, the striped sofa cover and the model's boots. With only the minimum of detail, the figure already looks solid, with his weight nestling into the soft seating.

Introducing detail

With deft strokes, the artist begins to model basic facial features. Folded fabrics take shape, with cast shadows and highlights indicated with strokes of paint. Though broadly painted, details such as collars, cuffs, pockets and seams give form and definition to the clothing.

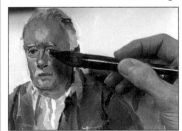

Keeping colours fresh
When laying gouache, make a single stroke in one direction only. This deposits the paint on the surface without disturbing the underlying colour.

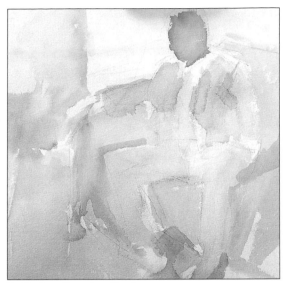

Blocking in positive and negative shapes

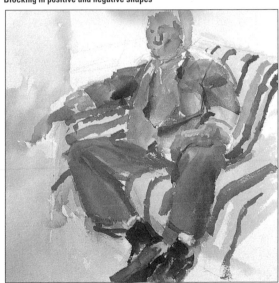

Introducing stronger and richer colours

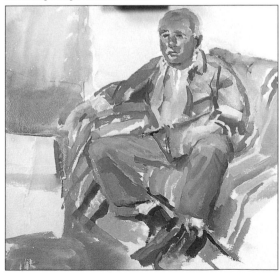

Detailing the features and clothing

What shall I paint?
FACES & FIGURES
Painting a person

"Don't try for a likeness too early. It is so easy to get bogged down with detail before the figure has any real substance."

FROM START TO FINISH

Allowing for rest breaks, the painting was brought close to fruition over a period of about five hours. The sequence below shows how the portrait evolved from the sketch plan and loose washes, until the finished painting (opposite) finally emerged. It is worth noting that the artist resisted the temptation to paint the model's features until the very end of the session.

Valerie Wiffen
PORTRAIT OF SIMON
Gouache on paper
38 x 38cm (15 x 15in)

Painting skin tones
In this case, so-called white skin is more like a warm grey with mauve-tinted shadows. Always look carefully at flesh tones and try to identify the colours objectively.

Painting eyes
Don't allow the eyes to dominate. If you paint them with pure white paint, your model can appear to be ·staring unnervingly out of the picture.

Painting hair
Hairstyle contributes to the sitter's appearance. There is no need to paint every wisp of hair, but here the artist was able to introduce sufficient detail to convey the age and character of her model.

Painting hands
For most painters, hands are a source of consternation, because they appear to be such complex structures. Paint them simply, as planes separated by rows of knuckles, remembering that these joints are only capable of hinging in one direction.

"There is nothing like a degree of success for building confidence, and with confidence comes the enthusiasm to do better still. So don't be overcritical when evaluating your own work. Look for the positive aspects of your painting, and try to recognize your achievements as well as your shortcomings."

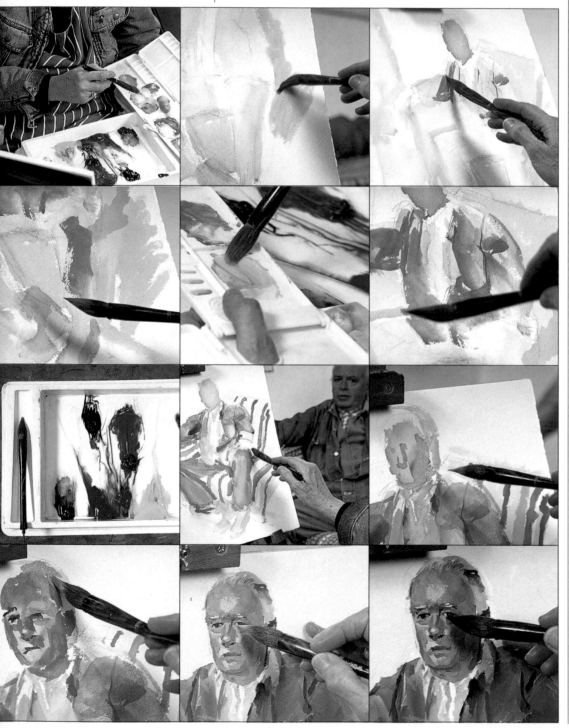

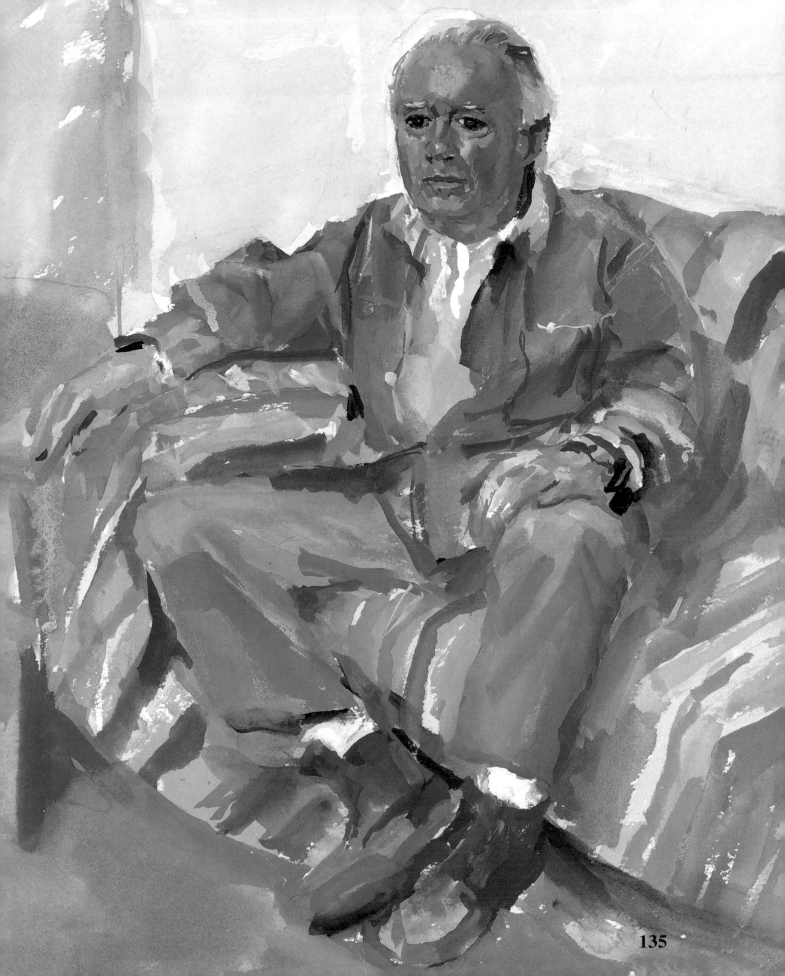

135

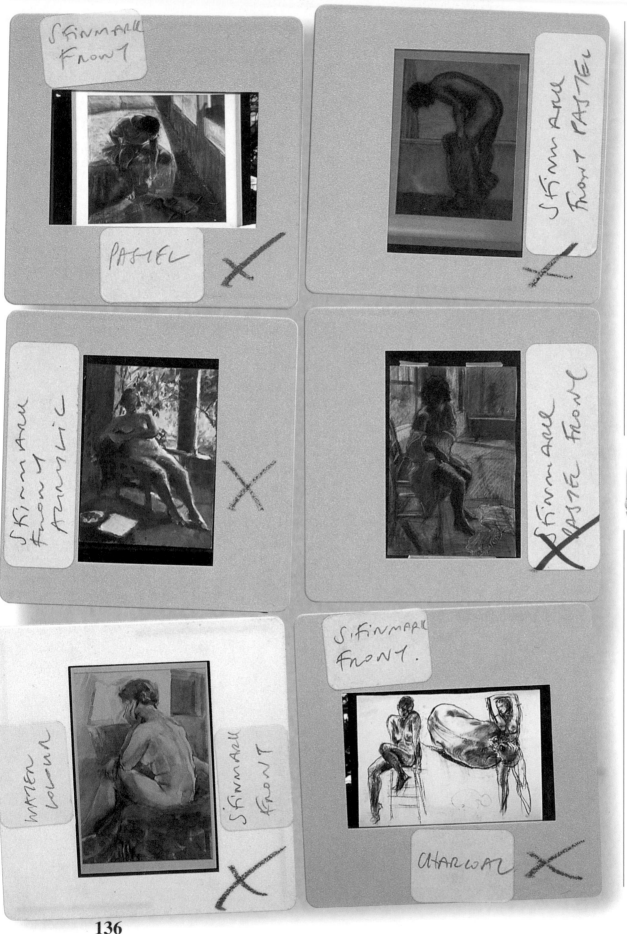

The handwritten labels on the slides read:
- SFINMARK FRONT / PASTEL
- SFinnArk Front PASTEL
- SKinnArk front Arrylic
- SFinnArk PASTEL FRONT
- WATER COLOUR / SFinmArk FRONT
- SiFINMARK FRONT. / CHARCOAL

Sharon Finmark
TRANSPARENCIES
OF FIGURE STUDIES
AND PAINTINGS
FROM THE ARTIST'S
COLLECTION
*Various media
on paper*

Figures in context

Furniture and simple props can be employed to make an eye-catching pose look plausible. Bedrooms and bathrooms make appropriate settings for nude or semi-clothed figures.

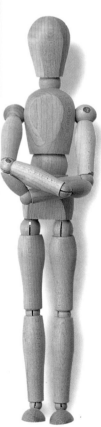

☛ SEE ALSO
Figure painting
in the studio 138
Painting a
friend 128
Painting hands
and feet 144
Putting life into a
painting 118

What shall I paint?
FACES & FIGURES
Working with models
Experimental poses

Experimenting with poses

For long figure-study sessions, artists generally ask the model to take up conventional seated or standing poses. But you can extend your repertoire with ten-minute sessions, to enable the model to adopt a more dramatic pose – or to let you practise capturing the essence of a figure in motion, using a rapid sketchy style.

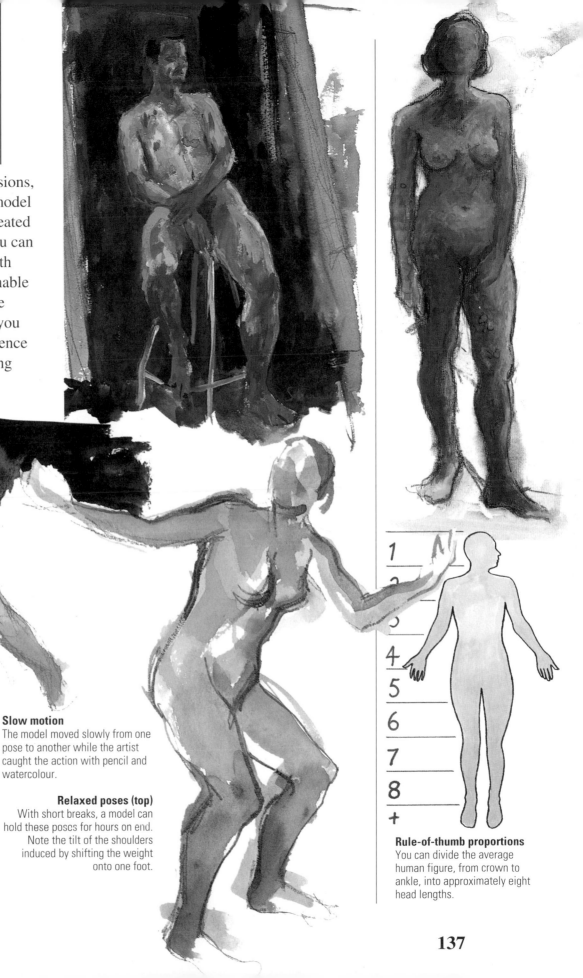

Slow motion
The model moved slowly from one pose to another while the artist caught the action with pencil and watercolour.

Relaxed poses (top)
With short breaks, a model can hold these poses for hours on end. Note the tilt of the shoulders induced by shifting the weight onto one foot.

Rule-of-thumb proportions
You can divide the average human figure, from crown to ankle, into approximately eight head lengths.

137

Figure painting in the studio

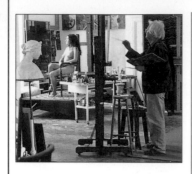

For many amateur artists, making a studio painting of a nude model is a relatively ambitious project, but one to which most aspire. To Ken Howard, well known for his back-lit life studies, it is a familiar process, but his painting featured here goes a step further. This particular picture is a sophisticated combination of three themes that have already been covered in this book – figure painting, room interior and still life. Making all these elements work successfully in one picture brings us to the core of this artist's approach to painting.

"Painting is the process of keeping everything working in a proper relationship. Keep your eye on the total picture, bringing everything along together right up to the last mark. That is the key."

This is an important theme that we will return to again and again as the work progresses.

WORKING WITH A MODEL

Hiring a professional model is a luxury few painters can afford, but there's no need to go to such lengths if there are close friends or family who are willing to sit for you. Particularly when using amateur models, it's essential to choose a comfortable pose that your subject can hold for extended periods. You should also allow for regular breaks, marking the key points of the pose with masking tape so that your model can take up the same position. Be sure to keep your workroom warm, and to provide somewhere where your model can change in private.

Ken Howard
PAULA
Oil on canvas
60 x 50cm (24 x 20in)

The following sequence covers approximately three hours' work, and was executed in a 'one-wet' session. The finished painting opposite was the result of a further two-hour session.

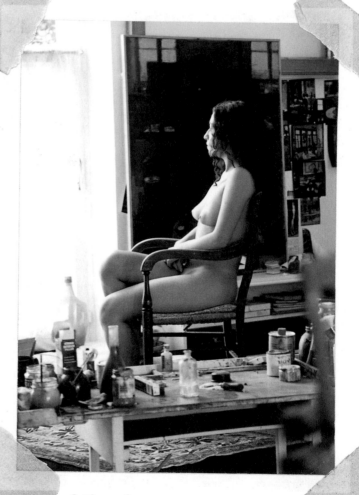

Setting up the pose
It pays to think about how you want to pose your model before he or she arrives. That way you won't waste valuable time arranging your props and lighting. In this painting, the model is posed against the diffused light from a window, with a dark-tone picture hanging behind her to provide dramatic contrast to her profile. A table, which is positioned to break the foreground, holds a selection of jars and bottles that add sparkle and colourful detail to the picture.

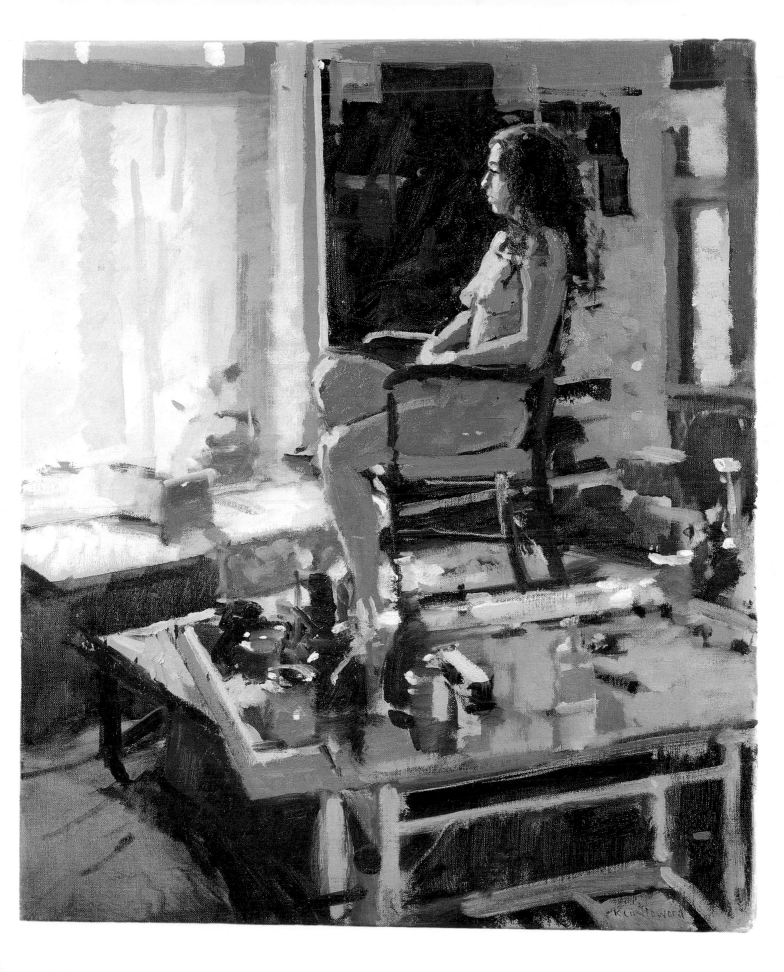

What shall I paint?
FACES & FIGURES
Figure painting
in the studio

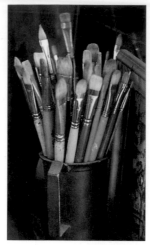

PAINT, BRUSHES AND CANVAS

"There is no reason to be afraid of using oils. If you want to be afraid of something, be afraid of watercolour or gouache – there's no turning back or scraping off with these paints."

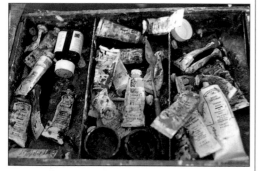

Paints
Oil paint is Ken Howard's preferred medium.

As with much of Ken Howard's work, this is in essence a tonal painting made with a limited palette, in this case cadmium lemon, cadmium red, French ultramarine, Naples yellow, raw umber, black and white. He uses glaze medium to accelerate the drying while preserving the transparency of the paint, and rinses his brushes in a jar of pure turpentine.

Brushes
This picture was painted with hog-hair flats and filberts, plus the occasional decorator's brush.

"The palette of colours an artist uses is a bit like the key a composer might choose when writing music. The composer wouldn't write every piece of music in the same key and no artist uses the same palette for every picture. Each time you come to a painting you should be trying to do something better or different."

"I prefer to work with relatively large brushes. If you start using small brushes during the early stages of a picture, you lose spontaneity and freshness."

Ken Howard stresses the importance of keeping paintbrushes clean.

"While I am working on a particular painting I reserve specific brushes for the different colours I am using. It is a mistake to keep using the one brush, because even when you have rinsed it in turps there is still a minute amount of paint left in the bristles which gets transferred along with the next colour you put on the canvas. Using several brushes is the only way to keep your colours looking fresh."

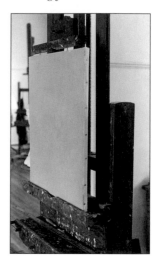

The canvas
The support for this work is a sized linen canvas, measuring 60 x 50cm (24 x 20in), coated with a white oil primer. A neutral ground colour was applied to provide the important mid tone.

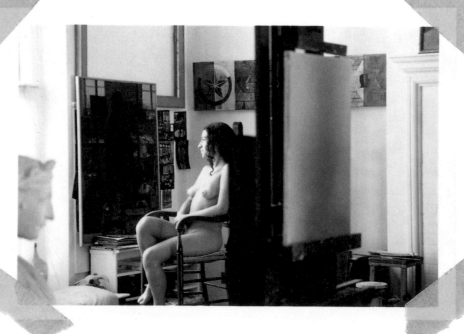

"If you are a tonal painter, you are constantly working between the darker and lighter ranges of tone. The half-tone ground of the canvas is the vital key tone."

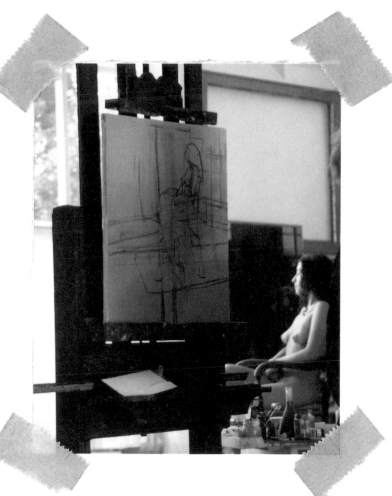

Gauging proportions and relationships
Use the model's head to gauge the proportions of her body. At the same time, establish the relationship between the different parts of the figure, using key vertical and horizontal grid lines that run through the picture.

UNDERDRAWING

"I have met a lot of good draughtsmen who could not paint, but I have never met a good painter who could not draw."

From the earliest stages of a painting, Ken Howard is concerned with working out proportions and relationships. When faced with a blank canvas, he likes to 'get his eye in' by drawing with charcoal. This allows him to check the proportions of the figure, and to work out how the various elements of the painting relate to each other.

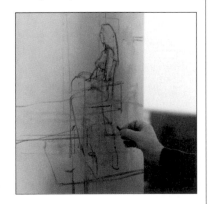

Drawing with charcoal
Don't make the mistake of thinking you can simply fill in the finished charcoal drawing with colour. As you make each mark with paint, you should be relating it back to your mental grid, constantly improving on the drawing as you add colour and tone to the painting.

LAYING IN

The next stage of the painting is the vital 'laying in' of the full range of tones and key colours, establishing a firm foundation upon which the picture is built. Tonal balance is all important at this point, but you should also be aware of how colours relate. Having identified and mixed a colour, look to see where that colour appears elsewhere in the picture, and brush that in too. This has the effect of unifying a painting.

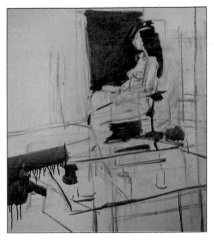

Blocking in the dark tones
To define the model's profile and hair, the darker areas of the picture are blocked in with broad washes of paint thinned with turpentine.

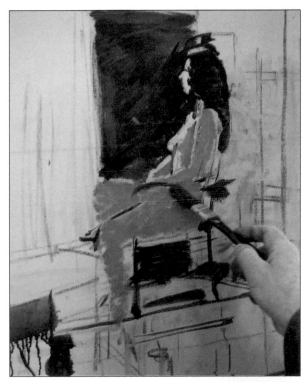

Painting flesh tones
Warm flesh tones are applied to the figure, followed by the neutral grey wall behind the model, then red-brown brush strokes for the chair.

Inserting highlights
Now the lighter tones and highlights are introduced, including the curtained window.

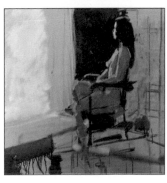

What shall I paint?
FACES & FIGURES
Figure painting
in the studio

☛ SEE ALSO
Experimenting with poses 136
Painting hands and feet 144

The image on the canvas begins to clarify, much like looking through a camera lens while the picture is slowly brought into focus. A painting can often look its best at this early stage because it seems to breath life and spontaneity.

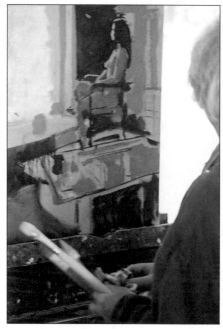

Painting the foreground
The foreground begins to emerge. The shadows beneath the table are painted in with a brush, then lifted off with a rag to suggest reflected light.

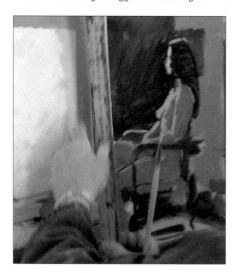

Painting straight edges
A long ruler is used to guide the brush when painting the straight edges of the window frame.

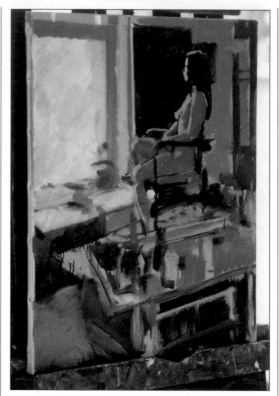

Introducing detail (above)
Dashes of colour and tone are added to represent the bottles and other objects in the foreground.

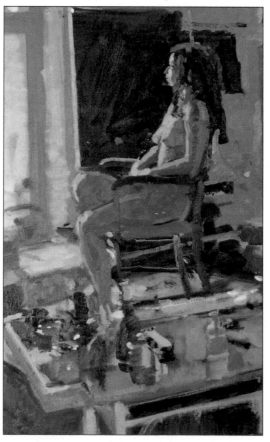

FOCUSING ATTENTION

There is more than one approach to painting. Some artists will work up the entire painting in detail until the whole picture is finished to the same degree. Alternatively, a painter can focus the onlooker's attention on what he or she considers to be the important elements of the picture. This is achieved by concentrating on the focal points and painting the peripheral parts of the picture in less detail. This is the approach favoured by Ken Howard.

"I have a point in a picture where I want the eye to linger, because I believe that is the way one sees in reality. If you look someone in the eye, the rest of their face is out of focus, a sort of impression. That is the way I like to paint."

As you work, it pays to compare mixed colours with the lighter and darker areas of the painting to avoid becoming absorbed in detail at the expense of the overall picture.

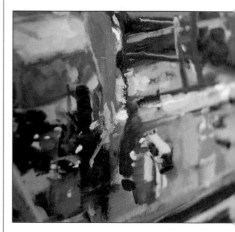

The still-life elements
The still life in the foreground is one focal point that receives special attention. Small dabs or streaks of paint suggest reflections, highlights and areas in shadow.

Features and flesh tones (left)
As the painting progresses, more work goes into the model's features, and flesh tones are strengthened to give solidity to the figure.

An individual approach

From his own experience as a tutor, Ken Howard is of the opinion that people teach themselves to paint.

"There are no fixed rules that you can pass on – there is no method that suddenly makes it possible to draw or paint. As a teacher, all you can do is explain your approach to painting and encourage people to observe with a painter's eye. Teaching art is about sowing seeds in people's minds – seeds that inspire them to search for their own way.

Some students have told me that the most encouraging thing I have taught them is that I too can get myself in a mess, but then find my way out again.

So don't become discouraged if you lose your way. Painting is all about losing and finding, even if that means taking a palette knife and scraping the painting back to the canvas."

A tonal painting made with a limited palette.

Cadmium lemon,

Cadmium red

French ultramarine

Naples yellow

Raw umber

Black and white

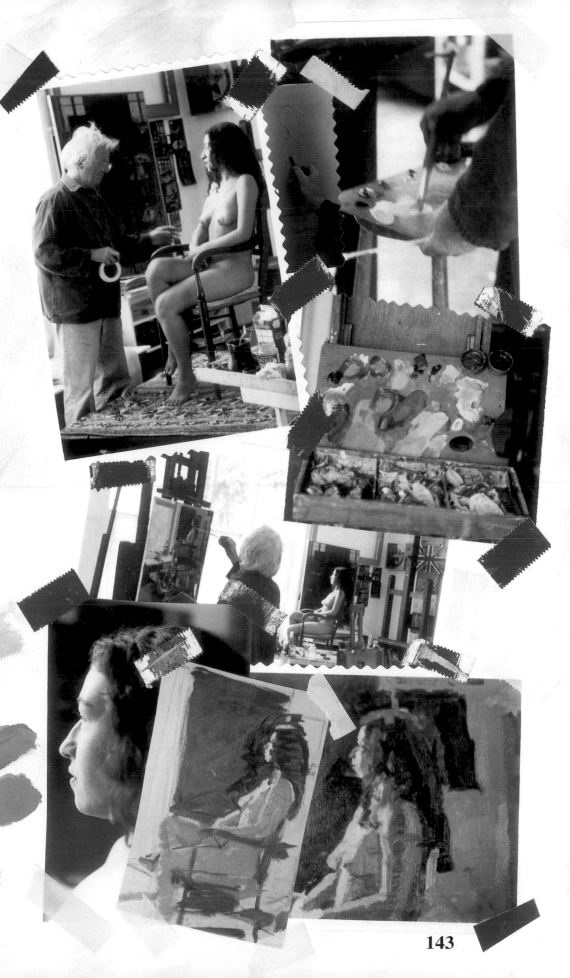

143

What shall I paint?
FACES AND FIGURES
Close observation
Shape and proportion

Painting hands and feet

Like faces, hands and feet have distinctive characteristics – fleshy, slim, elegant, pale, dark, young or elderly – that contribute significantly to a likeness of your sitter and towards the success of your painting. When making figure drawings and paintings, pay attention to the size and proportion of hands and feet in relation to the rest of the body.

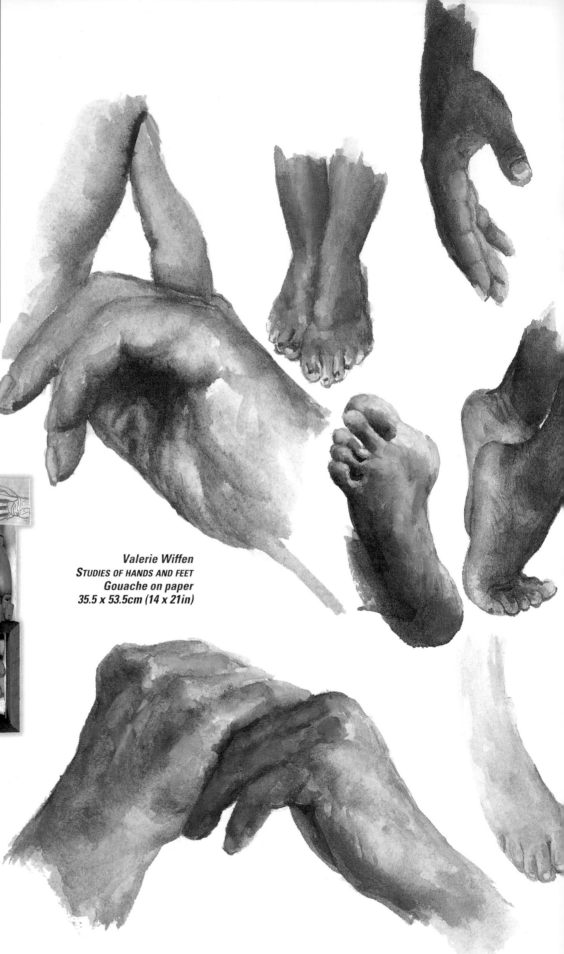

Valerie Wiffen
STUDIES OF HANDS AND FEET
Gouache on paper
35.5 x 53.5cm (14 x 21in)

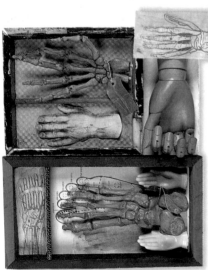

Making colour studies
Working mostly from live models, Valerie Wiffen has created a sketch-book page of colour studies in gouache. Making similar studies will help you to appraise the complex shapes and proportions of hands and feet, and give you the experience to develop a visual shorthand for painting them convincingly when creating full-figure portraits.

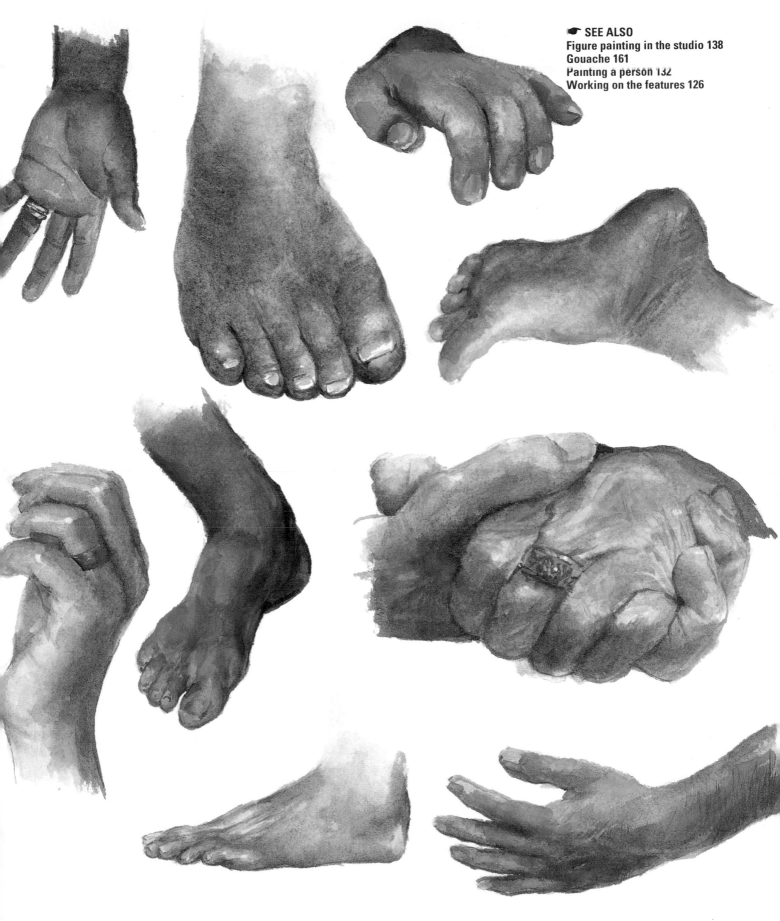

☞ SEE ALSO
Figure painting in the studio 138
Gouache 161
Painting a person 132
Working on the features 126

145

What shall I paint?
WILDLIFE
Rendering animals on the move
Studying animal characteristics
Painting fur and feather

Painting your pets

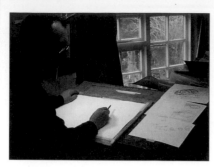

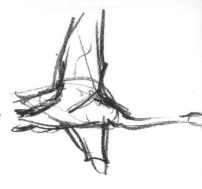

Sketching from life
The wildlife artist Peter Partington favours a soft graphite pencil.

"The point of a pencil glides effortlessly across the paper, and you can use it to suggest a wide variety of textures. I find it the ideal tool when working at speed."

Wildlife artists often specialize in naturalistic drawings and paintings of animals and birds. It takes dedication and experience to render wild animals in their natural habitat, but you will find that domestic pets can be challenging and rewarding subjects, too – though they can be just as uncooperative!

With fur and feather featuring strongly, animals and birds offer a wealth of colour and texture. And they have a natural talent for striking quite stunning sculptural poses.

Before you launch into a full-scale painting, develop a few ideas for possible compositions by studying your pets' habits and by recording their daily lives with rapid sketches or reference photographs.

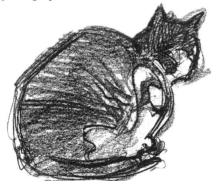

Working with unreliable models
Animals and birds are notorious for refusing to cooperate. There is no point in trying to control their habits, you simply have to work round them. One obvious way is to paint your pet while it is resting, but even then it pays to get the essentials down as quickly as possible. Also, most animals will settle quietly for a short period while they are feeding. If you want to progress to something more exciting, you have to find ways of rendering animals on the move.

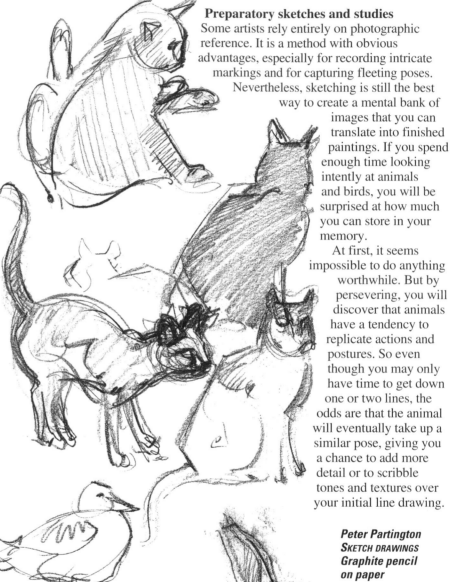

Preparatory sketches and studies
Some artists rely entirely on photographic reference. It is a method with obvious advantages, especially for recording intricate markings and for capturing fleeting poses. Nevertheless, sketching is still the best way to create a mental bank of images that you can translate into finished paintings. If you spend enough time looking intently at animals and birds, you will be surprised at how much you can store in your memory.

At first, it seems impossible to do anything worthwhile. But by persevering, you will discover that animals have a tendency to replicate actions and postures. So even though you may only have time to get down one or two lines, the odds are that the animal will eventually take up a similar pose, giving you a chance to add more detail or to scribble tones and textures over your initial line drawing.

Peter Partington
SKETCH DRAWINGS
Graphite pencil on paper

PAINTING YOUR CAT'S PORTRAIT

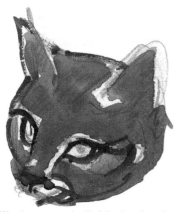

Just like humans, individual animals have distinctive characteristics, which enable you to distinguish your pet from perhaps hundreds of similar animals in the district.

Here, the cat is singled out as a worthy subject for portraiture – but making similar observations and studies will enable you to create an intimate picture of any animal.

Study the features and the overall shape of the animal's head. The average cat has large triangular ears, set high on a rounded head. Except for certain exotic species, cats have a short, almost flat, muzzle.

The relatively large eyes are on a line that divides the cat's face in half. Divide the lower half in two to define the top of the triangular nose, which more or less spans the space between the cat's eyes.

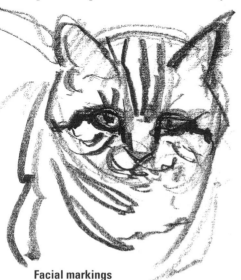

Facial markings
The fur is grouped into ridges that run vertically across the forehead. Some breeds of cat have striped markings that follow these ridges.

Eyes
The leaf-shape eyes are outlined in black. The eyelid casts a deep shadow across the iris; the distinctive pupil changes shape in response to the light.

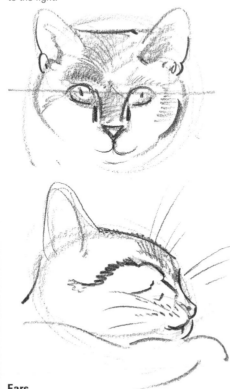

Ears
With velvet like fur on the outside and smooth skin protected by delicate hairs on the inside, a cat's ears face forward for most of the time. There are intricate folds where the lower ear joins the head.

Eyebrow hair
Cats have bushy eyebrow hair that grows in a direction that is different from the surrounding fur.

Whiskers
The cat's whiskers are coarse hairs that sprout from among the shorter and softer fur that covers the muzzle.

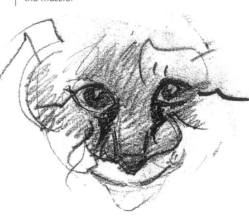

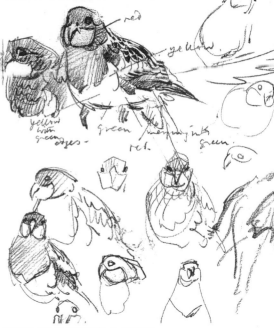

TRY PAINTING A BIRD

Even more than animals, caged birds present the challenge of capturing rapid movement. Feathers are fascinating and often colourful, providing endless possibilities for pattern and design.

Birds' eggs, too, are perfect examples of nature's ability to create wonderfully subtle colours and textures. If you come across abandoned eggs, you will find them fascinating subjects for detailed studies and paintings.

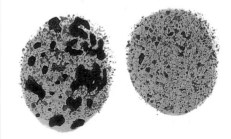

Rendering plumage
A bird's plumage comprises different-sized feathers arranged in groups or tracts that overlap one another. As a general rule, the feathers get smaller towards the breast, and longer towards the back. The longest ones are the primary flight feathers that form the wingtips and tail.

A quick way to re-create this layering is to draw a diamond grid, which you then fill in to suggest the coloured tips of individual feathers. Keep a close eye on local colour and the effects of light.

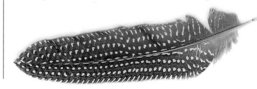

147

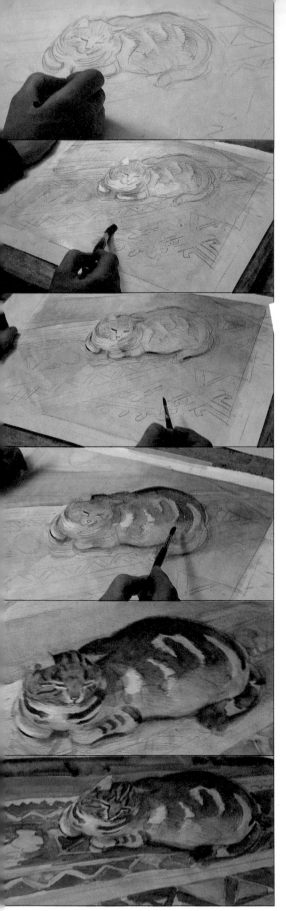

What shall I paint?
WILDLIFE
Painting your pets

☛ **SEE ALSO**
Coloured pencils 182
Painting a face 120
Papers 173
Watercolour paint 161
Wildlife painting 43

A CAT AT REST

Peter Partington takes up the cat theme by painting a brindled tabby who – though not actually asleep – is perfectly relaxed and enjoying the heat from the stove nearby. She is lying on a faded Persian rug that adds colour and pattern to the painting.

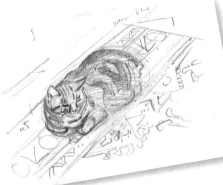

Preliminary drawings
Before embarking on the painting, the artist made two or three pencil studies from different angles. He also made colour notes and drew a diagram of the patterned carpet. Armed with this information, he retired to the studio.

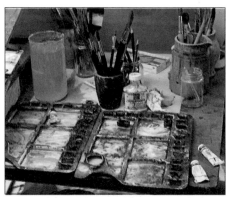

Materials and equipment
The featured painting was made on 300gsm watercolour paper, lightly taped to a drawing board. Most of the work was carried out with watercolour, but details and textures were added with coloured pencils. For this painting, the artist used just two brushes – a No.16 round for the broad washes, and a No.10 round for painting details.

"Tabby cats make wonderful subjects for painting. The linear markings help describe the contours of the body, giving the image a strong three-dimensional quality."

The artist starts by drawing in the main elements of the composition, including the cat's markings, then applies a warmish blue-grey wash mixed from cobalt blue and light red. Some areas of paper are left white for highlights.

Shadows and local colour are introduced to give form to the composition, and to indicate the tabby cat's striped markings. Colours are allowed to merge, to good effect.

The artist then begins to strengthen the tones and work up the surface of the fur, using a blue-grey mixed from cobalt blue and raw sienna. It's best to apply the paint in the direction of the fur, blotting the highlights with soft tissue paper to lift out areas of colour.

Peter Partington develops the cat's features and facial markings with the smaller paintbrush, and introduces a hint of burnt umber in order to warm the fur around the nose and cheeks.

Finally, the carpet is worked up to balance the foreground. Once the painting has dried thoroughly, the last touches and textures are added, using coloured pencils.

Painting fur
There's no need to include every hair when painting a cat's coat. It is more important to look for distinctive markings that help to describe the animal's form and character. You may find it pays to concentrate most detail around the cat's face and head, keeping the rest of its markings sketchy and free-form.

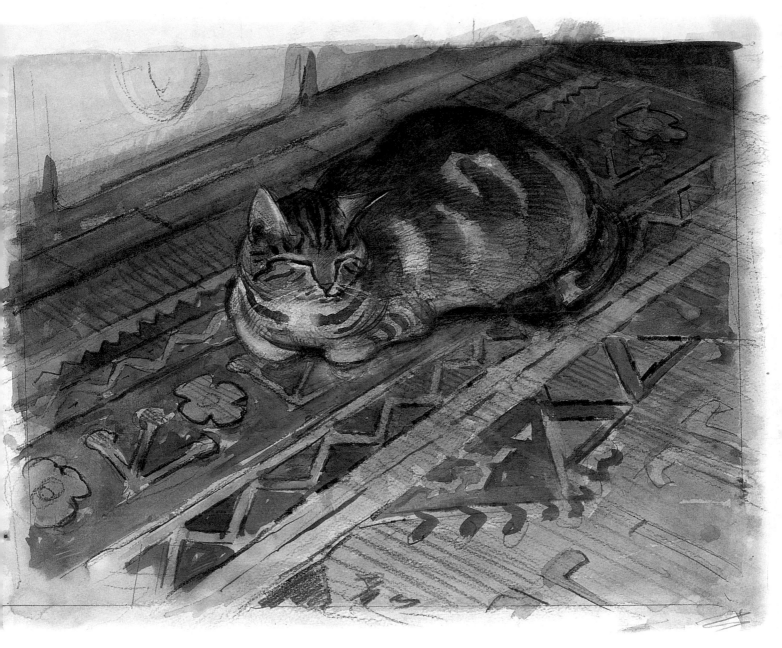

Peter Partington
Mrs Tabs
Mixed media on
watercolour paper
32.5 x 43cm (12½ x 17in)

Fur absorbs and reflects light

When depicting fur in a drawing or painting, look for changes of tone caused by the way the fur absorbs and reflects the light. As a general rule, when the hairs are pointing towards you, fur looks dark in tone. When they are lying flat and pointing away from you, the fur appears glossy and lighter in tone.

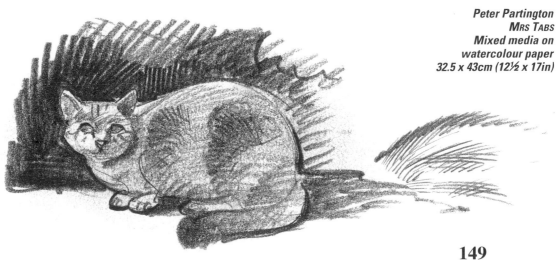

149

What shall I paint?
WORKING FROM IMAGINATION
Tracing and copying
Enlarging and reducing

Getting your ideas onto paper and canvas

There's a popular misconception that 'real' artists balk at the idea of tracing an image onto canvas or paper. Nothing could be further from the truth. For centuries artists have sought ways of accurately transferring images onto a flat surface – and although a great deal of cunning technique was (and still is) often employed to achieve a successful result, the notion that it might be construed as 'cheating' never entered their heads.

"A picture is something which requires as much knavery, trickery and deceit as the perpetration of a crime".
EDGAR DEGAS (1834–1917)

Camera obscura
Using cameras to establish a basic image for painting is not a new idea. With advances in lens making in the sixteenth century, it became possible to project an image onto a flat surface inside a darkened chamber, so that an artist could make a tracing from it.

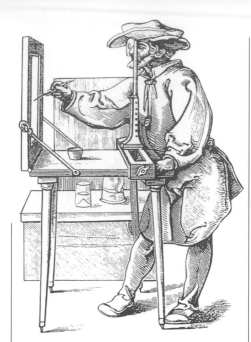

Drawing machines
In the past, inventive artists devised ways of tracing the outlines of three-dimensional objects onto sheets of glass.

Tracing wheel
Used to punch a design onto a support.

Pricking and pouncing
One of the most widespread methods of transferring images was to make a full-size drawing or 'cartoon' and then, following the lines with a toothed wheel, punch a series of closely spaced holes through the paper. The perforated drawing was laid onto the support and 'pounced' by tapping with a cloth bag filled with fine charcoal or chalk. The pouncing forced the powdered material through the holes, leaving a replica of the pricked image on the support.

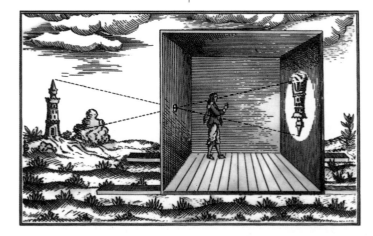

☞ SEE ALSO
Composing a picture from imagination 152

TRACING

Tracing is a simple way of copying drawn or photographic images onto a paper or canvas support. You can buy flat sheets and rolls of good-quality tracing paper that have sufficient transparency and strength to enable you to work easily.

Tracing paper
Tape tracing paper over your original and lightly trace the image, using a sharp pencil or fine felt-tip pen. Scribble across the back of the tracing with a soft graphite pencil; then tape the tracing, graphite side down, onto your support. Transfer the linework by drawing over the traced lines with a pencil, and then remove the tracing to reveal the image marked out in graphite on the support.

Using transfer paper
As an alternative to graphite, sandwich a sheet of carbon paper or dark-red rouge paper between the tracing and the support. Rouge paper is a specialized paper used by professionals to transfer designs. Its main advantage is that unwanted linework can be erased easily. You may find the lines created by carbon to be a little too opaque and permanent.

Tracing on a light box
You can trace an image directly onto paper or unstretched canvas, using a photographer's light box designed for viewing transparencies. This type of box comprises a fluorescent strip light mounted beneath a sheet of translucent glass or plastic. The light is bright enough to throw a clear image through reasonably thick paper or canvas.

CHANGING SCALE

Artists frequently need to change the proportion of the original image to fit a larger or smaller sheet of paper or canvas support. There are several methods for enlarging, transferring and manipulating images, some of which are mentioned here.

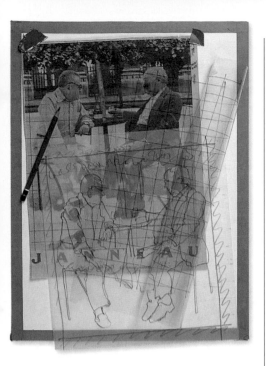

Gridding-up

To make an accurate enlargement or reduction, draw a squared grid across the original image. If you don't want to mark the original, draw your grid on a tracing-paper overlay or on a sheet of transparent acetate.

Draw a similar grid of larger or smaller squares on the support. To plot the grid across the width of the support, count the number of squares in one row drawn across the original (say nine squares), then align the tip of your ruler or tape measure with one edge of the canvas and the tenth division with the other. Make a pencil or charcoal mark against divisions one to nine, then use a T-square to draw a row of vertical lines across the support from each mark.

Create the grid of squares by drawing a series of horizontal lines with the same spacing and at right angles to the first set of lines. Finally, copy the image square by square onto the canvas support.

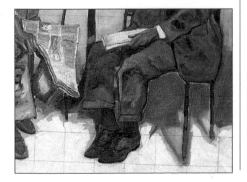

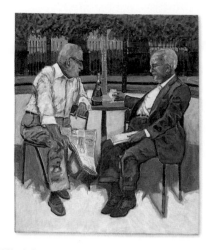

Work in progress
The painting above is based on a cutting from a newspaper (left). The artist has enlarged and cropped the proportion of the original image and transferred it to the canvas using the gridding-up method. The original drawing and grid lines are gradually obliterated as the painting progresses (below left).

Scanners and digital cameras

For relatively little money, you can buy a scanner that will copy flat artwork and photographs onto a computer, where it is possible to change the scale and recrop the image before printing it.

You can now also transfer pictures taken with a digital camera directly into the computer's memory.

Using a photocopier

If you have access to a photocopier, enlarging and reducing pictures couldn't be simpler. Most modern machines will print copies up to 400 per cent larger or 75 per cent smaller than the original.

Projecting pictures

To throw an image onto a sheet of paper or small canvas, use a photographer's enlarger or a table-top overhead projector. Adjust the focus, then draw the main elements on the support with a soft pencil or charcoal.

Working with large projections

You can use a slide projector to fill a large canvas, or buy an artists' tracer projector to blow up flat artwork and printed photographs. Ensure that the projector and canvas are aligned accurately and mounted securely, to prevent distortion and movement while you are transferring the image.

Working in a dimly lit room, either copy the image in line or block in the major areas of tone and colour with paint before proceeding with the painting under ordinary lighting conditions.

Alternatively, continue to build up more and more detail, using the projection as a guide – but remember to switch off the projector and turn on the lights from time to time to check the progress of the painting.

Tiling with photocopies
Very large assemblies can be created by taping photocopies or computer printouts together. These can then be gridded or traced and transferred to the support.

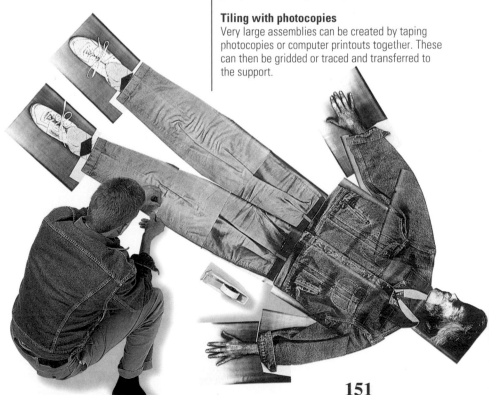

151

Composing a picture from imagination

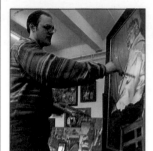

Researching the location

If you have made a habit of collecting pictorial reference, you could begin by sifting through your files to see if there's anything you might use as a starting point for your painting. Alternatively, you may prefer to start from scratch and look for a location that offers a wealth of diverse material.

Most of the paintings in this book have been made either from life or by using direct photographic reference. Although the artists may have reinterpreted the subjects to some extent, they are more or less faithful representations of what the artists could see in front of them. However, it makes a stimulating change to construct a picture from imagination, using a variety of reference material, such as sketches, photographs and magazine cuttings, as a basis for the composition.

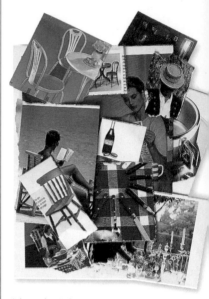

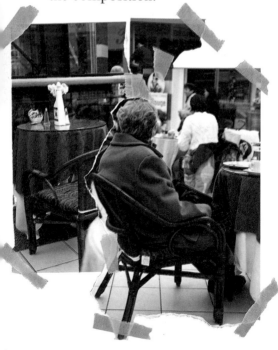

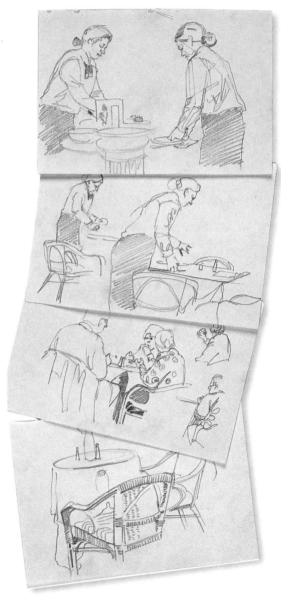

On-the-spot observation and back-up references
Alastair Adams constructed his painting from a series of references. You will never use all the images you gather on location, but it pays to accumulate as much reference as you can, including sketches, photographs and magazine cuttings.

Alastair Adams wanted to paint a café or bistro scene, which would give him the opportunity to include groups of people and individuals engaged in a variety of activities. He tried out a number of small intimate locations – which had plenty of atmosphere, but not enough going on. Most of them were also dimly lit, making it virtually impossible to take reference shots.

Eventually he decided on a dining area in a shopping mall, which supplied all his needs. It was a large open interior with a good source of natural light where an artist could sit unnoticed while he watched, sketched and photographed the numerous characters that passed through. In no time, he could retire to the studio with more than enough reference to begin the painting.

Working on the composition

By the time you get to the studio, you probably have a fairly strong image of the painting in your mind's eye. Some artists will make a preliminary drawing, using the reference gathered on location to jog their memory. Alastair Adams prefers to incorporate his reference material by enlarging and reducing tracings of his drawings and photographs on a photocopier, then tapes the images to an enlarged drawing of the interior.

Working on tracing paper gives him complete freedom to redraw interiors, figures and inanimate objects to suit his composition. Not only can he change the scale, he can flop the tracing paper so that a person is facing in the opposite direction, modify a pose by combining details from different shots of the same person, or compose a group of seated figures.

When combining disparate images, it is important to correct the perspective as you construct the composition. Here, the artist's viewpoint is from a seated position, so the heads of all the seated figures share that same eyelevel. Only the standing waitress appears at a different level.

"I start by re-creating the setting, using the background as an empty stage for my characters, which I arrange to balance the composition and to suggest depth in the painting by providing close-up detail in the foreground."

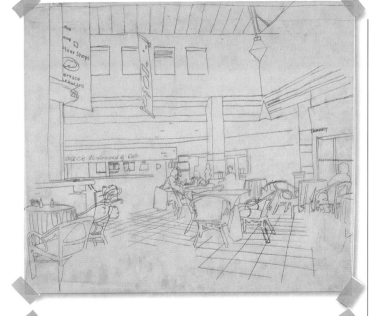

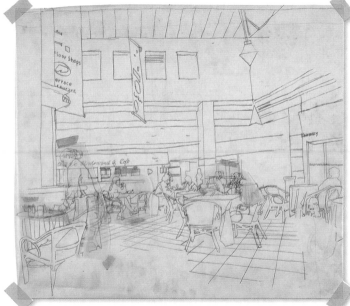

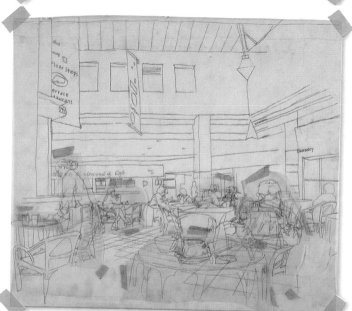

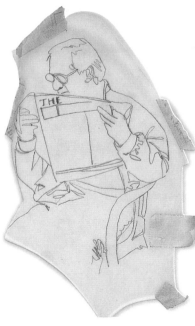

Working on tracing paper
This sequence (left) shows how Alastair Adams built up a preparatory collage of tracing-paper overlays as a basis for his composition. Being translucent, tracing paper allows the artist to impose layer upon layer without completely obscuring the underlying structure and detail.

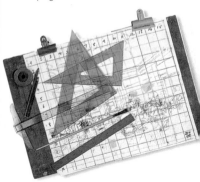

Transferring the image
Having finalized the composition, the artist makes an enlargement of the collage to match the size of the support, then draws a squared grid on the enlargement and an identical grid on the support. By copying the image exactly, square by square, he can re-create the composition on the support as an underdrawing for the finished painting.

153

What shall I paint?
WORKING FROM IMAGINATION
Composing a picture
from imagination

Materials and equipment

The finished picture was painted in a fairly limited palette of acrylic colours – titanium white, cadmium yellow light, cadmium yellow medium, cadmium red medium, quinacridone crimson, dioxazine purple, phthalo green-blue shade and phthalo blue-green shade.

For fine detail, the artist used Nos.3 and 5 round synthetic-bristle brushes, designed specifically for applying acrylic paints. When manipulating thicker paint, he prefers relatively stiff natural-hog brushes, in this case Nos.2, 4 and 6 flats.

The painting was made on a sheet of medium-density fibreboard (MDF), which does not buckle when wet paint is applied. The board has a smooth surface and is stiff enough to allow the paint to be built up quite thickly.

Having transferred the underdrawing to the board, the artist coated it with a clear acrylic primer that allows the natural colour of MDF to be used as a warm mid-tone ground colour.

A protective coat of varnish
To maintain their rich colouring and prevent the paint absorbing dust, Alastair Adams invariably protects his pictures with a coat of varnish.

Flesh tones
Flesh tones are based on white mixed with cadmium red medium or crimson and cadmium yellow light or cadmium yellow medium. To prevent these combinations becoming too warm and pink, the artist also adds purple or green to neutralize the mixes.

Painting signs
In this type of situation, there are always a number of printed signs and graphic images. It is essential to include them in order to convey the atmosphere of the location, but if you attempt to make them too legible they can detract from the main subject matter. It is better to suggest lettering and symbols with simple brushstrokes and spots of colour.

Keeping colours fresh
The artist manages to keep his colours fresh and uncontaminated by building up an image with distinct patches of colour laid side by side. This method also prevents a painting becoming fussy and overworked.

Painting neutrals
The neutral areas of the painting comprise a number of subtle greys and off-whites. They were created by adding complementary colours to a basic white mix – for example, white with cadmium yellow light and a small amount of purple.

The neutral colours just below the glazed atrium had to be kept cool so that they would recede and suggest depth in the painting. They are made with greens and blues mixed with crimson and cadmium red, and just a hint of cadmium yellow light.

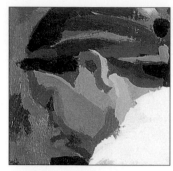

Flesh tones

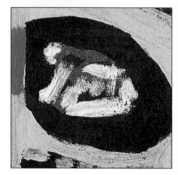

Signs

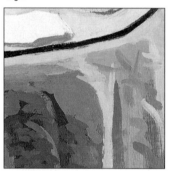

Fresh colours

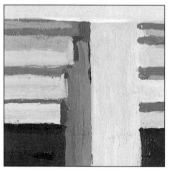

Neutral colours

The finished composition
The action takes place within the lower two-thirds of an almost-square format. This mass of colour and detail is balanced visually by the neutral colours, geometric planes and simple linear patterns of the shopping-mall walls and skylights.

The painting is divided vertically by a concrete pillar that directs the viewer's gaze towards a foreground dominated by an elderly gentleman reading a news-paper. Foreground detail serves to add depth to the painting and encourages the eye to linger until it is eventually led away by a curving chair back, towards the waitress clearing the table on the left of the picture. Her activity is crucial in counterbalancing the passive, almost contemplative postures of the other characters in the painting. The relatively large area of neutral-coloured floor creates a calm balance, giving the eye a rest before it alights upon a young woman sipping her coffee and groups of people finishing their meals or engaged in conversation.

Though small in scale, these figures are beautifully realized, with sufficient detail and animation to make them believable – yet kept simple enough to ensure they recede into the background.

☞ SEE ALSO
Acrylic paint 162
**Collecting resources
and references 18**
**Getting your ideas
onto paper and canvas 150**
Imaginative painting 44
Paintbrushes 167
**Painting space, depth
and distance 116**
**Putting life into
a painting 118**
Rooms and interiors 30

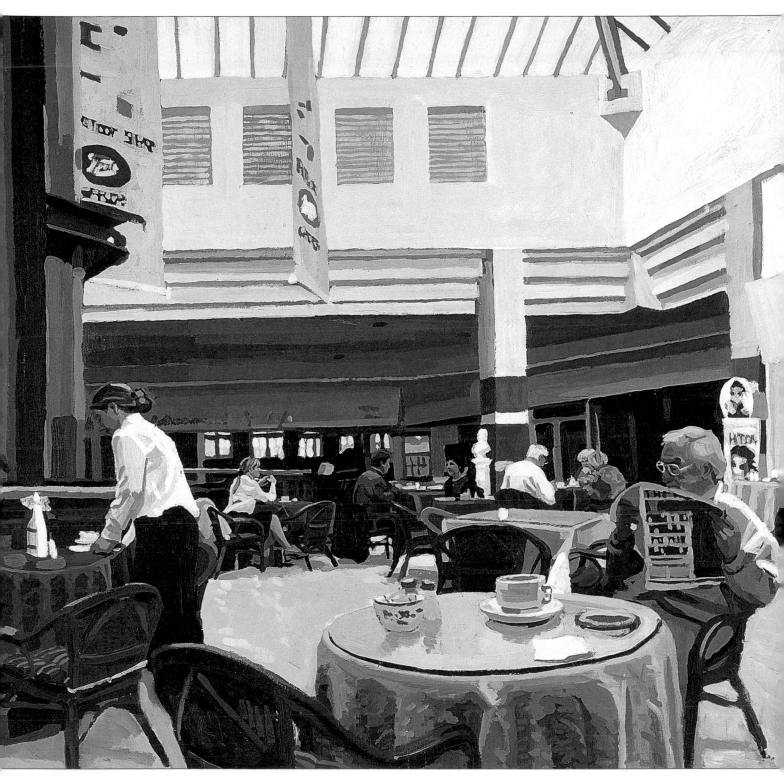

Alastair Adams
CAFÉ SCENE
Acrylic on board
51 x 54.5cm (20 x 21½in)

Empathy with the characters
We are not directly engaged with any of the figures in this painting – we are merely spectators. Yet as onlookers, we cannot help speculating whether the man reading a newspaper may perhaps be waiting for his wife or a friend to return from shopping; or if the waitress is taking advantage of a temporary lull in her busy day's work to clear the tables.

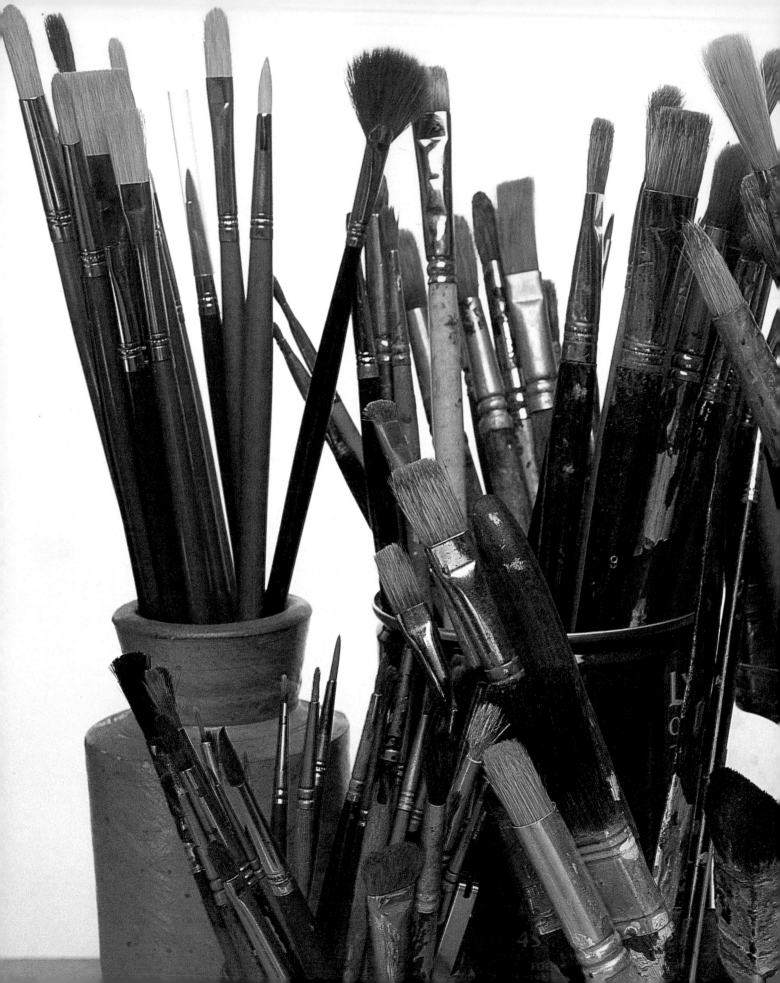

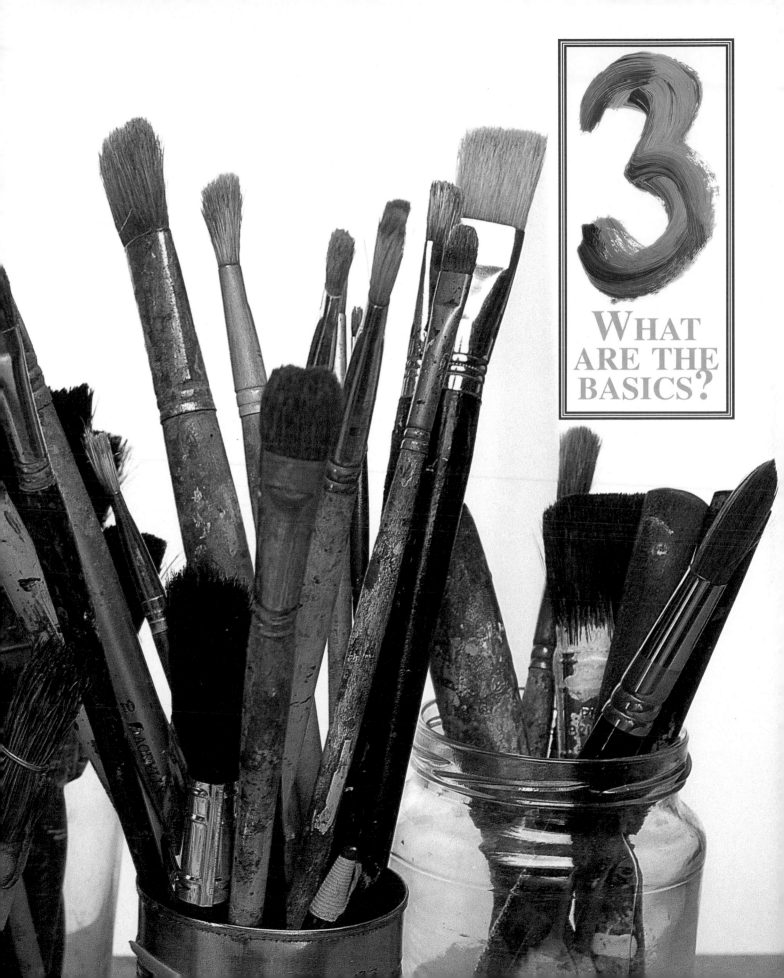

3

WHAT
ARE THE
BASICS?

COLOUR

Knowing how to mix and use colours is crucial to the success of your painting. Yet many artists find selecting, mixing and using colours a bewildering process. Understanding the basic principles of colour theory and knowing how to apply colours in practice will help boost your confidence.

THE COLOUR WHEEL

One of the most important 'tools' for the artist is the colour wheel. This is a simplified version of the spectrum, bent into a circle. It is an arrangement of the primary colours (red, yellow and blue) and secondary colours (orange, green and violet) from which all others – including greys and browns – are mixed.

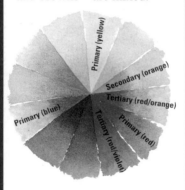

Primary colours
The primary colours are equidistant on the colour wheel. A primary colour is one that cannot be made by mixing other colours.

Secondary colours
A secondary colour is obtained by mixing two primaries. Thus, blue and yellow make green, red and yellow make orange, and red and blue make violet.

Tertiary colours
A tertiary colour is made by mixing a primary colour with the secondary next to it on the colour wheel. If you combine red with its neighbour to the right (orange), you get red-orange; if you combine red with its neighbour to the left (violet), you get red-violet.

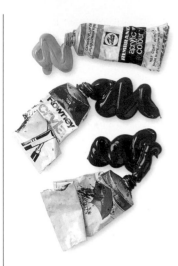

MIXING COLOURS
In theory, by mixing the primary colours in varying proportions, you can produce every other colour known. In practice things are not that simple, because the pigments used to manufacture paints are not as pure as light.

Mixing mud
According to basic colour theory, blue and yellow make green; but mixing just any old yellow and blue could have a very different result. Ultramarine blue, for example, has a reddish undertone, and lemon yellow a greenish one; combined, they make a muddy green.

Mixing clean colours
To mix a clean green, it is important to choose the exact colours – here phthalo blue and lemon yellow – for the particular shade you want.

Solid or broken colour
You can mix the required colour on your palette, or combine two colours on the surface of your painting.

Fully mixing two colours produces a solid third colour.

Partly mixing paint on the canvas creates interesting broken colour.

WARM AND COOL COLOURS
All colours have familiar associations. Reds and yellows conjure up sunlight and warmth; and we connect blues and greens with water, foliage and shadow. Taking advantage of these associations allows you to create a distinct atmosphere in your painting.

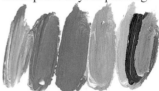

Neutral colours
Pure neutrals are mixtures of black and white, and are neither warm nor cool. However, most so-called neutrals are the result of mixing two or more colours, and therefore have a temperature bias depending on the proportions of the colours in the mix.

Depth and space
Because the eye perceives cool colours as being further away than warm ones, contrasts of warm and cool are used to create an illusion of receding space in landscapes.

Colour and tone
Tone refers to the relative lightness or darkness of a colour.

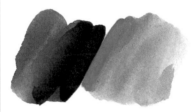

Comparative tones
Some colours are by nature lighter in tone than others. Cerulean blue is light in tone, while Prussian blue is darker.

Tints and shades
When white is added to a colour to lighten it, the resulting mix is referred to as a tint of that colour. Shades are darker tones of a colour, achieved by adding black.

Intensity

Intensity (also referred to as chroma or saturation) refers to how bright or strong a colour is. Vivid, pure colours are strong in intensity; pale, greyed colours are weak.

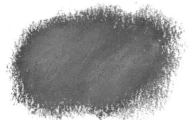

A vibrant, intense colour, such as cadmium red, becomes less intense when white is added, turning it pink. The intensity of a colour can also be reduced by mixing it with its complementary, which shifts the colour towards grey.

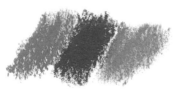

Using intensity to create contrast

Juxtaposing neutrals with intense colours makes the intense saturated colours appear more brilliant.

Counterchange

Counterchange is the placing of light shapes against dark, and vice versa. It creates lively, interesting pictures, because the reversals of light and dark provide intriguing contrasts. Counterchange also gives movement and rhythm to a picture, leading the viewer from light to dark and back again.

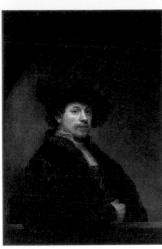

Chiaroscuro

The term chiaroscuro describes the effect of light and shade in a painting or drawing, especially where strong tonal contrasts are used.

Harmonious colours

There is a harmonious relationship between colours that lie on the same section of the spectrum or colour wheel – between yellow and green, for example.

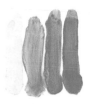

Colours with similar characteristics will harmonize when placed together in a painting.

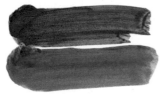

Close harmonies

The closest relationships are between shades of one colour, or between a primary colour and a secondary which contains that primary, such as blue and blue-green or blue and blue-violet.

Hue

Hue is another word for colour, and refers to the generalized colour of an object. The term is used to describe close or similar colours: for example, cadmium red, alizarin crimson and alizarin scarlet are close in hue.

Complementary colours

The colours opposite one another on the wheel are contrasting partners, called complementary colours. There are three main pairs, each consisting of one primary colour and the secondary composed of the other two primaries. Thus, red is the complementary of green, blue of orange, and yellow of violet. These relationships extend to pairs of secondary colours, so that red-orange is complementary to blue-green, blue-violet to yellow-orange, and so on.

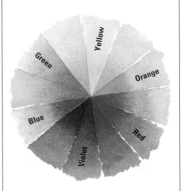

Colours directly opposite one another on the colour wheel are contrasting partners. They are known as complementary colours.

Vibrant complementaries

When complementary colours are juxtaposed, they enhance each other, producing a vibrant visual sensation; each colour seems brighter when placed against its neighbour than it would standing alone.

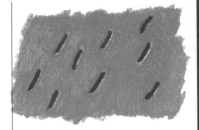

Using complementary accents

A harmonious scheme can also be enlivened by the introduction of complementary accents. Brilliant accents have a powerful effect, even when used in small amounts. A small touch of red in a green landscape, for example, can add zest to a painting.

Split complementaries

Near or 'split' complementaries are often more pleasing to the eye than true ones. Split complementaries are those which are separated by the true complementary; for example, violet is the true complementary of yellow, while blue-violet and red-violet are its split complementaries.

Mixing complementaries

When complementary colours are mixed together, they form neutral greys and browns. Depending on the colours used, and their proportions, it is possible to create a wide range of colourful neutrals.

PAINTS

Throughout this book, much is made of the importance of choosing the best medium for the work you want to create, and of using media that will suit your personal approach to painting. There is no 'right' medium for the job – each one offers advantages and disadvantages. Listed here are the main painting media in their various forms.

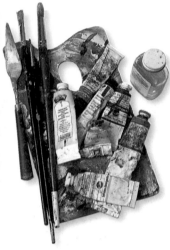

OIL PAINT

Oil paint consists of dry pigments ground in a natural drying oil such as linseed, or a semi-drying oil such as safflower or poppy. Some brands of paint are matured and then remade with more pigment to achieve the right consistency, but most are made with additives, such as stabilisers and driers, to improve stability and, in some cases, to improve consistency.

Buying oil tubes
Oil-paint tubes range from 5ml (0.17 US fl oz) to a generous 200ml (6.66 US fl oz). The most useful size is probably 37ml (1.25 US fl oz), though a larger tube of white – say 56ml (1.86 US fl oz) – tends to be more economical, since white is used more than most other colours.

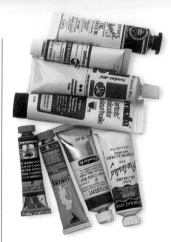

Artists' colours
Artist-quality oil paints offer the widest range of colours combined with maximum colour strength. They contain a high concentration of pigment, very finely ground with the best-quality oils.

Artists' oils vary in price, depending on the initial cost of the pigment. In some brands, they are classified according to 'series', typically from 1 (the cheapest) to 7 (the most costly). Earth colours are the least expensive, while cadmium colours may cost four times as much. Some pigments, such as lapis lazuli, are prohibitively expensive, and most manufacturers now replace it with modern synthetic pigments.

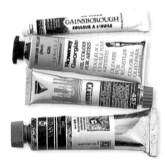

Students' colours
Because they are made in larger quantities and the colour range is relatively limited, student-quality paints are cheaper than artists' oils. In the best-quality ranges, the more-expensive pigments, such as cadmiums and cobalts, are replaced with cheaper but permanent alternatives. These colour names are suffixed with the word 'hue'. Students' colours may have lower pigment levels and contain small amounts of fillers, such as chalk, which slightly weaken the colour strength of the paint.

ALKYD PAINTS
Alkyd paints are made from pigments bound in an oil-modified synthetic resin.

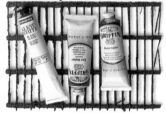

These paints handle like traditional oil paints, but dry faster, typically touch dry within 18–24 hours.

When primed with oil or acrylic primer, any supports that are suitable for oil and acrylic paints may also be used for alkyds.

WATER-MIXABLE OIL PAINTS
This type of paint is made from modified linseed and safflower oils. As a result, the paint can be thinned with water instead of the usual solvents, such as turpentine or white spirit. The appearance, consistency and working characteristics are similar to those of conventional oils.

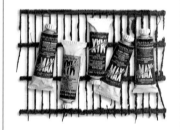

Water-mixable oil colours have other practical advantages over traditional oils – it is quicker to clean up, and water is cheaper than turpentine. A limited range of mediums is available to allow you to modify the characteristics of the paint.

Hog brushes are most often used when paint is to be applied thickly; synthetic brushes are recommended for washes and glazing techniques.

All brushes can be washed out with soap and water.

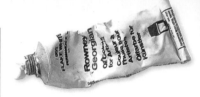

WHITE PAINT
The most important pigment in the oil painter's palette is white – it is used more than any other colour. Several whites are available, each with different properties, although as a general rule titanium white is the most common.

Flake white
Flake white, which is also known as lead white or silver white, is a comparatively quick-drying, durable and flexible paint. It is frequently used for underpainting, and accelerates the drying of other colours mixed with it. Since it contains lead, it is harmful if swallowed – so must be kept out of the reach of children.

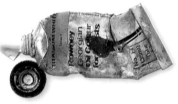

Titanium white
The strong covering power of titanium white (also known as permanent white) is useful for mixing tints and for creating highlights. It dries slowly to a soft chalky film. Titanium white is classed as non-hazardous.

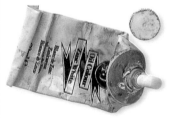

Zinc white
This paint has a pure, cold-white appearance that is the most transparent. It is most suitable for tinting and glazing. Zinc white dries slowly to a relatively brittle film. It is classed as non-hazardous.

OIL-PAINT STICKS

Oil-paint sticks combine the richness of oil colour with the freedom and directness of pastels or charcoal. They are made by combining artist-quality pigments with highly refined drying oils, which are then blended with special waxes that enable the mix to be moulded into stick form.

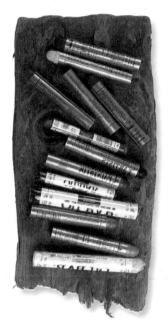

The chunky sticks glide across the support, making expressive flowing lines. Some brands are thixotropic – they become creamier in texture when applied with slight pressure, then harden again on the support.

Different colours can be blended together on the support, using either a brush or a painting knife. Alternatively, special colourless sticks are available: these aid the blending process and increase the transparency of the colours.

The paint can also be brushed out on the support, using the same solvents and mediums employed with tube oil colours. Also, you can improve the flow of colour by dipping the end of a stick into a medium or solvent before applying it to the support. You can even apply the paint in thickly impasted layers and then model it with a paintbrush or knife. The paint remains workable for several hours.

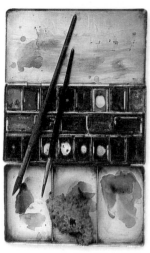

WATERCOLOUR PAINT

Watercolour paints comprise very finely ground pigments bound with gum-arabic solution. The gum enables the paint to be diluted with water in order to make thin transparent washes of colour that will adhere to the paper. Glycerine is added to the mixture to improve solubility and prevent the paint cracking. A wetting agent, such as ox gall, ensures the even flow of paint across the paper.

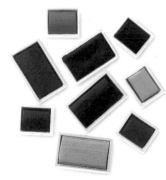

Pans and half pans

These small slabs of solid paint slot neatly into enamelled-metal boxes made with recesses to hold the pans in place. The lid doubles as a palette for mixing colours.

You can either buy boxes that contain a range of preselected colours or fill an empty box with your own choice of pans. Colour is released by stroking the solid paint with a wet paintbrush.

Watercolour in tubes

Tubes of colour are available in a number of sizes. The smaller tubes are designed primarily to fit into portable watercolour boxes, but larger tubes are more economical. Tubes can be bought singly or in preselected sets. Choosing your own tubes allows you to select precisely the colours you need.

Artists' paints

Artists' paints contain a high proportion of permanent, finely ground pigments. The colours are transparent and luminous, they mix well, and there is a wide range. Like oils, watercolour paints are often classified by 'series', usually from 1 to 5, according to the availability and cost of the pigments.

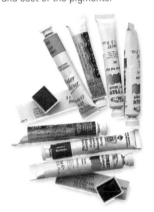

Students' paints

Student-quality paints are sold at a uniform price. The pigments are not as pure as those used for better-quality paint, and more fillers and extenders are added. The selection of colours is relatively small compared with artists' ranges.

Transparent pigments

Highly transparent colours permit the white reflective surface of paper to shine through. These colours have an attractive airy quality, which is perfect for capturing the illusion of atmosphere, space and light.

Some transparent colours, such as alizarin crimson, are highly staining: they penetrate paper fibres and cannot be removed without leaving a trace of colour. Some earth colours, cadmiums and modern organic pigments also tend to stain. If you intend to 'lift' or sponge out areas of colour, choose non-staining pigments where possible.

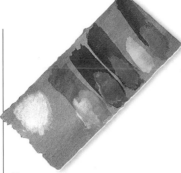

Opaque pigments

In watercolour, so-called 'opaque' colours are actually transparent when thinly diluted, but impart a degree of opacity to other colours they are mixed with. If used carelessly, opaque pigments create cloudy colours that lack brilliance and luminosity.

Body colour

Traditionally, paler tones are produced by adding more water to the paint; pure white is achieved by leaving areas of paper unpainted. However, most watercolourists take a more pragmatic approach and use opaque paint when it seems appropriate for a particular stage in a painting – when creating highlights, for example. Transparent water-colours can be rendered opaque or semi-opaque by mixing them with Chinese white or gouache to produce what is called body colour.

GOUACHE

The opacity of gouache and its matt chalky appearance when dry are very different from the pure, transparent quality of watercolour – but the equipment, supports and techniques used are similar for both media.

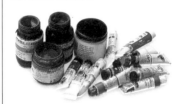

The best-quality gouache paints contain a very high proportion of pigment. The colours are therefore pure and intense, and create clean mixes. The less-expensive paints contain an inert white pigment, such as chalk, to impart smoothness and opacity. Gouache is sold in tubes, pots and bottles.

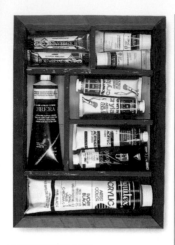

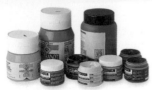

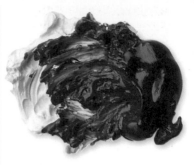

ACRYLIC PAINT

Acrylic paints dry rapidly through evaporation of the water contained in the binder. As the water evaporates, the acrylic-resin particles fuse to form a flexible and water-resistant paint film that does not yellow with age. Once dry, an acrylic painting on canvas can be rolled up, stored and restretched years later, with less danger of the paint surface cracking. Another advantage is that all colours dry at the same rate. As with oils and watercolours, acrylics are available in both artists' and the cheaper students' qualities.

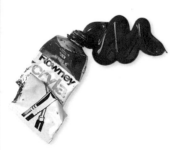

Acrylics in tubes
The thickness of tube paint varies from brand to brand, but in general it has a soft, buttery consistency similar to that of oil paint. It retains the marks of a painting knife or brush, and is excellent for working with impasto techniques.

Acrylics in jars
Smoother and more fluid than tube colour, acrylic paint sold in jars is easily thinned with water and/or medium. This makes it ideal for watercolour techniques and for covering large areas of flat colour. The paint dries to a smooth, even film that sometimes has more of a matt finish than tube colour. The paint comes in wide-top tubs and jars, or plastic bottles with nozzles.

Liquid acrylics
Liquid acrylics flow readily from the brush and are similar to brilliant drawing inks. They are supplied in bottles with dropper caps, and are suitable for wash techniques and fine-pen work. Liquid acrylics are made with an alkali-base resin, and can be removed using an alkali cleaner.

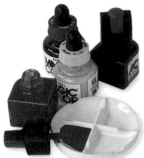

Iridescent colours
Iridescent acrylic paints can be used singly, or mixed with regular acrylic colours to give them luminescent surface qualities. They are used to best effect on a dark background, especially black. Also available are iridescent mediums, which can be mixed into any of the ordinary colours to pearlize them.

Fluorescent colours
These absorb ultraviolet light and emit visible light of a longer wavelength. As a result, they appear to 'fluoresce', or glow. However, this effect fades rather rapidly because the dyes are not stable. Fluorescent colours are not recommended for paintings intended to last for any length of time.

CHROMA COLOURS

Chroma colour is similar to acrylic paint in that it is fast-drying, thins with water and becomes waterproof when dry. It can be applied using any technique and onto virtually any support, with a brush, dip pen, painting knife or airbrush.

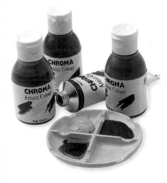

Due to their high pigment loading, Chroma colours tend to be strong and vivid, even when thinly diluted. The tonal values do not change as the paint dries.

By adding water to pot or tube colours, Chroma can be used like coloured inks; the effect may be either opaque or transparent, according to the degree of dilution. Chroma is capable of producing subtle translucent washes which, unlike traditional watercolour washes, do not change appreciably on drying.

Chroma colours dry insoluble, so it is possible to lay wash over wash without any danger of previous applications being disturbed. Once dry, however, Chroma colours cannot be lifted out to create highlights, as is the case with watercolour paints.

Used straight from the tube or pot, Chroma is similar to gouache in that it is highly opaque and dries to a velvety matt finish.

EGG TEMPERA

Tempera is a water-based paint made by mixing egg yolk with pigments and distilled water. As this mixture dries on the painting surface, the water evaporates, leaving a hard thin layer of colour that is extremely durable.

Prepared egg-tempera colours are available from a few manufacturers, although formulations vary.

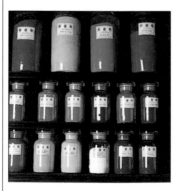

Because the colour range of ready-made paints is limited, many artists working in tempera prefer to prepare their own paints from the vast range of colour pigments available.

READING A PAINT TUBE

Although there may appear to be a bewildering amount of coded information on a standard tube of paint, it is quite simple to decipher.

The ability to 'read' a tube will help you choose the right paint.

The tube below is a composite, but the various items of information on it can be found on different tubes of paint. Each manufacturer's catalogue provides further details about its brands.

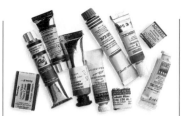

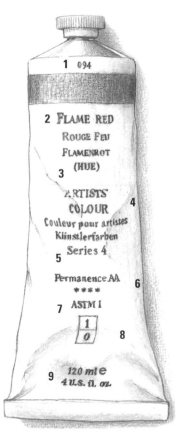

1 Product code
This refers to the manufacturer's catalogue data or ordering code.

2 Colour
Most names of colours are common to all brands, but some colourmen give certain colours a proprietary name – Winsor Violet or Rowney Turquoise, for example.

3 Hue
The suffix 'hue' indicates that a synthetic pigment has been substituted for a traditional one because the latter is either no longer available or too expensive, or has been withdrawn due to possible health hazards. In some cases, a pigment name in brackets – such as (phthalo) – is added, to indicate the basic pigment used.

4 Quality
This name refers to the quality of the paint – artists' colour being the top quality. Students' colour is not quite as good, and is often known by trade names, such as Georgian (Daler-Rowney) or Gainsborough (Grumbacher).

5 Series
A series number denotes the quality and cost of the pigment used. This typically ascends from 1 (the cheapest) to 5 or 7 (the most expensive).

6 Permanence
The permanence of the colour is indicated by alphabetical, star and/or ASTM ratings.

7 ASTM ratings
The ASTM (American Society for Testing and Materials) ratings provide accelerated testing of artists' colours; it simulates 20 years of gallery exposure.

ASTM codes for lightfastness:
ASTM I – excellent lightfastness
ASTM II – very good lightfastness

8 Transparency
Some manufacturers also display transparency ratings of O (opaque), TL (translucent), or TP (transparent).

9 Content
The statutory declaration of tube-content weight is given in millilitres (ml) for Europe and US fluid ounces (US fl oz) for the United States.

DILUENTS

Diluents, or 'thinners', are liquids used for diluting paints so that they can be applied more easily to the support, and for cleaning brushes and palettes.

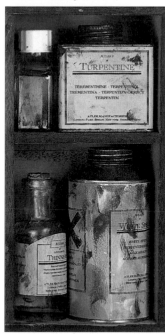

Turpentine
Double-distilled or rectified turpentine is the traditional diluent for oil paint. Ordinary household turpentine, sold in hardware shops, is not suitable, because it leaves a gummy residue that yellows badly, and the paint remains sticky. Turpentine evaporates from paint mixes at a relatively slow rate.

White spirit
White spirit (refined petroleum spirit) is perhaps more popular than turpentine as a diluent for oil paints, mainly because it is cheaper. Also, white spirit is less viscous, and does not deteriorate in storage.

In the past, white spirit had a tendency to cause a white bloom on the surface of oil paintings, but with improved formulation this problem has been eradicated.

Odourless thinners
Low-odour paint thinners are available for those painters who object to the strong smell of both turpentine and white spirit. Low-odour thinners do not deteriorate in storage.

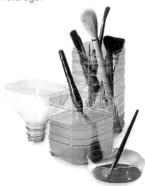

Water
The majority of artists thin water-soluble paints (acrylics, gouache and watercolours) with ordinary tap water. However, some water-colourists prefer distilled water for mixing colours, as it can discourage granulation.

When painting, don't skimp on water. Use as large a container as practicable. If the container is too small, the water becomes murky from washing brushes and may spoil the transparency of your colours.

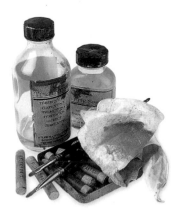

Diluents for oil pastels
Turpentine and white spirit dissolve oil pastels, and can be used for blending colours and obtaining painterly surface effects. Your initial pastel drawing can be modified, using a brush dipped in the diluent and worked over the surface, but it may stain the paper.

MEDIUMS

Mediums are added to paint to modify its characteristics. Different mediums are required for watercolour, acrylics and oil paints.

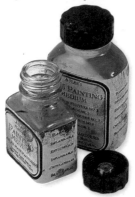

MEDIUMS FOR OIL PAINTS

There are several types of medium for oil paints – some based on traditional recipes, others on modern laboratory research. These mediums are variously formulated to improve the flow of the paint, alter its consistency, or produce a matt or gloss finish. Some are slow-drying; others contain agents to speed up the drying rate. A similar range of mediums is available for water-mixable oil paints.

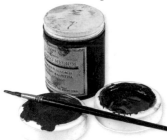

Glazing mediums
Glazing is a technique for applying translucent overlays of paint. To increase its flow and transparency, paint for glazing should be thinned with a glazing medium. Fast-drying synthetic glaze mediums speed the drying process.

Turpentine mediums
Conventional oil paint can be used either straight from the tube or diluted with thinners. However, some artists will add linseed oil to the diluent when painting to keep fat-over-lean.

You can make your own slow-drying mixture of refined linseed oil and white spirit or turpentine. Pour the two liquids into separate containers, so that you can add more oil as paint layers are built up. The normal proportions are 1 part oil to at least 2 parts diluent, with increasing amounts of oil added in the final layers (up to a maximum of 50 per cent oil).

MEDIUMS FOR WATERCOLOUR

Gum arabic, ox gall and glycerine are all constituents of watercolour paints. When used as additional mediums, they modify the working properties of the paint.

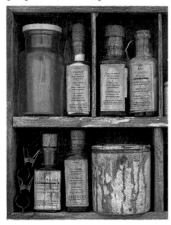

Gum arabic
A pale-coloured solution of gum arabic in water increases both the gloss and transparency of water-colour paints. Diluted further, it improves paint flow. Too much gum arabic makes paint slippery and jelly-like, but in moderation it enlivens the texture and enhances the vividness of the colours.

Ox gall
Ox gall is a straw-coloured liquid which, when added to water in a jar, improves the flow and wetting of watercolour paints. It is particularly suitable for wet-in-wet techniques.

Glycerine
You will find glycerine useful when working outdoors in dry conditions. A few drops added to water will counteract the drying effects of wind and hot sun.

MEDIUMS FOR ACRYLICS

Used alone, acrylic paints dry to a flat eggshell finish. However, adding an acrylic medium to the paint gives the colours brilliance and depth.

Other mediums can be used to alter consistency and finish, to help thinly diluted paint maintain its adhesion, to improve the paint's flow and 'brushability', and to control its drying rate.

Add mediums to the paint a little at a time, and mix well with a palette knife. You can further dilute the paint with water. For an even result, always mix colours before adding a medium.

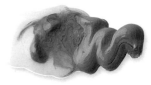

Gloss medium
Acrylic gloss medium thins the paint, and enhances colour luminosity. The paint becomes more transparent, allowing thin glazes to be built up with colours of exceptional depth and brilliance. The surface dries to a soft sheen.

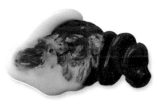

Matt medium
Depending on how much matt medium you add to it, acrylic paint will dry either semi-gloss or with a non-reflective matt finish. Matt medium also increases the transparency of the paint.

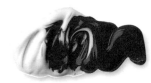

Gel medium
This paste-like substance thickens paint in order to create prominent textured brushstrokes and impasto effects. Since gel medium increases the adhesive qualities of paint, you can use it to create colourful three-dimensional collages.

Retarding medium
This retards the drying time of acrylic paint, enabling you to move paint around on a surface and to blend colours slowly and smoothly. Adding too much retarder makes paint sticky and unpleasant to use. Add a very small amount of water to increase fluidity.

Flow improver
Flow improver, or water-tension breaker, thins acrylic colours without reducing their strength or affecting the finish of the dried paint. It allows flat, even washes to be applied over large areas.

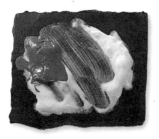

Iridescent tinting medium
This is a special-effects medium containing mica-coated flakes. When mixed with acrylic colours, it produces an iridescent quality.

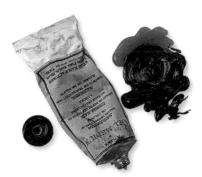

ALKYD MEDIUMS FOR OIL COLOURS

Alkyd is a translucent synthetic resin that has been oil-modified to make it suitable as a paint medium.

Good-quality alkyd mediums speed the drying process and form a flexible virtually non-yellowing film. They come in various consistencies, from a liquid gel, suitable for glazing and blending, to a stiff gel for impasto.

PRIMERS AND GROUNDS

The primer, or ground, not only seals and protects the painting support but also provides a base that readily accepts the application of paint. Some artists prefer to paint on a toned or coloured ground because they find white canvas, board or paper inhibiting. By covering the support with a wash of neutral colour, you create a more sympathetic surface on which to work.

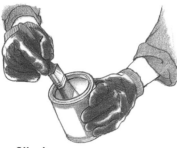

Oil primer
The traditional, and best, primer for oil painting, particularly on stretched canvas, is oil-based lead-white primer. This primer is flexible enough to stretch and contract with the canvas as it responds to changes in temperature and humidity. It dries to form a durable base, which does not absorb too much oil from the paint.

Alkyd primer
This is an alternative to oil primer. It is flexible, non-yellowing and fast-drying. Each coat can be over-painted after 24 hours.

Acrylic primer
Acrylic primer is flexible, durable, water-thinnable, fast-drying and inexpensive. It can be used to prime canvas, board, paper and other surfaces, and can be applied directly to the support without the need for an isolating layer of size. It dries in a few hours.

Acrylic primer is the ideal surface for acrylic paints, providing a bright undercoat which brings out the vividness of the colours and gives added luminosity to thin washes. The best quality acrylic primers can also be used with oil paints.

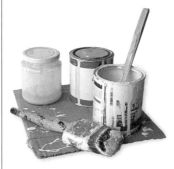

Emulsion paint as primer
An economical primer, often used by students, is ordinary matt household emulsion paint, which provides a sympathetic semi-absorbent ground. However, household paint should not be used as an artist's material – cheap emulsions have a limited life span.

Toned ground
A white ground can give a false 'reading' of tones and colours, especially during the early stages of a painting. Most colours appear darker on a white surface than they do when surrounded by other colours – and this creates a tendency to paint in too light a key. If you work on a neutral mid-toned ground, you will find it much easier to assess colours and tones correctly, and you can paint towards light or dark with equal ease.

If the colour of the ground is allowed to show through the overpainting in places, it acts as a harmonizing element, tying together the colours that are laid over it.

The colour chosen for a toned ground will depend on the subject, but it is normally a neutral tone somewhere between the lightest and the darkest colours in the painting. The colour should be subtle and unobtrusive, so that it does not overwhelm the colours in the overpainting. Diluted earth colours, such as Venetian red, raw sienna or burnt umber, work very well, as do soft greys and greens.

A toned ground must be dry before you can paint over it. An oil ground takes a day or two to dry; an acrylic ground is dry in minutes. So long as it is applied thinly, you can use acrylic paint for the toned ground and work over it with oils.

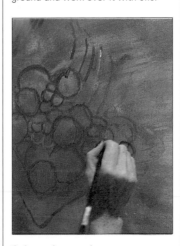

Coloured ground
Some artists choose bold colours for their grounds, deliberately to affect the overpainting. A deep-red ground, for example, will enliven a predominantly green landscape. A green ground will help to tone down warm flesh colours.

Transparent ground
With a transparent ground (also known as imprimatura), the paint is heavily diluted and applied as a thin wash. A transparent ground allows light to reflect back through the succeeding colours, retaining their luminosity. It is used where trans-parent or semi-transparent colour is to be applied.

Apply diluted ground colour with a large decorator's brush or a lint-free rag. Loose, vigorous strokes give a more lively effect than a flat stain of colour. After a few minutes, rub the wash with a clean rag, leaving a transparent stain.

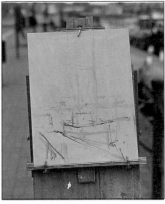

Opaque ground
Opaque toned grounds are used as a base for relatively thick opaque overpainting, where the light-reflecting qualities of a white ground are not so important.

Mix a little tube colour into a white primer before applying it. Alternatively, mix the colour with white paint, dilute it a little, and brush a thin layer over the priming. Never mix oil paint with an acrylic primer, or vice versa.

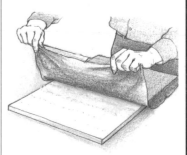

Textured ground
To create a textured surface finish, lay and then press a piece of coarse fabric, such as an old piece of sacking, into the final coat of primer.

VARNISH

A layer of varnish protects a painting from damage caused by scuffing, humidity, dust and atmospheric pollutants. It also enhances the depth and lustre of the colours.

Natural varnishes

Natural dammar varnish, composed of dammar resin and mineral spirits, enhances colours with high gloss. It may bloom in damp conditions. Natural mastic varnish, with mastic resin and turpentine, dries to a high gloss. However, this type of varnish does have a tendency to darken, crack and bloom.

Synthetic varnishes

Synthetic-resin picture varnishes, such as those made from ketone, are preferable to traditional natural-resin varnishes. Modern varnishes can be relied upon to be non-yellowing and tough, yet flexible enough to withstand any movement of the canvas without cracking.

Varnishing oil paintings

An oil painting must be completely dry before picture varnish is applied. Drying can take anything from six months to a year, or even longer for thickly impasted paint. Oil paint expands and contracts as it dries, and premature varnishing may cause cracking.

However, you can apply retouching varnish as soon as the paint is touch-dry, which normally takes only a few days or weeks. This will protect the surface until it is dry enough for final varnishing.

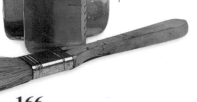

VARNISHING ACRYLIC PAINTINGS

Always use a good-quality proprietary acrylic varnish, which dries quickly to a clear film. You can buy gloss or matt varnish, or mix the two to create a pleasing semi-matt finish.

Acrylic paintings can be varnished as soon as the paint is dry, which normally means waiting until the next day.

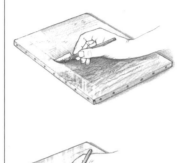

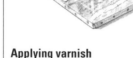

Applying varnish

Ensure the painting is free from dust and grease, then apply the first thin coat of varnish with a broad soft-haired brush, preferably a varnishing brush. Stroke the surface smoothly and evenly, working in one direction only, to avoid creating air bubbles.

Leave to dry overnight, then apply a second coat at right angles to the first – unless you are using a matt varnish, in which case brush in the same direction as before. Leave the picture in a horizontal position, protected from dust and hairs, until the varnish has dried hard.

SIZE

Size seals the pores and spaces between the fibres of the support, making it less absorbent. This prevents the binder in the primer and paint layers from sinking into the support, which may cause paint layers to sink, flake and crack.

GLUE SIZE

Rabbit-skin glue has traditionally been used for sizing oil-painting supports. It comes in the form of granules, and is available in most art-supply shops. The glue size is made by soaking dry glue with water, then gently heating it.

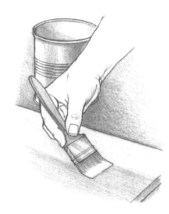

Applying size

Size is applied warm. Thin boards should also be sized on the reverse and edges, to prevent warping. Leave to dry for 12 hours, then sand lightly.

When sizing canvas, allow it to dry for a few hours, then check that it has not stuck to the stretcher. If it has, carefully prise it free with a palette knife.

For sizing canvas:

You need 36g (1¼oz) glue to 1.1 litres (2 pints) of water.

For rigid panels:

Use a stronger solution of 72g (2½oz) of glue to 1.1 litres (2 pints) of water. This recipe will make enough size to cover a support measuring about 120 x 180cm (4 x 6ft).

CMC

A modern alternative to traditional glue size is carboxymethylcellulose (CMC). It is also easier to use and preferred by vegetarians.

Dissolve the granules in warm or cold water (using an 8 per cent solution by volume) and apply with a stiff brush. There is no heating involved – and no smell, but CMC is probably not as effective as rabbit-skin glue.

Gelatin size

Gelatin is a liquid size, sold in small bottles, that can be brushed onto watercolour paper that is too absorbent. It makes it easier to apply washes. The size is dry in a few minutes.

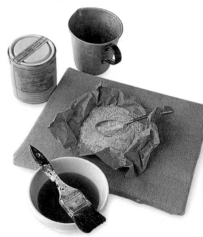

PAINTBRUSHES

Artists' opinions differ widely on the merits of paintbrushes. Some use a whole range of sizes and shapes for a single painting, others get by using one or two. Some painters advocate using only brushes of the best quality, others see no advantage in spending a lot of money on equipment when they can produce perfectly satisfactory work with cheaper alternatives. Included here are all of the common paintbrush materials, shapes and sizes you will find on offer at the average art-materials shop.

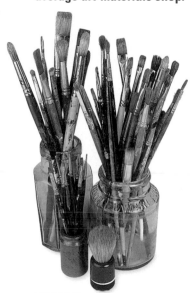

BRISTLE

Tough and springy bristle brushes are particularly suitable for oil painting because they can manipulate thick paint and are robust enough to be worked against the textured surface of canvas. The finest bristle comes from the Chunking region of China.

Synthetic-bristle

Manufacturers have developed synthetic-bristle paintbrushes specifically for acrylic painting (many artists also find them ideal for oils). These brushes are easy to clean, and are built to withstand the tough handling demanded by acrylics.

SABLE

Sable hair is obtained from the tail of the sable marten, a relative of the mink. Sable brushes are undoubtedly the best choice for watercolour painting.

Soft-hair brushes are not vital in oil painting, but they are useful for applying fine details during the final stages of a painting and for applying thinly diluted colour.

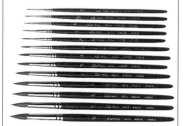

Kolinsky sable

These top-quality brushes are very expensive. They are immensely strong, yet supple and springy.

Synthetic sable

Sable-type synthetics are a golden yellow colour, and are made from polyester filaments. These brushes can be a little stiff and unsympathetic, with less colour-holding capacity than genuine sable.

Squirrel hair

Softer and cheaper than sable, squirrel hair does not point well and has little resilience. However, this type of hair offers an adequate and less-costly alternative to large-size sable wash brushes.

Ox hair

Ox hair is strong and springy, but quite coarse. It does not point well, but is good for square-cut brushes.

Goat hair

Soft but sturdy, goat hair is ideal for laying broad washes.

Combination hair

It is possible to buy brushes made from various combinations of animal hair, or from a mixture of synthetic and natural hair.

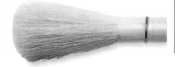

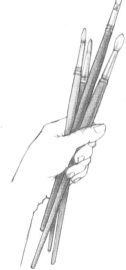
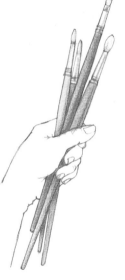

SOFT-HAIR BRUSH

1 Head
The head should point well. When loaded with water, it should return to its original shape.

2 Belly
The belly should hold a lot of colour, and release the paint slowly and evenly.

3 Ferrule
A seamless cupro-plated nickel ferrule is strong and will not corrode.

4 Handle
This should be lacquered to protect it from water, chipping or cracking. Brush size, series and type are embossed on the handle.

BRISTLE BRUSH

1 Head
The best bristles have split ends, known as 'flags'. These give a softness to the very end of the brush and help the bristles to hold plenty of paint.

2 Ferrule
This holds the bristles together and shapes them into rounds, riggers, filberts, flats and fan blenders. Good-quality ferrules are firmly crimped onto the handle.

3 Handle
The length of an oil-brush handle allows the artist to work at a distance from the canvas, and helps to balance the weight of the tip and ferrule. The characteristic handle shape, with the wood thickening just below the ferrule, is designed to prevent the heads of brushes touching when you are holding more than one brush in your hand.

BRUSH SHAPES

Brushes come in a wide range of sizes and shapes. Each is designed to make a different kind of mark, but some are more versatile than others. Selecting a brush depends on the effects you wish to achieve.

Round brushes

A round brush, perhaps the most common and versatile paintbrush, has a tapered head with a large 'belly' that has good paint-holding capacity. When applying heavily diluted paint, round brushes make soft strokes, and are ideal for blocking in the basic composition during the initial stages of a painting. When loaded with thick paint, these brushes make bold, vigorous marks.

Round soft-hair brushes come to a point, ideal for painting delicate lines and details, but hog-hair brushes are incapable of coming to such a fine point.

Spotter brushes

A retouching or spotter brush has a fine point, with a relatively short head that provides extra control. Spotters are used mainly by miniaturists and botanical artists, for painting precise details.

Rigger brushes

A long-haired round brush is known as a designer's point, writer or rigger (from when the brush was used for painting the finely detailed rigging on sailing ships). The long shape gives the brush an extra-fine point and good colour-holding properties.

Mops and wash brushes

These brushes are used for laying in large areas of colour quickly. Wash brushes are generally wide and flat, while mops have large round heads. Both types of brush are available with synthetic or natural hair.

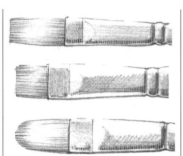

Flat brushes

Long flat brushes have square tips. Their long bristles are flexible and hold a lot of paint. When used flat, they make long fluid strokes and are useful for filling in large areas and for blending colours. When used with the tip edge-on, a flat brush makes fine lines.

Flat watercolour brushes are also known as 'one-strokes'.

Brights

Short flat brushes are often referred to as 'brights'. They are basically the same shape as long flats, but they have shorter, stiff bristles that dig deeper into the paint, leaving strongly textured rectangular marks. They are useful for applying thick, heavy paint to produce impasto effects. With their shorter bristles, brights are somewhat easier to control than flats.

Filberts

Filberts are a compromise between flat and round brushes. Being shaped to a slight curve at the tip, they produce soft, tapered strokes, and are useful for fusing and softening edges.

Fan blenders

Where a smooth, highly finished result is required, fan blenders are used to feather wet paint, to soften brushstrokes and to effect smooth gradations of tone. They are available in sable as well as synthetic and hog bristle.

BRUSH SIZES

Brush sizes are broadly similar within each country, but they are not universally standard from one country to another.

Watercolour brushes

All watercolour brushes are graded according to size, ranging from as small as 00000 to as large as a No. 24 wash brush. The size of a flat brush is generally given by the width of the head, measured in millimetres or inches.

Oil-painting brushes

Most types of oil-painting brush come in a range of sizes, from 000 (the smallest) to around 16 (the largest). The range of sizes given for bristle brushes is not comparable with similar figures given for soft-hair brushes.

SPECIALS

Good-quality brushes, although more expensive, will not shed hairs as readily as cheap ones.

Household brushes

Decorators' brushes are inexpensive, hard-wearing and extremely useful for applying broad washes of colour.

Shaving brushes

Traditional-style shaving brushes are a reasonable alternative to using soft blending brushes.

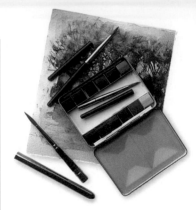

Oriental brushes

Oriental brushes are made with natural hair set into hollow bamboo handles. They are inexpensive and versatile brushes, with thick tapered heads that make broad sweeps of colour. When wet, the head can be drawn up to a very fine point for painting delicate lines. New brush heads are coated in starch size; remove this by soaking and teasing the hairs in a jar of water for a minute or two.

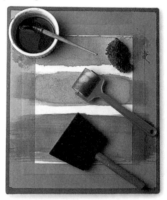

Portable brushes

Small retractable brushes, plus a 'travelling' set of pans, are ideal for making colour sketches when painting outdoors.

Foam brushes

Foamed-plastic brushes can be used to apply any type of paint, including enamel, emulsion, stain, tempera, and solvent-based household paints. Foam brushes are hardwearing and easy to clean.

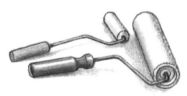

Paint rollers

When working on large-scale paintings, you can apply broad strokes with a roller. Rollers are often used to apply acrylic primer; they keep the paint moving and deliver an even coat. For smaller supports, use a small radiator roller.

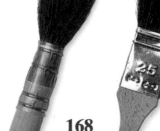

Mop and wash brush

PAINTING KNIVES

Painting knives can be used instead of brushes to apply thick paint. Painting knives should not be confused with palette knives, which have stiffer blades and are mostly used for mixing paint on the palette.

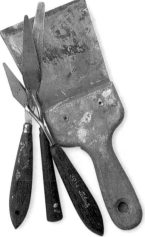

A painting knife has a relatively short flexible blade, fitted with a cranked handle that prevents your knuckles accidentally brushing against the canvas when applying paint. Choose a stainless-steel knife when painting with acrylics. There are also easy-to-clean plastic knives.

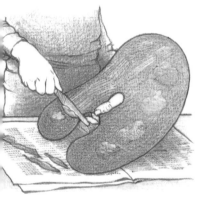

Palette knives

Palette knives are used for mixing colours, scraping palettes clean and removing wet paint from a picture when making alterations. This type of knife has a straight blade with a rounded tip. The long edges of the knife are ideal for removing wet paint, and the tip is used to pick up and mix dabs of paint on the palette.

ACCESSORIES

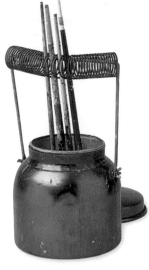

Brush washers

These metal containers come in various sizes, and have a coiled handle for keeping brushes suspended in the cleaning agent while soaking. This prevents the tips being pressed against the bottom of the container.

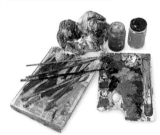

Brush wipes

An old telephone directory is handy for wiping excess paint off your brushes prior to cleaning. Simply wipe the brush across a page, then tear it off and throw it away, leaving the next page ready for use.

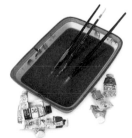

Water tray

Lay brushes used for acrylic paints in a shallow tray of water, with the bristles resting in the water and the handles propped up on the edge.

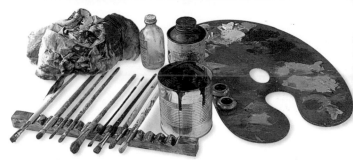

Brush holder

If you use a lot of brushes, this simple home-made device will keep them all neatly at hand and prevent them from rolling off the table onto the floor.

PALETTES

Palettes provide a surface upon which you can mix water-based paints and oils. If you don't want to purchase one of the many ready-made palettes, you can make your own or use old plates and saucers.

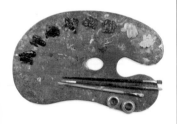

Thumbhole palettes

Thumbhole palettes are designed to be held in one hand and supported on the forearm. They are available in a range of sizes, either rectangular (called 'oblong'), oval or kidney-shaped. Palettes veneered in mahogany are expensive, but plywood or melamine palettes are more economically priced. Before investing in a palette, try several for comfort; the better ones are well balanced and less tiring when working for long periods.

New wooden palettes should be sealed by rubbing linseed oil into the grain. This prevents the wood absorbing oil from the paint, thus causing it to dry out too quickly on the palette.

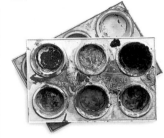

Recessed palettes

Recessed palettes are available in china, plastic and aluminium. They are used primarily for mixing thin dilutions of paint.

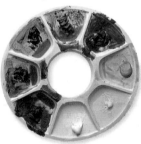

Slanted-well tiles

These ceramic palettes are divided into several recesses or wells, so that a number of separate colours can be laid out without them flowing into one another. The wells slant to allow diluted paint to collect at one end, ready for use.

Some tiles have a row of small circular recesses below the slanted wells; neat paint is squeezed into these recesses and then moved to the larger slanted wells where it is diluted with water or mixed with other colours.

Tinting saucers

These small round ceramic dishes are used for mixing larger quantities of paint. Some saucers are divided into four separate recesses.

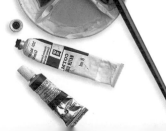

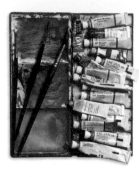

Integral palettes

Enamelled-metal paintboxes designed to hold pans or tubes of paint are particularly useful when working outdoors. When opened out, the lid doubles as a palette. Some boxes also have an integral hinged flap for mixing and tinting, and a thumb ring in the base.

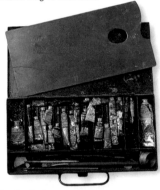

Pochade box

A pochade box is useful for painting in oils on location. It incorporates a box that holds paints and equipment with a slide-out palette.

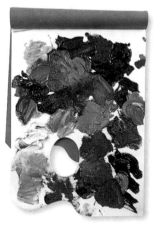

Disposable palettes

Made of oil-proof paper, disposable palettes are bound into pads. At the end of a painting session, the used sheet is torn off and thrown away.

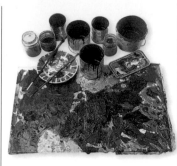

Improvised palettes

In the studio, many artists prefer to use a homemade table-top palette that simply rests on a convenient surface close to the easel. Any smooth non-porous material is suitable – such as a sheet of white laminate or melamine board, or a sheet of glass laid over white or neutral-coloured paper.

Old cups, jars or tins are perfectly adequate for mixing, and can be covered with clingfilm to discourage the paint drying between sessions.

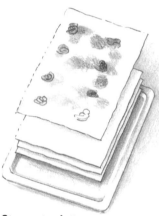

Stay-wet palette

Special palettes have been developed to keep acrylic paint moist and workable. They comprise a lidded plastic tray lined with a sheet of absorbent paper soaked in water. A membrane is laid on top. Colours squeezed out onto the membrane take up moisture from the absorbent paper below.

ACCESSORIES

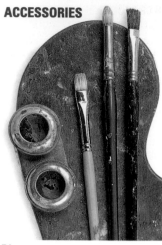

Dippers

Designed for holding oils and solvents, dippers are small open metal cups that clip onto the edge of a thumbhole palette. You can buy single or double dippers. Some have screw caps to prevent spillage or evaporation of solvents.

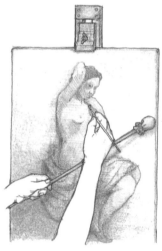

Mahlstick

A mahlstick has a long handle with a pad at one end. With the pad resting against the canvas stretcher, the stick is used to steady the painting arm when executing detailed, controlled work.

PALETTE LAYOUT

Get into the habit of laying out colours on the palette in the same systematic order each time you paint. This will help you locate each colour conveniently and quickly.

Some artists arrange colours in the order of the spectrum, with red, orange, yellow, green, blue and violet running across the palette; white and earth colours are arranged down the side of the palette. Other painters set out their colours from light to dark, or align warm colours (reds, oranges and yellows) on one side, and cool colours (blues, greens and violets) on the other.

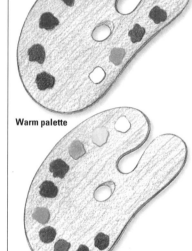

Warm palette

Light-to-dark palette

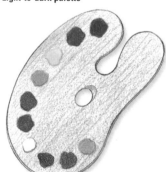

Spectrum palette

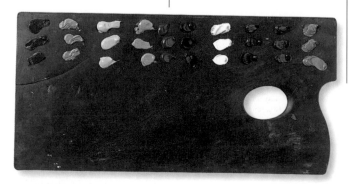

Oblong wooden palette

A clean and clear colour layout, with the ideal amount of paint set out on the palette.

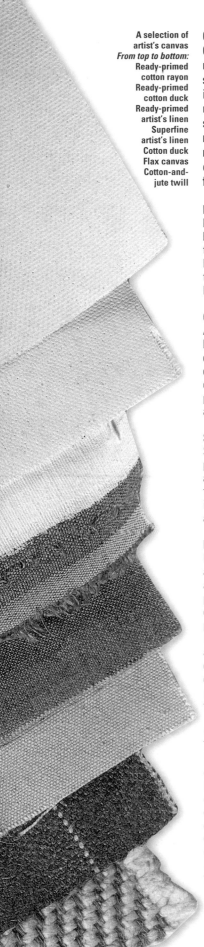

A selection of artist's canvas
From top to bottom:
Ready-primed cotton rayon
Ready-primed cotton duck
Ready-primed artist's linen
Superfine artist's linen
Cotton duck
Flax canvas
Cotton-and-jute twill

CANVAS

Canvas is the most widely used painting support. When stretched and primed, canvas is taut but flexible and has a unique receptiveness to the stroke of the brush. The two most common fibres for making canvas are linen and cotton, although synthetic fibres are also used.

Linen canvas

Linen is considered the best canvas because it has a fine even grain that is free from knots. Good-quality linen has a tight weave of even threads; avoid cheap linen, which is loosely woven.

Cotton canvas

A good-quality cotton duck is the best alternative to linen, and is much cheaper. However, the weave of cheap cotton quickly becomes obscured by layers of primer and paint, leaving the surface rather flat and characterless.

Synthetic fibres

Synthetic fabrics, such as rayon and polyester, make exceptionally strong and durable canvases that are both flexible and stable. These canvases invariably come ready-prepared with acrylic primer.

Ready-primed canvas

Most of the ready-prepared canvas and boards available in art shops are primed for use with oil or acrylic paint. If you paint in acrylics, don't buy supports that have been prepared specifically for oils – the linseed oil in the primer repels acrylics, and the paint eventually comes away from the support. You can paint with oils on an acrylic-primed canvas, provided you use thinned paint

Canvas weights

The weight of canvas is measured in grams per square metre (gsm) or ounces (oz) per square yard. The higher the number, the greater the density of threads. Better-grade cotton canvas, known as cotton duck, comes in 410gsm (12oz) and 510gsm (15oz) grades. Lighter-weight canvases of between 268gsm (8oz) and 410gsm (12oz) are recommended for practice painting only.

ACCESSORIES

As well as the canvas of your choice, you need a range of accessories in order to make your own stretched supports.

Stretcher bars

Wooden stretcher bars are sold in most art-supply shops and come in different lengths. They have premitred corners with slot-and-tenon joints. The face side of each stretcher bar is bevelled to prevent the inner edge of the stretcher creating 'ridge' lines on the canvas.

Stretcher bars come in varying widths and thicknesses, depending on the size of support you wish to make. For a work under 60 x 60cm (24 x 24in), use 45 x 16mm (1¾ x ⅝in) stretcher bars. For larger works, use 57 x 18mm (2¼ x ¾in) bars.

Wedges

You will also need eight wedges or 'keys' for each stretcher. These fit into slots on the inside of each corner of the assembled stretcher. If the canvas sags at a later date, then the wedges can be driven in further with a hammer to expand the corners and make the canvas taut again.

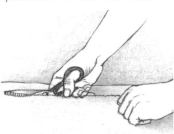

Canvas-straining pliers

Canvas-straining pliers are especially useful for stretching ready-primed canvases. They grip the fabric firmly without any risk of tearing. The lower jaw is bevelled to provide good leverage when pulling fabric over a stretcher bar.

The correct tension is achieved by lowering the wrist as the canvas passes over the back of the frame.

Pinking shears

Use pinking shears to cut canvas. Their serrated blades prevent the edges of the canvas fraying.

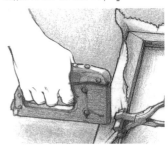

Staple gun

When fixing canvas to a stretcher, use a heavy-duty staple gun that takes non-rusting staples with a depth of at least 10mm (⅜in).

Stretcher bars and wedges

171

STRETCHING CANVAS

Stretch your own canvas if you want to work on a painting that is a different proportion from any of the standard ready-prepared supports. You will also save money by making up your own canvas supports.

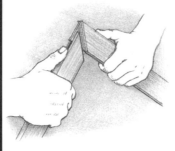

Assembling the stretcher frame

Slot the stretcher bars together, checking that all the bevelled edges are at the front. Tap the corners gently with a wooden mallet or a piece of wood to achieve a close fit. Use a set square or woodworker's try square to check that all the corners of the assembled frame make right angles.

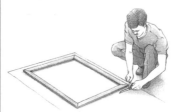

First fixings

Working on a large table or on the floor, lay the frame bevel-side down on the canvas. Cut the canvas to fit the frame, allowing a margin of about 50mm (2in) all round for stapling.

Ensure that the warp and weft threads of the canvas run parallel with the sides of the frame. Fold the canvas round to the back, and secure it with a staple at the centre of one of the long stretcher bars.

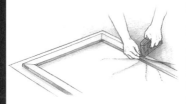

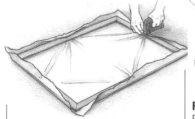

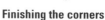

Stapling the four sides

Stretch the canvas firmly and evenly across the frame, and secure it with a staple to the opposite stretcher bar. If necessary, use canvas-straining pliers to grip the cloth and pull it taut over the frame.

If you intend to apply glue size, don't stretch the canvas as tight as a drum; make sure it is taut, but allow for possible shrinkage.

Repeat the process on the two short sides, securing the canvas with a single staple in the centre of each stretcher bar. Make sure the canvas weave lies parallel with the edges of the frame.

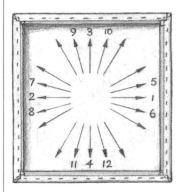

Securing the canvas

Following the sequence shown in the diagram, add two more staples to each of the four stretcher bars – one on either side of the central staples. The staples should be spaced evenly at 50mm (2in) intervals. Continue adding pairs of staples to each side, gradually working towards the corners. Insert the final staples about 50mm (2in) from each corner.

You can buy ready-primed and stretched supports, which consist of a piece of canvas mounted on a stretcher. These supports are convenient, but expensive compared with the cost of stretching, sizing and priming your own canvas.

Finishing the corners

Pull the canvas across one corner of the stretcher and fix with a staple. Then tuck in the flaps on either side and fix with staples. Don't staple across the mitre join, or you will find it impossible to tighten the canvas later on.

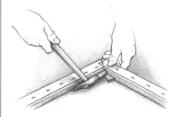

Fold and fix the diagonally opposite corner, followed by the remaining two. If necessary, hammer the folds flat to produce a neat corner.

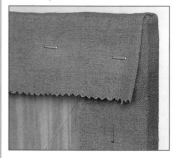

Inserting wedges

Finally, insert two wedges in the slots provided in each of the inner corners of the frame – the longest side of each wedge should lie alongside the frame. Tap the wedges home. The canvas is now ready for sizing and priming.

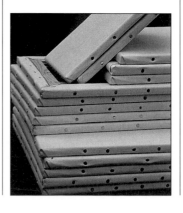

BOARDS AND PANELS

Man-made boards are cheaper to buy and prepare than stretched canvas; they are also easier to store and transport, and provide a more durable support than canvas.

Hardboard

Hardboard is inexpensive, strong and lightweight. Tempered hardboard is suitable for oil paints and primers, and does not require sizing. For acrylic painting, however, use untempered board, which has no greasy residue.

Hardboard is smooth on one side and rough on the other. The smooth side is the one most often used for painting, but needs sanding lightly to provide a key for a primer.

The rough side is only suitable for heavy impasto work, as the texture is very mechanical and regular.

Hardboard is prone to warping, particularly in humid climates, but priming the front, back and edges of the board reduces this risk. Paintings larger than 45cm (18in) square should be braced with a framework of wood battens (see below).

Plywood

Plywood comes in various thicknesses, with a smooth surface on both sides. To keep the sheet stable, size and prime it on the front, back and edges. Large sheets should be battened or 'cradled' by gluing wooden battens to the back of the board.

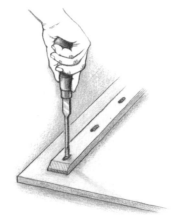

Cut two battens 50mm (2in) shorter than the width of the board. Bevel the ends, and stick the battens to the back of the board with wood glue. Fix them to thick boards with woodscrews.

Chipboard

Chipboard is made from wood particles compressed into a rigid panel with resin glue. Chipboard panels make reasonably stable supports, but they are heavy to transport. Another disadvantage is that the corners and edges may crumble – and being absorbent, they need to be well primed.

Medium-density fibreboard

MDF is made from pressed wood fibre, and is available in a wide range of thicknesses and standard board sizes. It is a dense, heavy, but very stable material, and has fine, smooth surfaces.

Cardboard

Some painters use brown cardboard as a mid-tone ground. However, cardboard should be sized on both sides and on the edges, to prevent warping and to help prevent impurities in the board leaching into the paint. A finished painting must be framed under glass if it is to last.

Mounting board

Heavy mounting board, or paste-board, is available in a range of colours. It has a smooth surface suitable for painting in acrylics and gouache, particularly when thin washes and glazes are applied. Always choose acid-free conservation boards for work that is intended to last.

Gesso panels

Gesso panels are the traditional support for egg-tempera painting; they can also be used for oil, acrylic and watercolour. Ready-prepared gesso panels can be bought from specialist art stores, though they are expensive. Gesso boards have an exceptionally smooth brilliant-white finish that enhances the translucence of tempera colours.

Canvas boards and panels

Commercially prepared canvas boards and panels consist of acrylic-primed cotton canvas mounted on rigid board. They come in a range of standard sizes and surface textures, and are a good choice for beginners. Being lightweight, canvas boards are ideal for painting outdoors.

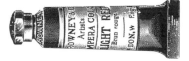

PAPERS

In one form or another, paper is used as a support for just about every medium, including watercolour, acrylics, pastels and oils.

WATERCOLOUR PAPERS

Although they are primarily intended for watercolour, artists use these splendid papers for drawing and painting in whatever medium takes their fancy.

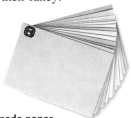

Handmade paper

The very best watercolour papers are handmade from 100 per cent cotton. These papers are lively to use, durable, and have a pleasing irregular texture. They are costly, but worth the expense.

Machine-made paper

Although inexpensive to produce, machine-made papers are less resistant to deterioration and sometimes distort when wet. Some machine-made papers have a rather monotonous mechanical surface grain.

Mould-made paper

European mills produce paper on cylinder-mould machines. The paper fibres are formed into sheets with a random distribution, close to that of handmade papers. This type of paper is durable, extremely stable, and is unlikely to distort under a heavy wash.

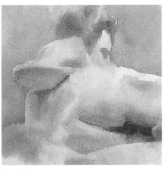

Smooth paper

Hot-pressed paper

Hot-pressed paper has a hard, smooth surface suitable for precise, detailed work. Most artists, however, find this surface too smooth and slippery; and the paint tends to run out of control.

Cold-pressed paper

This is also referred to as 'Not', meaning not hot-pressed. It has a semi-rough surface, equally good for smooth washes and fine brush detail. This is the most popular and versatile of the three surfaces, described here, and is ideal for less-experienced painters. It responds well to washes, and has enough texture to give a lively finish.

Rough paper

This has a more pronounced tooth (tiny peaks and hollows) to its surface. When a colour wash is laid on it, the brush drags over the surface and the paint settles in some of the hollows, leaving others untouched. This creates a white sparkle that illuminates the colour.

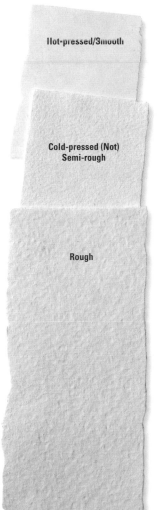

Hot-pressed/Smooth

Cold-pressed (Not) Semi-rough

Rough

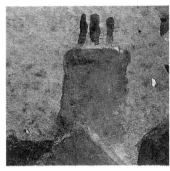

Rough paper

Weight

The weight (thickness) of water-colour paper traditionally refers to the weight of a ream (500 sheets) of a given size. The weight may be expressed in pounds (imperial measure), but the more accurate metric equivalent of grams per square metre (gsm) is now common.

Lightweight papers (less than 300gsm/140lb) tend to buckle and wrinkle when washes are applied, and need to be wetted and stretched on a board before use. There's no need to stretch heavier grades unless you intend to flood the paper with washes.

Paper sizes

Sizes of papers differ from country to country, and art suppliers still commonly describe paper in imperial sizes. The following table is a guide to imperial sizes and their metric equivalents.

Medium
22 x 17½in (559 x 444mm)
Royal
24 x 19in (610 x 483mm)
Double Crown
30 x 20in (762 x 508mm)
Imperial
30½ x 22½in (775 x 572mm)
Double Elephant
40 x 26¼in (1016 x 679mm)
Antiquarian
53 x 31in (1346 x 787mm)

Watercolour blocks

These consist of sheets of water-colour paper 'glued' together round the edges with gum. The block of paper is mounted on a backing board. When a painting is completed, it is separated from the block by sliding a palette knife between the top sheet and the one below. Although more expensive than loose sheets, watercolour blocks are convenient and dispense with the need for stretching paper.

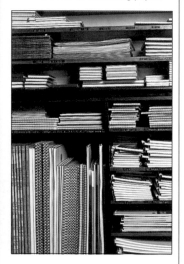

Watercolour boards

Watercolour board has a solid core faced with good-quality watercolour paper. The core provides extra strength and stability. Check that the core of the board, as well as the paper, is acid-free. Watercolour boards also perform well with pastel and charcoal.

Watercolour sheets

Watercolour paper is most commonly sold in sheet form. However, many mills supply their papers in rolls (which are more economical) and bound pads.

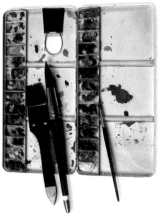

SIZED PAPER

Sizing controls the absorbency of paper and produces a more receptive working surface. All watercolour paper is sized to varying degrees. Heavy sizing produces a hard surface with little absorption and an extended drying time; this allows you to push the paint around on the surface. The colours remain brilliant, because they are not dulled by sinking into the paper.

Lightly sized papers are softer and more absorbent, with a shorter drying time. Alterations are more difficult because the paint sinks into the fibres of the paper. Absorbent papers are best suited to direct, expressive painting methods.

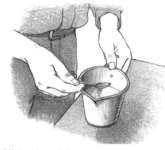

Mixing size solution

Internal sizing

When size is added at the pulp stage, it is contained within the body of the paper. This is known as internal or 'engine' sizing. Internal sizing makes the paper robust and prevents colour washes from bleeding beneath the paper surface, even when it has been abraded.

Surface sizing

Many watercolour papers are also surface-sized, by being passed through a tub of gelatine size (hence the term 'tub-sized'). Surface sizing not only reduces the absorbency of the paper but also limits the risk of fibre lift when removing masking material and lifting out washes of colour.

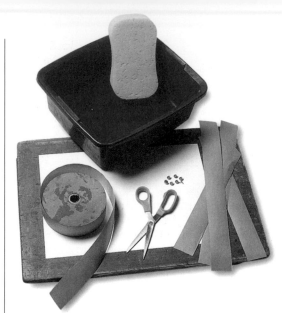

STRETCHING WATERCOLOUR PAPER

Lightweight watercolour paper needs to be prestretched on a drawing board to prevent it wrinkling and cockling when washes are applied. Before you begin, cut four lengths of gummed brown-paper tape 50mm (2in) longer than the sheet of paper to be stretched.

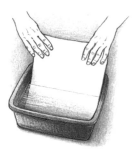

Immerse the watercolour paper in cold water for a few minutes, making sure it has absorbed water on both sides. Heavier papers may take up to 20 minutes.

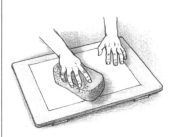

Run a dry sponge around the edges of the paper to remove excess water. Moisten each length of gum strip with a damp sponge immediately before use.

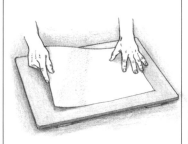

Hold the paper up by one edge and shake it gently to drain surplus water. Place the paper on the board and smooth it out from the centre to make sure that it is perfectly flat.

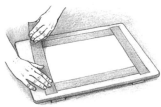

Beginning with the long sides, tape the paper to the board using the gummed strips; each strip should overlap the paper by half its width. Allow the paper to dry flat naturally, and leave the gummed strips in place until the completed painting is dry.

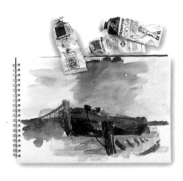

PAPERS FOR OILS AND ACRYLICS

Heavy paper with plenty of tooth makes a perfectly satisfactory support for small-to-medium-size oil or acrylic paintings. Thin light-weight papers will buckle when sized or primed.

Watercolour papers
Heavy rough-surfaced watercolour paper and handmade Indian paper are suitable for oils and acrylics. Their surface textures show to advantage when colour is applied in thin washes. For extra support, mount the paper on hardboard. Priming is required for oils.

Oil-painting paper
Sheets of paper textured to resemble canvas and primed ready for oil painting are available in fine or coarse grades. Cheaper-grade oil-sketching pads and blocks are convenient for sketching outdoors.

Acrylic-sketching paper
This comes in the form of spiral-bound pads of embossed acrylic-primed paper, convenient for small paintings and sketches.

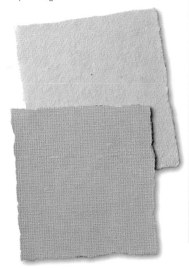

PAPERS FOR PASTELS

Some pastel artists like to work on primed hardboard, muslin-covered board or canvas, but most prefer to paint on one of the many tinted papers made specifically for pastel work.

The subtle textures hold the pastel particles to just the right degree. When the pastel stick is passed lightly over the surface, the colour of the paper shows through and gives an interesting broken-colour effect; when the pastel is pressed firmly into the tooth of the paper, solid patches of colour are obtained.

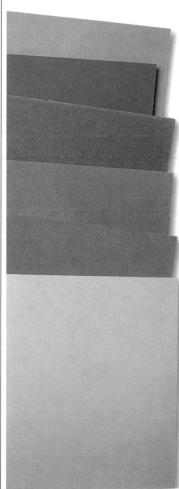

Papers for pastel work
From top to bottom
Mi-Teintes
Ingres
Velour
Sand-grain
Sansfix
Charcoal

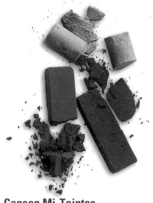

Canson Mi-Teintes
A lightly sized rag paper with a neutral pH, Canson Mi-Teintes is produced in France. It has a fairly soft surface, suitable for pastel, charcoal and chalk, and is available in a wide range of colours.

Ingres
A mould-made paper, Ingres is one of the most widely used papers for pastel work. It has a hard surface and a laid finish, with a neutral pH.

Velour paper
Also known as flock paper, this has a soft velvet-like surface, which gives a pastel painting a rich matt finish. It is best not to blend pastel colours too vigorously on velour paper, as this may spoil the nap of the surface.

Sand-grain paper
This has a pronounced tooth that is pleasant to work on. The rough surface of sand-grain paper is suited to a bold, vigorous style of painting, because it shaves colour off the pastel fairly rapidly.

Sansfix
The unique tooth of this paper, similar to very fine sandpaper, is made from a thin layer of fine cork particles, which eliminates the need for fixative. Similar in feel to Mi-Teintes paper, it has a light card backing and is acid-free. It is ideally suited to pastel work.

Charcoal paper
This inexpensive paper is useful for pastel sketches. However, it is rather thin and fragile, and you may find its regular linear surface texture too monotonous.

Watercolour papers
Good-quality watercolour papers are excellent for pastel painting, because they stand up to a lot of wear. Choose a Not (medium surface) or rough surface; hot-pressed papers are too smooth for pastels. It is best to use a tinted paper, as white paper makes it difficult to judge the tones of your colours.

Tinting papers
You can tint white watercolour paper by rubbing crushed pastels into the tooth of the paper with a damp rag. Use the same technique to modify coloured pastel papers.

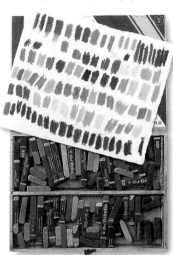

PAINTING TECHNIQUES

In the previous section of this book ('What Shall I Paint?'), artists describe the various techniques they use to produce their paintings. In that context, it was not always practical to describe the techniques in detail, so they are included here for further clarification. It is worth noting that many artists are not purists, and will adapt and combine techniques in order to create exactly the effects they are looking for.

UNDERPAINTING

The underpainting provides a foundation from which a painting can then be developed. Its main purpose is to determine the composition and the relationships of colours and tones at an early stage of the work.

Thin paint is used to block in roughly the main shapes and tones, before adding the details and surface colour.

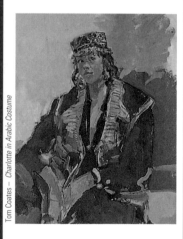

Tom Coates – Charlotte in Arabic Costume

Monochrome underpainting
Traditionally, the underpainting is monochrome, using neutral greys and browns. These colours form a solid base from which to model the figure.

Complementary underpainting
Alternatively, you can use complementary or contrasting colours for the underpainting to enhance subsequent layers of paint.

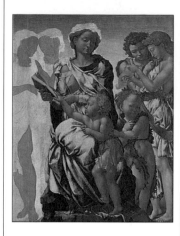

FAT-OVER-LEAN

The term 'fat-over-lean' is synonymous with 'flexible-over-inflexible'. 'Fat' describes paint that contains a higher percentage of oil, and is therefore flexible; 'lean' paint has little or no extra oil added, and is thinned with turpentine or white spirit, making it comparatively less flexible.

Lean paint may dry faster than fat paint, and thin layers dry faster than thick ones. If a lean or thin layer is applied over a fat or thick layer, the paint beneath dries more slowly and contracts as it does so, eventually causing the hardened paint on top to crack.

To ensure that a painting will have a sound structure, start with paint thinned with a diluent. The next layer may consist either of undiluted tube paint or of paint mixed with diluent and a little oil. Any successive layers should contain increasing amounts of oil – but they should not contain less oil or medium.

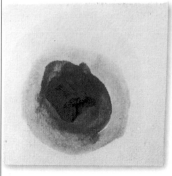

Removing excess oil
Some painters like to take excess oil out of their colours to make a stiffer paint. The safe way to do this is to squeeze the paint onto absorbent paper, which will remove only a small amount of oil. Don't leave the paint on the paper for too long in case it removes too much oil.

GLAZING

Glazing is a method of optical mixing, in which the colours blend in the viewer's eye. Each successive glaze modifies the underlying colour, without obscuring it completely. It is this incomplete fusion of the colours, combined with the effects of reflected light, that gives glazing its luminous quality.

Glazing with oil paint
With a slow-drying medium such as oils, glazing can be a laborious process; each colour must be completely dry before the next is applied, otherwise they simply mix together and become muddied. Paint for glazing should be thinned with a glazing medium, in order to increase its flow and transparency. Fast-drying synthetic glaze mediums speed the drying process.

Glazing with acrylics
The principle of glazing in acrylics is the same as for oil painting, but acrylic is even better suited to the technique, since you don't have to wait long for each layer to dry. And because dry acrylic paint is insoluble, it is possible to build layer upon layer without picking up the colour beneath.

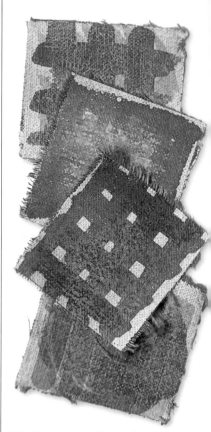

Glazing over other paints
Save time by glazing with oils over an underpainting done in egg tempera, alkyds or acrylics, all of which dry in minutes rather than days. Acrylics must be applied thinly, otherwise the oil-paint layer may lack adhesion. There is also a danger of cracking. Although oil paint can be applied over acrylic, the reverse is not possible.

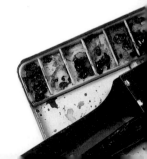

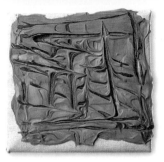

SCUMBLING

Scumbling is a way of modifying colour while retaining the liveliness of the paint surface. A thin film of dry semi-opaque colour is loosely brushed over a dry underlayer, creating a delicate veil of colour. Because the underlayer is only partially obscured, it shimmers through the scumbled paint.

Scumbling technique
Load the brush with neat or slightly diluted paint, and wipe it on a rag or onto your palette to remove any excess. Lightly scrub the paint onto the support with free, vigorous strokes, to produce a very thin film of colour.

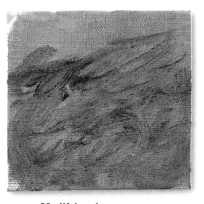

Modifying the temperature
A warm or hot colour can be modified by scumbling with a cool or cold colour.

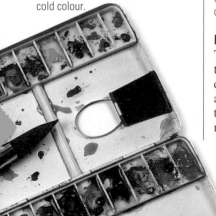

DRY BRUSHING

The dry-brush technique is most successful when applied to distinct textures, such as the coarse weave of canvas or previous brushstrokes that have dried.

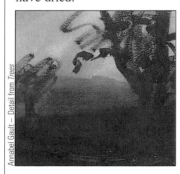

Annabel Gault – Detail from *Trees*

Dry-brush technique
A small amount of neat colour is picked up on a brush and skimmed lightly over the support. The paint catches on the raised 'tooth' of the canvas or the textured paint surface, leaving tiny specks of the ground, or the underlying colour, showing through.

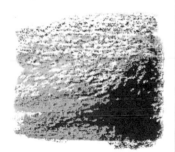

Dry brushing with watercolour
The dry-brush technique is invaluable in watercolour painting, because it can suggest complex textures with an economy of means. Moisten your brush with very little water, then take up a small amount of paint on the tip. Remove excess moisture by flicking the brush across a paper tissue or a dry rag before lightly skimming the brush over the dry paper.

BLENDING

The consistency of oils, and their prolonged drying time, enables an artist to blend the area where two colours or tones meet, so that they merge imperceptibly.

Blending with broken colour
Blending can be achieved simply by dragging one colour over the edge of the next, so that both colours are roughly knitted together, with the marks of the brush still evident.

Smooth blending
Alternatively, you can stroke one colour into the next, using a soft-hair brush or fan blender, until you achieve a smooth, highly finished transition in which the marks of the brush are invisible.

OPTICAL MIXING

Instead of mixing a colour on the palette, you can lay small specks of pure colour side by side on the picture surface. When the painting is viewed from an adequate distance, the colours appear to blend and suggest a completely different colour. Optical mixing creates colours with a vibrant, luminous quality.

IMPASTO

Create a highly textured surface by applying paint thickly with a brush or painting knife.

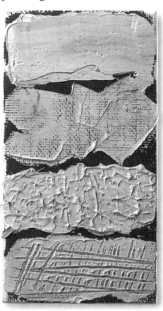

Knife painting
Utilize the flat base of the blade to produce a smooth surface (top). Holding the knife at a slight angle to the surface gives a thinner covering and allows the texture of the canvas to show through (second row). Make a brisk patting motion with the tip of the blade to create a rough, stippled texture (third row). Scratching through a layer of wet paint with the tip of the blade reveals the colour beneath (bottom).

Tonking
If a painting done in oils or acrylics becomes overworked or clogged with too much paint, the excess can be removed by a process known as 'tonking'.

Place a sheet of absorbent paper, such as newspaper or toilet tissue, over the wet paint. Gently smooth the paper down with the flat of your hand, then peel it off the surface, lifting the excess paint along with it.

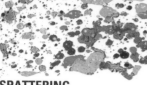

TEXTURES AND EFFECTS

Inventive artists have always sought to create a wider armoury of textures and effects than is possible using conventional paintbrushes. Here is a selection of techniques that will help enrich your paintings.

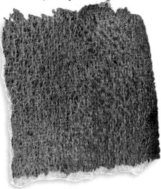

GRANULATION

Granulation is a naturally occurring texture that imparts a beautiful subtle texture to a wash. The relatively coarse pigments in some watercolours settle in the hollows of the paper as the wash dries out.

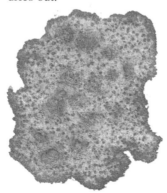

FLOCCULATION

A similar grainy effect is produced by pigments that flocculate. Instead of dispersing evenly, the pigment particles in some watercolour paints are attracted to each other.

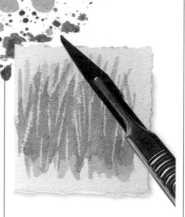

SPATTERING

Spattering (flicking paint onto a support) adds interest to a large area of flat colour. It is an effective means of suggesting textures such as sea foam, sand and pebbles.

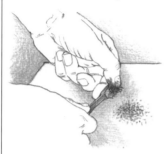

Using a toothbrush

Dip an old toothbrush into fairly thick paint and, holding it horizontally above the painting surface, quickly draw a thumbnail through the bristles. This releases a shower of fine droplets onto the painting. You can use scrap paper to mask off parts of the painting.

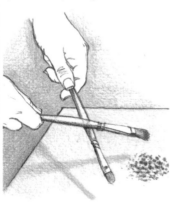

Using two brushes

Load a paintbrush with colour and tap it sharply across your out-stretched finger or across the handle of another brush. This produces a relatively dense spatter, with large droplets of paint.

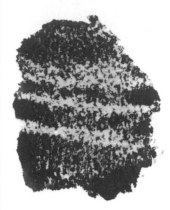

SCRATCHING OUT

Create fine linear highlights in watercolour by scratching through a painted surface when it is dry. You can use a razor blade or a sharp, pointed knife. Work gently to avoid tearing the surface of the paper.

Pale highlights

Make paler marks by scratching paint that is not quite dry, using the tip of a paintbrush handle or a sharpened stick.

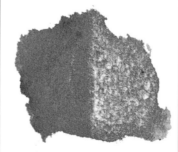

Diffused highlights,

To suggest reflections from moving water or ocean waves, scrape the painted paper gently with the side of the blade or rub the surface with a piece of fine sandpaper.

WAX RESIST

A broken texture can be created by drawing with a wax candle or coloured crayon, then overpainting with watercolour. The wash of colour is repelled by the wax (which coagulates in droplets), but it soaks into the unwaxed areas of the paper.

Oil resist

A similar but more subtle texture is created by painting turpentine or white spirit onto well-sized paper. Allow the paper to dry, then apply a wash of watercolour over the top. The paint and oil separate, creating an interesting marbled surface.

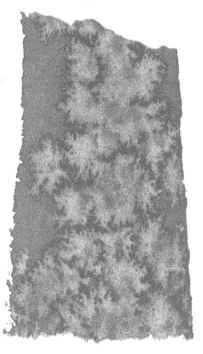

MAKING TEXTURES WITH SALT

Unpredictable textures can be induced by scattering grains of coarse rock salt into wet watercolour – as the salt crystals soak up the paint around them. When the picture has dried, brush off the salt to reveal a pattern of pale crystalline shapes.

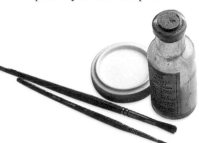

MASKING FLUID

Masking fluid is a rubbery solution which, when dry, resists overlays of water-colour. Apply masking fluid with a brush or dip pen where you want light areas or highlights to appear in your picture. Continue painting right over the masking fluid; then, once the washes have dried, rub off the masking fluid with an eraser to reveal the white of the paper or the previously laid colour.

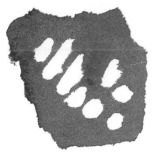

Masking white paper
Before you start painting, paint spots of masking fluid onto the paper. When the paint has dried, rub the surface to reveal the white paper.

LIFTING OUT

Soaking up watercolour while it is still wet creates soft diffused highlights. Apply a generous wash of colour, and then lift out areas of colour with absorbent tissue paper or a damp sponge, or a paint-brush dipped in clean water then squeezed out.

Lifting out is a technique that's often used by landscape painters to suggest soft billowing clouds.

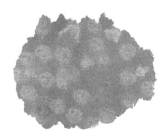

Lifting out dry paint
Lift out dry watercolour by gentle coaxing with a damp sponge, brush or cotton bud.

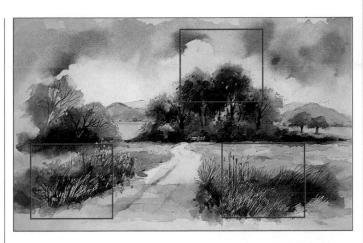

Putting texture to good effect

Here we see a watercolour painting in progress. The artist is employing a variety of techniques to add textures to the picture and create the illusion of depth. The top illustration shows the painting about half finished. The detail, top right, shows how absorbent tissue can be used to lift out colour from areas of the sky. Texture has been introduced to the foreground (detail bottom right) by scratching through the paint surface with a knife. The detail below shows how masking fluid can be used to delineate flowers and grasses, as in the left-hand foreground of the painting. (See also pages 88–93.)

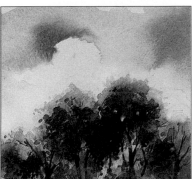

Lifting out

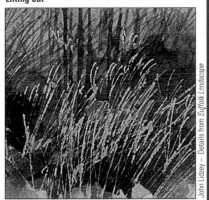

Scratching out

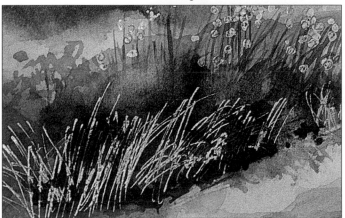

Masking-fluid technique

John Lidzey – Details from *Suffolk Landscape*

WASHES

Colour washes are thin, usually broadly applied, layers of transparent or heavily diluted paint.

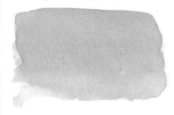

FLAT WASHES

Watercolourists apply washes of colour in the process of building up a painting, and frequently overlay one wash with another. A flat wash is also used to tint white paper as a background for body colour or gouache.

Painting a flat wash

To create a flat wash, wet the paper evenly, using a sponge or large brush to apply the water. Then load a brush with dilute paint, and draw a single stroke across the painting. Paint a second stroke just below the first, slightly overlapping it to pick up the wet edge.

Continue for as far as you want the wash to extend, reloading the brush with colour as required. It is essential to work reasonably quickly, to ensure the wash merges into an area of flat, even colour.

GRADED WASHES

The method of applying a graded wash is the same as for a flat wash, except that with each successive brushstroke the brush carries more water and less pigment

It takes a little practice to achieve a smooth transition in tone, with no sudden jumps. The secret is to apply a sufficient weight of paint so that the excess flows very gently down the surface of the paper, to be merged with the next brushstroke.

VARIEGATED WASHES

If you plan to merge one colour with another, mix your chosen colours beforehand.

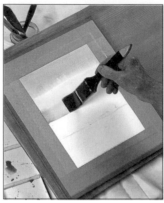

Painting a variegated wash
Apply the first line of colour along the top of the paper. Wash your brush, then apply the second colour, partly overlapping the first wash. Allow the colours to run together naturally.

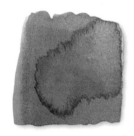

BLOOMS

Blooms or backruns are created by flooding a wet wash into another, slightly drier, wash.

As the second wash spreads, it dislodges some of the pigment particles beneath. These particles collect at the edge of the wash as it dries, creating a pale flowerlike shape with a dark crinkled edge. A similar effect is created by dropping clean water from a brush onto the first semi-dry wash.

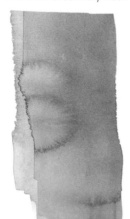

WET-IN-WET

This is a watercolour technique that encourages paints to merge and blend, creating areas of texture and variegated colour.

Apply diluted colours to either a damp sheet of paper or an area of still-wet paint, allowing them to run out over the wet surface to create soft hazy edges and joins. You can tilt the paper to encourage the washes to run in a certain direction, but minimum control is an essential part of the wet-in-wet technique.

WET-ON-DRY

Superimposing washes of relatively thin colour on other dry washes results in resonant areas of colour. This is due to light passing through each transparent wash to the white paper beneath, and then being reflected back through the colours. The dry surface of the paper 'holds' the paint, so that brushstrokes do not run out of control.

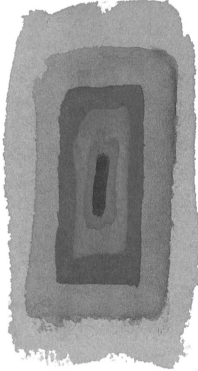

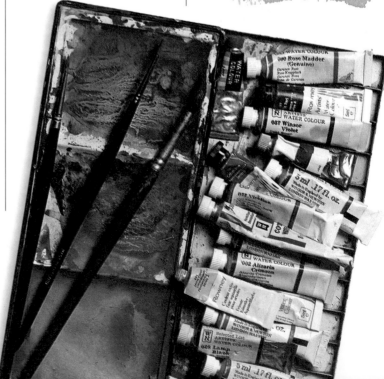

PASTELS

Pastels are made from finely ground pigments mixed with a base such as chalk or clay and bound together with gum to form a stiff paste. This is then cut and shaped into sticks and allowed to harden.

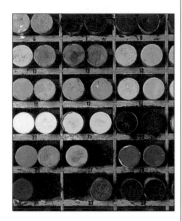

SOFT PASTELS

Soft pastels are the most widely used of the various pastel types, because they produce the wonderful velvety bloom that is one of the main attractions of pastel art. They contain proportionally more pigment and less binder, so the colours are rich and vibrant.

HARD PASTELS

These contain less pigment and more binder than soft pastels, so although the colours are not as brilliant, they do have a firmer consistency. Hard pastels can be sharpened to a point with a blade and used to produce crisp lines and details. They do not crumble and break as easily as soft pastels, nor do they clog the tooth of textured papers.

Hard pastels are handy for the preliminary stages of a painting, when you are outlining the composition. They are also used for adding details and accents in the latter stages, sometimes in combination with other drawing and painting media.

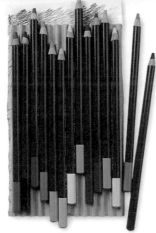

PASTEL PENCILS

Thin pastel sticks can be bought encased in wooden shafts, like pencils. Pastel pencils are clean to use, do not break or crumble like conventional pastels, and provide more control. They are suitable for line sketches and small-scale work, and can be used in conjunction with hard and soft pastels.

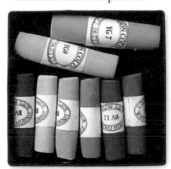

DRAWING AND PAINTING WITH PASTELS

Pastels are both a painting and a drawing medium. Working with the side of the stick creates broad strokes that can be blended and smudged, or built up in thickly impasted layers. When drawing with the tip, you can make thin lines and crisp marks that create a very different feel.

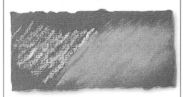

Blending pastels

One of the attractions of a powdery medium such as pastel is that it can be blended easily to create soft velvety tones and make subtle gradations from dark to light.

To create an area of blended tone, apply the pastels to the paper and then lightly rub the surface, with a rag, tissue or paper stump, to blend the marks together and create an even tone.

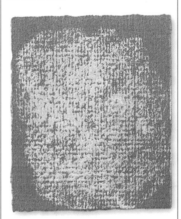

Scumbling with pastels

Scumbling modifies a colour (a tinted paper or a layer of pastel) by applying a thin semi-opaque layer of another colour over it. Apply loose circular strokes, using the side of the stick, to create a thin veil of colour that does not entirely obliterate the one underneath. Scumbling not only creates subtle colour effects; it also gives a very attractive surface texture. Use it to give depth and luminosity to your colours, and to soften and unify areas of the drawing.

Oil Pastels

Soft pastels are known for their velvety texture and subtle colours, whereas oil pastels make thick, buttery strokes, and their colours are more intense.

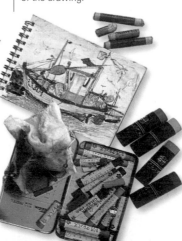

OIL PASTELS

Oil pastels are made by combining raw pigments with animal fat and wax; this makes them somewhat different in character from the more friable pastels, which are bound with gum.

Blending oil pastels

The colours can be applied to the support and then spread and blended with a brush, rag or tissue dipped in white spirit or turpentine.

Alternatively, you can blend oil pastel with a wet finger. Because oil and water are incompatible, your dampened finger will not lift the colour from the paper – it simply smooths and blends the surface of the pastel.

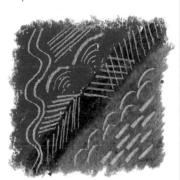

Sgraffito

Waxy oil pastel can be scratched with a sharp tool, creating distinct patterns and textures – a technique known as sgraffito.

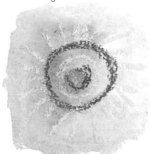

Wax resist

Watercolour paint will adhere to the paper but is resisted by waxy pastel marks. More-pronounced textures can be achieved by working on rough-surfaced paper.

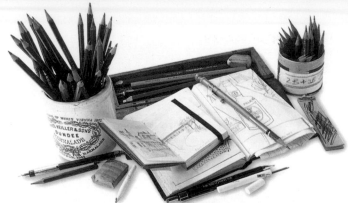

CONTÉ CRAYONS

Made from pigment and graphite bound together with gum and a little grease, Conté crayons are similar to pastels in consistency and appearance but are slightly harder. They are available in pencil form, and as traditional square-section sticks about 75mm (3in) long.

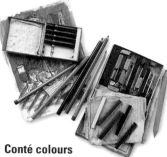

Conté colours

Conté crayons are made in a wide range of colours, but many artists still favour the restrained harmony of the conventional palette: black, white, grey, and the earth colours sepia, sanguine (terracotta red) and bistre (cool brown).

MAKING MARKS WITH CONTÉ

As with pastels, block in broad areas of tone with the side of the stick, and use a sharp corner for making expressive lines. When drawing, it's convenient to snap off small pieces of crayon, about 25mm (1in) long.

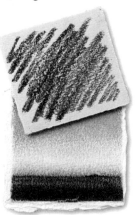

Blending Conté

Conté is soft enough to blend colours by rubbing them together with a finger, soft rag or paper stump.

CHARCOAL

Charcoal is made from vine, beech or willow twigs charred at high temperatures in airtight kilns. Willow is the most common type; vine and beech charcoal are more expensive, but make richer marks.

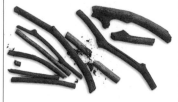

Charcoal sticks

Stick charcoal, which comes in 15cm (6in) lengths, varies in thickness and density. Soft charcoal is powdery, making it ideally suited to blending and smudging techniques. The harder type of charcoal is more appropriate for detailed linear work, as it does not smudge so readily. The one drawback with stick charcoal is that it is very brittle and fragile, and tends to snap when used vigorously.

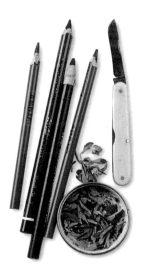

Charcoal pencils

These pencils are made from thin sticks of compressed charcoal encased in wood. They are cleaner to handle and easier to control than stick charcoal, and have a slightly harder texture. Only the point can be used, so they are not ideal for creating large areas of tone. Charcoal pencils come in hard, medium and soft grades; the tips can be sharpened, like graphite pencils.

PENCILS

Pencils are used for sketching and underdrawing, and many artists add pencil textures and detailing to their finished paintings, especially watercolours.

GRAPHITE PENCILS

Drawing pencils come in a range of grades, from 'H' for hard to 'B' for soft. The hardness of the lead is determined by the relative proportions of graphite and clay used: the more graphite, the softer the pencil. Typically, hard pencils range from 9H (the hardest) to H, and soft pencils range from 9B (the softest) to B. Grades HB and F are midway between the two.

A very soft pencil makes rich black marks, and is excellent for rapid sketches and expressive line-and-tone drawings, especially on textured paper. Harder leads are more suitable for precise lines and details, because they can be sharpened to a fine point.

Although a single pencil of grade HB or 2B gives you considerable scope for expression, many artists use several grades of pencil in one piece of work, creating a rich interplay of line and tone.

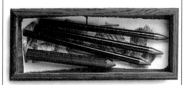

Graphite sticks

These are made of high-grade compressed and bonded graphite formed into thick, chunky sticks. They glide smoothly across the surface of the paper, lending themselves to bold, expressive drawing. Marks can be varied by using the point, the flattened edge of the point, or the side of the stick.

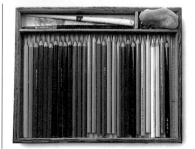

COLOURED PENCILS

Coloured pencils are made from a mixture of pigment, clay and filler, bound together with gum. The coloured sticks are soaked in wax, before being pressed into rods and encased in wood.

Water-soluble pencils

These offer all the advantages of coloured pencils, but include a water-soluble ingredient in the lead, so that it is possible to thin out their colour into a transparent wash.

You can apply the colour dry, then loosen the pigment particles and create a subtle watercolour effect, using a wet brush or sponge.

If you dampen the paper first, the marks made by water-soluble pencils bleed slightly and produce soft broad lines.

MAKING LINEAR MARKS

The weight, quality and nuance of a pencil line can be varied and controlled by the grade of pencil chosen, its sharpness, the degree of pressure applied, and the texture of the paper surface.

Shading

Continuous gradations of tone can be created by shading with soft pencils. These areas are first drawn in broadly, working from the lightest to the darkest tones or vice versa. The marks are then carefully blended together using a paper stump, your fingers or an eraser.

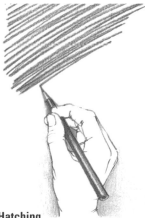

Hatching

Areas of tone can be built up with hatching – roughly parallel lines drawn close together. These can be straight and mechanical or free and sketchy. Altering the direction of the lines describes shape and form.

Crosshatching

In crosshatching, lines are criss-crossed on top of one another to create a fine mesh of tone. The lines may run in any direction – vertical, horizontal or diagonal.

Crosshatching

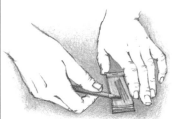

Sharpening pencils

Sandpaper blocks, consisting of small tear-off sheets of sandpaper stapled together, are handy for putting fine points on pencils and graphite sticks.

PAPER STUMPS

Paper stumps, also called torchons, are used for blending or shading charcoal, pastel or soft-graphite drawings. They are made of tightly rolled paper, and taper to a point for working on small details.

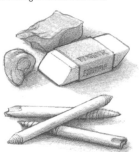

ERASERS

Not only can you rub out pencil drawings with an eraser, but you can also use it to create highlights by lifting out areas of tone.

Plastic or putty erasers are best, as India rubber tends to smear pencil work and can damage the paper surface. Putty erasers are very malleable; they can be broken off into smaller pieces and manipulated into any shape, including a point.

PEN AND INK

Depending on the type of ink you use, you can tint a pen drawing with watercolour, leaving the linework intact, or dissolve an ink drawing into free-flowing washes, using a wet paintbrush.

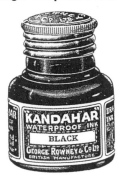

WATERPROOF INKS

Black waterproof Indian ink is the first choice of many artists when making monochrome drawings, but there are also about twenty coloured waterproof inks to choose from.

Waterproof inks are essential if you intend to apply a wash or tint on top of a line drawing; otherwise the linework will run. These inks are denser than non-waterproof varieties, drying to a slightly glossy finish that gives the work a precise, painted quality. The shellac that is added to the ink to make it waterproof also makes it clog easily, so be sure to clean brushes and pens thoroughly after use.

NON-WATERPROOF INKS

These contain no shellac, and are primarily used for laying washes over waterproof-ink drawings. They can be used for line drawings, too, as long as you don't want to overlay them with washes.

Non-waterproof inks sink into the paper more than waterproof types do, and dry to a matt finish. They can be diluted with distilled water, not only to improve their flow but also to produce a range of lighter tones. The inks can also be mixed with each other, but it is advisable to stick to the range of a single manufacturer, because different brands of ink vary in consistency and in the surface finish that they produce when dry. Pigment in ink settles at the bottom of a jar if left unused for some time, so jars should be shaken before use.

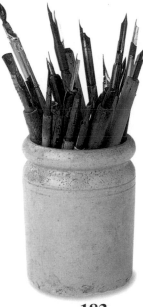

Dip pens
Dip pens with metal nibs have long been the traditional tool of pen-and-ink artists and illustrators. Inexpensive and versatile, these pens comprise a holder and an interchangeable steel nib.

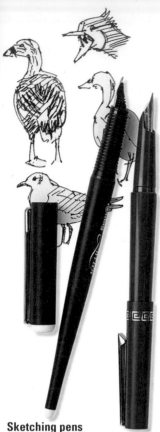

Sketching pens

Although they resemble ordinary fountain pens in appearance, sketching pens have flexible nibs (designed specifically for drawing) that deliver ink smoothly from prefilled ink cartridges to the paper.

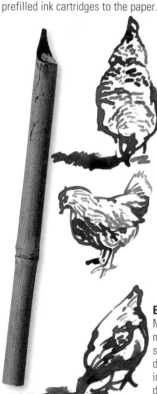

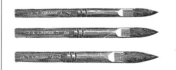

Line and wash

The combination of crisp finely drawn lines and fluid washes has great visual appeal, capturing the essence of the subject with economy and restraint. The secret is to work rapidly and intuitively, allowing the washes to flow over the 'boundaries' of the drawn lines and not be constricted by them.

The traditional method is to start with a pen drawing, leave it to dry, and then lay in light fluid washes of ink or watercolour on top. Alternatively, washes can be applied first to establish the main tones, with the ink lines drawn on top after the washes have dried.

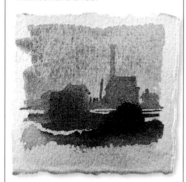

Brush drawing

The brush is a very flexible drawing tool. A soft brush with a good point can, in a single stroke, convey line, rhythm, and even the play of light on a subject. You can change direction easily with a brush, twisting and rounding corners where a pen or pencil might falter. It is best to experiment with different types of brush on both smooth and textured papers, and compare the different marks they make.

Bamboo and reed pens

Many artists prefer bamboo or reed pens. They make relatively broad and slightly irregular strokes, which makes them ideal for bold line drawings. Some of their appeal probably lies in the sheer pleasure that can be derived from drawing with such a 'primitive' instrument.

PROTECTING DRAWINGS

The best way to preserve drawings is to spray them with fixative, a thin colourless varnish that binds the particles of pigment to the surface of the paper.

AEROSOL OR ATOMIZER

Fixative is sold in aerosol-spray form, or you can apply it to the work using a mouth diffuser, known as an atomizer. A metal atomizer, which has a plastic mouthpiece, is stood in a bottle of fixative. Blowing through the atomizer distributes a fine spray of fixative onto the drawing. Atomizers are ideal for spraying small areas, but it takes practice to get used to them, and they need regular cleaning to prevent clogging.

Aerosol sprays give an even coat, and are more convenient to use when covering a large area.

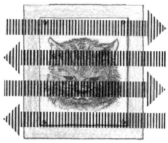

Applying fixative

Pin your finished work to a vertical surface and hold the spray can or atomizer at least 30cm (12in) away from the image, pointing directly at it. Begin spraying just beyond the left side of the picture. Sweep back and forth across the picture with a slow, steady motion, always going beyond the edges of the picture before stopping. Keep your arm moving so that the spray doesn't build up in one spot and create a dark patch or start to drip down the paper.

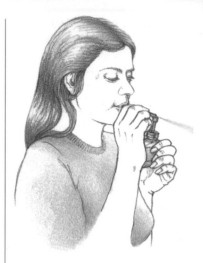

Fixing a pencil drawing

Spraying a drawing with fixative requires a delicate touch; it should be applied sparingly, as a couple of light coats are better than one heavy one. It is worth practising on pieces of scrap paper until you discover how to produce a fine uniform mist without getting any drips on the paper. If you hold the spray too close, it will saturate the surface and may run and streak your work. Always work in a well-ventilated area, to avoid inhaling too much of the spray.

Fixing charcoal

It is advisable to spray charcoal drawings fairly liberally with fixative to prevent them from smudging.

Fixing pastels

Apply fixative sparingly to pastel paintings; too much fixative will darken the colours.

Protecting oil pastels

Unlike other pastels, oil pastels do not require fixing, because the blend of pigments, fat and wax never fully dries. For the same reason, it is inadvisable to apply varnish over oil pastels; should you need to remove the varnish at a later date, it will take most of the oil-pastel colour off the surface with it. To prevent smudging, store oil-pastel pictures in mounts.

THE LANGUAGE OF ART

As with most specialized subjects, art has its own peculiar terminology. Listed here are some of the more unfamiliar terms that occur in this book or which the reader may encounter.

Acrylic paint
Any paint containing acrylic resin, derived from either man-made acrylic or propenoic (derived from petroleum) acid.

Alkyd resin
A synthetic resin used in paints and mediums.

Alla prima *(Italian for 'at the first')*
Technique in which the final surface of a painting is completed in one sitting, without underpainting. Also known as *au premier coup*.

ASTM
The American Society for Testing and Materials. An internationally recognized independent standard for certain paint qualities, adopted by most manufacturers.

Atmospheric perspective
The illusion of depth created by using desaturated colours and relatively pale tones in the background of a painting. Also known as aerial perspective.

Backrun
A dark irregular line of colour caused by water dispersing pigment particles in a laid wash. (See also bloom.)

Balance
In a work of art, the overall distribution of forms and colour to produce a harmonious whole.

Binder
A liquid mixed with powdered pigment to form a paint.

Bistre
A brown transparent pigment made by boiling beech-tree soot.

Bleeding
In artwork, the effect of a dark colour seeping through a lighter colour to the surface. Usually associated with gouache paint.

Blending
Smoothing the edges of two colours together so that they have a smooth gradation where they meet.

Blocking in
Applying areas of colour and tone with relatively broad brushstrokes.

Bloom
A roughly circular mark, similar to a backrun. Bloom is also a term for a cloudy white deposit on varnished surfaces that have been kept in damp conditions.

Body colour
Opaque paint, such as gouache, that has the covering power to obliterate underlying colour. 'Body' also refers to a pigment's density.

Brushwork
The characteristic way each artist brushes paint onto a support. Often regarded as a 'signature', it is used to help attribute paintings to a particular artist.

Casein
A milk-protein-based binder mixed with pigment to make paint. Most often associated with tempera.

Chiaroscuro
(Italian for 'light/dark')
Particularly associated with oil painting, this term is used to describe the effect of light and shade in a painting or drawing, especially where strong tonal contrasts are used.

Cissing
The effect caused when a water-based paint either does not wet the support enough to adhere effectively or is repelled by the surface. Also known as 'crawling' or 'creeping'.

Cockling
Wrinkling or puckering in paper supports caused by applying washes on a flimsy or inadequately stretched and prepared surface.

Collage
Artwork composed of pieces of paper, fabric or others items pasted onto a support.

Composition
The arrangement of elements by an artist in a painting or drawing.

Contre-jour
(French for 'against daylight')
A painting or drawing where the light source is behind the subject.

Copal
A hard, aromatic resin, used in making varnishes and paint mediums.

Crosshatching
Close parallel lines that crisscross each other at angles to model and indicate tone. (See also hatching.)

Dammar
A resin from conifer trees, used in making oil mediums and varnishes.

Dead colour
A term for colours used in underpainting.

Diluents
Liquids, such as turpentine, used to dilute oil paint. The diluent for water-based media is water.

Distemper
A blend of glue, chalk and water-based paint, used mostly for murals and posters but also sometimes for fine-art painting.

Dry brushing
A technique for applying the minimum of paint by lightly stroking a barely loaded brush across the surface of a painting or support.

Earth colours
These colours – umbers, siennas and ochres – are regarded as the most stable natural pigments.

Encaustic
An ancient technique of mixing pigments with hot wax as a binder.

Fat
Used to describe paints that have a high oil content. (See also lean.)

Filler
In painting, the inert pigment added to paint to increase its bulk (also called extender). Or the material used to fill open pores or holes in a support or ground.

Film
A thin coating or layer of paint, ink, etc.

Fixative
A solution, usually of shellac and alcohol, sprayed onto drawings, particularly charcoal, chalk and soft pastels, to prevent them smudging or crumbling off the support.

Flocculation
A grainy effect in paintwork caused by pigment particles settling in groups instead of dispersing evenly. (See also granulation.)

Flop
To turn over.

Format
The proportions and size of a support.

Fresco *(Italian for 'fresh')*
A wall-covering technique that involves painting with water-based paints on freshly applied wet plaster. Also known as *buon fresco*.

Fugitive colours
Pigment or dye colours that fade when exposed to light. (See also lightfast and permanence.)

Genre
A category or type of painting, classified by its subject matter – still life, landscape, portrait, etc. The term is also applied to scenes depicting domestic life.

Gesso
A mixture, usually composed of whiting and glue size, used as a primer for rigid oil-painting supports.

Glaze
In painting, a transparent or semi-transparent colour laid over another, different colour to modify or intensify it.

Grain
See tooth.

Granulation
A specked effect caused by coarse pigment particles settling in the hollows of textured paper. (See also flocculation.)

Gridding up
A method for transferring an image to a larger or smaller format. The original version is covered with a grid of horizontal and vertical lines, then each numbered square is copied onto its counterpart on a larger or smaller set of squares on a different support. Also known as squaring up.

Grisaille
A monochrome painting in shades of grey, or a grey underpainting.

Ground
A specially prepared painting surface.

Ground colour
Dilute or broken colour applied to a primed canvas or other support in order to reduce the glare from a white surface and create a more sympathetic background colour for a painting. (See also imprimatura.)

Gum arabic
A gum, extracted from certain acacia trees, used in solution as a medium for watercolour paints.

Hatching
A technique for indicating tone and suggesting light and shade in a drawing or painting, using closely set parallel lines. (See also crosshatching.)

Highlight
High-key area of tone, created by light reflecting back from a surface.

Hue
The name of a colour – blue, red, yellow etc. – irrespective of its tone or intensity.

Impasto
A technique of applying paint thickly with a brush or painting knife, or by hand, to create a textured surface. Also the term for the results of this technique.

Imprimatura
A coat of diluted colour, usually a wash, used to tone down or tint a white canvas or other support before painting.

Intensity
The purity and brightness of a colour. Also called saturation or chroma.

Key
Used to describe the prevailing tone of a painting: a predominantly light painting is said to have a high key, a predominantly dark one a low key. In modern mural painting, the key is the result of scratching and preparing a wall surface ready for the final layer of plaster.

Landscape format
A painting or drawing wider than it is tall. (See also portrait format.)

Laying in
See underpainting.

Lay figure
A jointed wooden manikin which, ideally, can be moved into almost any pose or attitude, for studying proportions and angles and for arranging clothing and drapery. Lay hands and horses are also available.

Leaching
The process of drawing out excess liquid through a porous substance.

Lean
Adjective used to describe paint thinned with a diluent such as turpentine or white spirit, which therefore has a low oil content. (See also fat.)

Lightfast
Term applied to pigments that resist fading when exposed to sunlight. (See also fugitive.)

Limited palette
A relatively small number of colours chosen by an artist for a painting, usually to retain greater control over the colour balance of a picture. (See also palette.)

Linework
The linear elements of a picture, produced by drawing with a pen, pencil or paintbrush.

Local colour
The actual colour of an object or surface, unaffected by shadow colouring, light quality or other factors; for instance, the local colour of a lemon is always yellow, even with a blue shadow falling across it.

Loom-state canvas
Canvas that has not been primed, sized or otherwise prepared beforehand for painting.

Medium
This term has two distinct meanings: (1) an additive (plural mediums) mixed with paint to modify characteristics such as flow, gloss or texture; (2) the material (plural media) chosen by an artist for working, such as paint, ink, pencil, pastel, etc.

Mixed media
In drawing and painting, this refers to the use of different media in the same picture (for example, ink, watercolour wash and wax crayon), or to the use of a combination of supports (for example, newspaper and cardboard).

Mixed method
The process of using oil glazes on top of a tempera underpainting.

Mural
Also sometimes referred to as wall painting, this term describes any painting made directly onto a wall. (See also fresco and secco.)

Negative shapes
The shapes between and around the principal elements or objects in a painting. (See also positive shapes.)

One-wet session
A single session during which an artist works on a painting without allowing the paint to dry. (See also alla prima.)

Opacity
The ability of a pigment to obliterate an underlying colour. Opacity varies from one pigment to another.

Open landscape
A view unobstructed by buildings or trees – usually a broad sweep of countryside.

Palette
As well as describing the various kinds of holders and surfaces employed for mixing paint colours, the term palette is also used to refer to the artist's choice and blends of colours when painting. (See also limited palette.)

Patina
Originally the green-brown encrustation on bronze, this now includes the natural effects of age or exposure on a surface, such as old yellowing varnish on an oil painting.

Pentimento
(Italian for 'repentance' or 'regret') In an oil painting, this is when evidence of previous painting shows through the finished work when the surface paint becomes transparent. The word also refers to unerased attempts to fix a line or contour in a drawing or painting.

Permanence
Refers to a pigment's resistance to fading on exposure to sunlight. (See also fugitive and lightfast.)

Pigments
The colouring agents used in all painting and drawing media. Traditionally they were derived from natural sources, but pigments are also man-made substances. The word is also used to describe the powdered or dry forms of the agents.

Plasticity
In a two-dimensional drawing or painting, plasticity describes figures, objects or space with a strongly three-dimensional appearance, often achieved by modelling with great contrasts of tone.

Plein air *(French for 'open air')* Term describing paintings done outdoors, directly from the subject.

Portrait format
A painting or drawing taller than it is wide. (See also landscape format.)

Positive shapes
The shapes created by the principal elements or objects in a painting. (See also negative shapes.)

Primer
Applied to a layer of size or directly to a support, a primer acts as a barrier between paint and support. It also provides a surface suitable for receiving paint.

Proportion
The relationship of one part to the whole or to other parts. For example, this can refer to the relation of each component of the human figure to the figure itself or to the painting as a whole.

Preliminary drawing
A study made to determine composition, tones and/or colours before embarking on a finished painting. (See also underdrawing.)

PVA
Polyvinyl acetate. A man-made resin used as a paint medium and in varnish. Not recommended for permanent work.

Recession
In art, this describes the effect of making objects appear to recede into the distance by the use of atmospheric perspective and colour.

Reduction
The result of mixing a colour with white paint.

Sanguine
A red-brown chalk.

Saturation
The intensity and brilliance of a colour.

Scumble
The technique of dragging one or more layers of dryish opaque paint over a bottom layer that partially shows through the overlying ones.

Secco *(Italian for 'dry')*
A technique of wall-painting on dry plaster or on lime plaster that is dampened shortly before the paint is applied.

Sfumato *(Italian for 'shaded off')*
Gradual, almost imperceptible transitions of colour, from light to dark.

Sgraffito *(Italian for 'scratched off')*
A technique of scoring into a layer of colour with a sharp instrument, to reveal either the ground colour or a layer of colour beneath.

Shade
Term for a colour darkened with black.

Shellac
A yellow resin secreted by the lac insect, used in making varnish.

Silverpoint
A drawing method now almost entirely superseded by the graphite pencil. A piece of metal (usually silver wire) was used to draw on a ground prepared with Chinese white, sometimes with pigment added to the ground. There was no possibility of erasure. Also called metalpoint.

Sinopia
A red-brown chalk used for the preliminary marking-out of frescoes; also the preliminary drawing itself.

Size
A weak glue solution used for making gesso and distemper, for stiffening paper and for making canvas impervious before applying layers of primer or oil paint.

Size colour
A combination of hot glue size and pigments.

Sketch
A rough drawing or a preliminary draft of a composition, not necessarily to be worked up subsequently. Sketches are often used as a means of improving an artist's observation and technique.

Study
A detailed drawing or painting made of one or more parts of a final composition, but not of the whole.

Support
A surface used for painting or drawing – canvas, board, paper, etc.

Tempering
In painting, mixing pigments with tempera to produce a hue.

Thixotropic
A property of stiff fluids that become liquefied when stirred, shaken or brushed.

Tint
Term for a colour lightened with white. Also, in a mixture of colours, the tint is the dominant colour.

Tinting strength
The power of a pigment to influence mixtures of colours.

Tone
The relative darkness or lightness of a colour, without reference to its local colour.

Tonking
Pressing a sheet of paper onto a painting then peeling it off again in order to remove thick paint.

Tooth
The surface texture, ranging from coarse to fine, of painting supports.

Traction
In oils, this is the movement of one layer of paint over another.

Traction fissure
This usually occurs when the principles of painting 'fat-over-lean' in oils have not been applied, leading to cracking of the top layer or layers of paint or varnish.

Tragacanth
A gum, extracted from certain plants of the *Astragalus* genus, used as a binding agent in watercolour paints and pastels.

Transparency
The state of allowing light to pass through, and of filtering light.

Trompe l'oeil
(French for 'deceive the eye')
A work of art – for example, a still life with extreme naturalistic details – that aims to persuade the viewer that he or she is looking at actual objects rather than a two-dimensional representation.

Underdrawing
A drawing made on a support in order to determine the positions of the main elements within a painting. (See also preliminary drawing.)

Underpainting
An early stage of a painting (sometimes in monochrome) used to establish the composition, overall tone and colour balance. Also known as laying in.

Value
An alternative word for 'tone'. The term 'tonal value' refers to the relative degree of lightness or darkness of any colour, on a scale of greys running from black to white.

Veduta *(Italian for 'view')*
An accurate representation of an urban landscape.

Vehicle
A liquid that carries pigments in suspension and makes it possible to apply them to a surface; sometimes called the base. The word is also used to describe a combination of medium and binder.

Verdaccio
An old term for green underpainting.

Volume
The space that a two-dimensional object or figure fills in a drawing or painting.

Wash
A thin, usually broadly applied, layer of transparent or heavily diluted paint or ink.

Wetting agent
A liquid – ox gall or a synthetic equivalent – added to watercolour paint to help it take evenly and smoothly on a support.

Wet-in-wet
A watercolour technique for mixing two or more colour washes on a support before the washes have had time to dry.

Wet-on-dry
A watercolour technique for applying a wet wash over another that has already dried on the paper.

Whiting
Ground and washed chalk, used in making gesso and whitewash.

Yellowing
This effect on oil paintings usually has one of four causes: excessive use of linseed oil; applying any of the varnishes that are prone to yellowing with age; or, most often, an accumulation of dirt that embeds itself into the surface of the varnish. Yellowing will also occur if oil paintings are kept in the dark.